'Clare is the voice of reason when it comes to pelvic health. She educates, empowers and offers practical tips to help women through all stages of their lives. As a currently pregnant woman, I shall be bookmarking the Bump, Birth and Beyond chapter for the foreseeable!'   DR SARA KAYAT

'As a gynaecologist I thought I was well-informed when it came to pelvic floor health, but after two appointments with Clare I realised how much more there was to know! Now everyone can have access to Clare's fantastic knowledge and skills. I'll be recommending this book to all my patients.'   DR ANITA MITRA

'Warm, wise and vitally important! Every woman should read this book. When you meet someone so passionate about the pelvic floor that they carry a plastic pelvis in their handbag, you sit up and listen. Within seconds of listening to Clare talk I had gained a whole new respect for my body. Clare is a woman on a mission [...] she compassionately and skilfully ensures that women are equipped with the tools to nurture a chronically overlooked part of their body that (quite literally) holds them together. This book is a much-needed handbook, a roadmap, a letter to our bodies.'
ANNA MATHUR, AUTHOR

'A revolutionary book that changes your entire view on the female body.'   CHESSIE KING

T0312415

'Pelvic floor health is a little discussed subject. Most women have no idea of its importance until they experience symptoms, most commonly post-natal or during the menopause. By this point they may well be too embarrassed to seek help. This book should change that by empowering women with knowledge and understanding so that they can seek the help they need.'

DR NAOMI MIDDLETON

'If there is one book that all females should read to have the foundational understanding to get to know their pelvic floor and learn how to keep it working at its best – this is it! I wish I'd had this information as a teenager and before my first child. Nothing is taboo and I have finished this book feeling like my body is a marvel to be cared for and honoured.'

DR MARTHA DEIROS COLLADO

Strong Foundations

WHY PELVIC HEALTH MATTERS

An empowering guide
to understanding your body

CLARE BOURNE

Thorsons

This book contains advice and information relating to health care. It should be used to supplement rather than replace the advice of your doctor or another trained health professional. If you know or suspect you have a health problem, it is recommended that you seek your doctor's advice before embarking on any medical programme or treatment. All efforts have been made to assure the accuracy of the information contained in this book as of the date of publication. This publisher and the author disclaim liability for any medical outcomes that may occur as a result of applying the methods suggested in this book.

Thorsons
An imprint of HarperCollins*Publishers*
1 London Bridge Street
London SE1 9GF

www.harpercollins.co.uk

HarperCollins*Publishers*
Macken House, 39/40 Mayor Street Upper
Dublin 1, D01 C9W8, Ireland

First published by Thorsons 2023

1 3 5 7 9 10 8 6 4 2

Text © Clare Bourne 2023
Illustrations by Liane Payne

Clare Bourne asserts the moral right to be identified as the author of this work
A catalogue record of this book is available from the British Library

ISBN 978-0-00-860422-6

Printed and bound in the UK using 100%
renewable electricity at CPI Group (UK) Ltd

All rights reserved. No part of this publication may be reproduced, stored in a retrieval system, or transmitted, in any form or by any means, electronic, mechanical, photocopying, recording or otherwise, without the prior written permission of the publishers.

This book is produced from independently certified FSC™ paper
to ensure responsible forest management.

For more information visit: www.harpercollins.co.uk/green

*For all the women out there who have allowed me
to support them on their pelvic health journeys.*

*For the next generation – may your pelvic health
journeys be more informed and empowered.*

*For my little family: David, Poppy and Jonas – thank you
for always being there and being my biggest supporters.*

***

*In loving memory of little Eliza King who we lost during
the time I was writing this book at just 7 months old.
Thank you for reminding me that I can do hard things.
Forever in our hearts x*

*I want to discuss before the book begins the use of language through-
out, and my desire to never exclude anyone when discussing pelvic
health. Pelvic health is for all, whatever your gender and I want everyone to learn more about it. However, I want to acknowledge that
throughout this book when using the words 'women', 'woman' or
'mother' I am referring to cis women with natal female anatomy. This
is in part due to my experience with treating this population group as
well as the scientific research being focused on cis women.*

*I identify that there needs to be more pelvic health information and
guidance for those who identify as trans men, trans masculine and
non-binary. We need more research that looks at supporting those of
all genders with their pelvic health. Though this book cannot help
everyone, I have included some resources in the Helpful Resources
section that I hope may be informative and supportive.*

Contents

Introduction

Welcome to the Journey

Welcome, my dear, to a journey of learning and discovery about your body and your pelvic health. It's probably either a part of your health that you haven't spent much time thinking about, or one that you have been abruptly introduced to at some point in your life. Whatever your story has been up to this point, you are welcome here and I hope the time we have together will be empowering and leave you feeling stronger in lots of ways.

Before we start, there are two things I want you to know:

1. You and your pelvic health are important, and worth investing time in.
2. Life, recovery and pelvic health are *not* linear.

When we are busy, which, let's face it, most of us are, it can be so hard to prioritise our health and wellbeing. However, I am absolutely certain that taking care of your pelvic health doesn't need to take hours. It just needs understanding and awareness of how to weave it through your existing day-to-day life. That is what we are going to do as we work through these pages together and I hope you will finish with a full toolkit to continue working on your pelvic health. I want to be honest with you though, these things don't always progress or go in the ways we always expect them to: a lovely linear, upwards trajectory. It can be much more of a rollercoaster – but it is so worth the ride. So, let's buckle up and crack on with our journey together.

WHAT IS PELVIC HEALTH?

Pelvic health is a phrase that can leave lots of us thinking, 'What does that mean?' You're not alone if you are a bit sceptical as to whether this is something you even need to think about. Our pelvic health is an important area of our overall wellbeing that we often take for granted – until something challenges it and we become acutely aware of how important it really is. So, let's break down what it is and why this book is going to help us all as, like all other areas of our health, we navigate different seasons of our life.

Our pelvic health incorporates the function of our pelvic floor muscles, our pelvic organs (bladder, bowels and uterus), as well as our abdominal muscles, breathing muscles and the pelvis itself. However, it is important to acknowledge at this stage that we should never view any one part of our body in isolation, and therefore you will hear me talking about how our pelvic health interacts with other parts of our health as we go through the chapters. I always love to consider the World Health Organization's definition of health, which is: 'Health is a state of complete physical, mental and social wellbeing and not merely the absence of disease or infirmity.' This helps to remind us that health is not only important when symptoms pop up but actually at all times.

The trouble with our pelvic health is that we are often not fully introduced to it, or its importance, until we fall pregnant. Someone mentions 'don't forget to do your pelvic floor exercises', maybe hands us a piece of paper and off we go to google 'how do I do pelvic floor muscle exercises and where even are they?!', or we just don't think about them again until maybe we do a big sneeze and out comes a wee we were not expecting. The outrage I hear from women, when they start to experience these unpleasant and often embarrassing symptoms, about why they were not told about the importance of their pelvic floor muscles earlier, is very understandable. Our information and education need to be better, *and* need to happen earlier than pregnancy. The average age of a pregnant woman is 31, so a significant amount of life passes before we are even introducing women to their pelvic health and pelvic floor muscles, and even then we are not doing it that well. There has been a call to change this, with some recent guidelines[1] stating: 'young women, aged between 12 and 17, should be taught about pelvic floor anatomy and pelvic floor muscle exercises as part of school curriculums' and that we should 'encourage women of all ages to do pelvic floor muscle training' as it helps to prevent symptoms. I hope we see this change in years to come, but what about the rest of us? My aim in this book is to help you understand your pelvic health in a new way, shine a light on areas you had no idea about, and think about pelvic health as something we can embrace for life, that can help to boost us forwards rather than drag us down like a ball and chain.

SO WHY HAVE I WRITTEN THIS BOOK FOR YOU?

A lot of the symptoms we may experience that relate to our pelvic health are still a bit 'taboo', making them very hard to open up about and share. I totally understand that, and there is no pressure from me to make you reveal all. All I want you to know is that if you are struggling, there *is* help; there are people out there like me, that talk about incontinence, sex and doing a poo like we talk about the weather, and you don't have to suffer in silence or feel lonely in your experience. Symptoms like incontinence, pain during sex, struggles to open our bowels and living with ongoing pain can have a huge impact on our mental and emotional wellbeing as well. Therefore, when we care for your pelvic health, we are caring for so much more than the physical structures of your pelvis. I am all about helping women to connect the dots about their health and understand how different parts influence each other: that is the foundation of this book.

MY STORY

My passion for pelvic health is shaped by my professional journey through my physiotherapy career, as well as my own personal journey with my own pelvic health in more recent years. So where did this love of talking about pelvic floors, wee and poo begin?! Back in 2009 I left university as a 21-year-old, convinced I was off to work in London and, over time, would be physio to the English Rugby team – every girl's dream, right? I did move back to London, which is my home, but at the time getting a physiotherapy job was as easy as winning the lottery. Competition was high, job vacancies were low, and it was a matter of taking what you could get. That is exactly what I did, and I was offered a junior position at Chelsea and Westminster Hospital. When you start out as a physiotherapist you need to gain experience in all areas of the profession, and so you rotate every few months into a new area. I took the job without any idea of what my first rotation would be, but guess what... that's right, it was in pelvic health. My first response was 'oh no'; I had not been taught anything about it during my university degree and can honestly say I knew nothing. Thankfully for me, and all the ladies I treated, I had the most amazing team around me who taught me everything I needed to know, and that was the beginning of my love story with pelvic health physiotherapy.

I got experience in lots of areas, including a year and a half in intensive care, during which time I took a month out to travel. I spent some time in the slums in Delhi where I again had the opportunity to work alongside women and educate them about their pelvic health. When I headed to India, I felt pretty disillusioned, for a variety of reasons, but I can honestly say my time there was a light-bulb moment. When I returned from my travels, I applied for a senior position in pelvic health, got the job, and let's just say the rest is history. Ten years on, here I am and my passion for this area of physiotherapy only grows.

An important part of this story includes my own motherhood journey, which started with the arrival of my gorgeous daughter 6 years ago. I'm not going to lie; I was pretty scared of giving birth, having heard quite a number of horror stories throughout my career, and had a good list of worst-case scenarios in my head that I didn't want to happen. On paper my daughter's birth was uncomplicated and a scenario I know many would dream of: it was quick, I was in the birth centre, I was in water for a lot of my labour and I had no major tearing. I'll be honest, I was on cloud 9 afterwards. However, I soon fell pretty quickly from that cloud when I started to notice symptoms of a prolapse, which was confirmed around 10 weeks postpartum. My world imploded. I was 28 years old, felt like I had aged 50 years and was living one of my worst postpartum nightmares. Fast-forward 6 years and I have been on quite a journey. I've been pregnant again, given birth to our wonderful son and got to a place where I live a life not dictated by prolapse symptoms or fear. However, it hasn't been easy, and it has further fanned the fire in my belly to support all women with their pelvic health journey and is one of the reasons I am delighted to be writing these words. So, if you are holding this book, with your own journey that you are struggling with, I want to say this: all your emotions are valid, and it is OK to find it incredibly hard. I just hope the words that you read will provide some hope, comfort and clarity in the moments you need them most.

HOW TO USE THIS BOOK

I have written this book to guide you through different life stages and help you to piece together your own pelvic health journey. I am so desperate for us to move away from only talking about pelvic health in the perinatal period, and to open up our understanding and awareness that our pelvic health journey started long before this time. To kick this off I want to introduce you to the pelvic floor continuum.

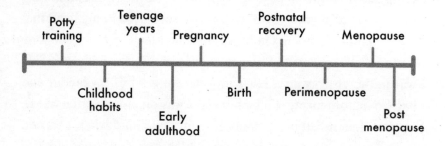

Most of us are introduced to the concept of pelvic floor exercises and our pelvic health around pregnancy, and are often aware of its importance postpartum. However, as the continuum shows, there are so many key life stages that can play a part and it is so vital for us to consider them all. Like other areas of our health, issues often don't arise from one isolated event; it is the culmination of smaller contributors over years. For most of us this is true of our pelvic health. Though often pregnancy and birth are the main focus, for good reason, when we break it down there is often more to the story. Reviewing each stage also helps us support the next generation better, if we have a better understanding of this lifelong journey we all go on. Throughout the book we shall discuss each part of the continuum and think about how they all play their part.

> Tell me and I forget, teach me and I may remember, involve me and I learn.
>
> **Benjamin Franklin**

I love this quote and feel it defines what I want this book to be for you. I want you to be fully involved in this process and understand what it means for you by allowing you to reflect on your own experience throughout. You will find 'Foundation Reflections' pages from Chapter 3 onwards, giving you the opportunity to jot down any thoughts or key learning points.

* * *

The book is split into four parts:

Part I: Understanding Our Foundations

We will start by learning about our anatomy, because without this knowledge it is very difficult to piece the other parts together. I will teach you more about the importance of your pelvic floor muscles and pelvic organs, and their roles in our life.

Part II: Where Did Our Story Begin?

We will then move on to learning about childhood and what can influence our pelvic health during this time, before moving into the teenage years and beyond. We will also discuss a few key pelvic health conditions that all women should be aware of, because, after all, knowledge is power.

Part III: Bump, Birth and Beyond

Though pelvic health is not only influenced by the perinatal period, this time does impact it in a variety of ways. Therefore, we will have an extensive look at this time in our lives, as well as at some of the symptoms we may face and - most importantly - what we can do to help.

Part IV: Moving Through Life – Perimenopause and Beyond

Finally, we will consider perimenopause and the transition through menopause, and what we can do to care for and protect our pelvic health - as well as empowering you with the knowledge you need in how to be active and exercise during this time.

* * *

This book is packed with the information I wish all women were given for all life stages, and I hope that you will find each section helpful in its own way and enjoy the chance to reflect along the way. Though I have designed *Strong Foundations* to flow through the life phases, I appreciate there may be some topics you are keen to read about straight away if you are struggling, so do dip in and out as you need. This is for you, on your journey, and my main hope is that you end this book with a new passion, understanding and desire to care for your pelvic health. Thank you for joining me; let's get this fascinating and exciting journey started.

PART I

Understanding Our Foundations

CHAPTER 1

Dear Body

Let's learn about:

- Understanding your body and how it functions better
- The pelvic health squad and how they function
- The wonder that is the bowels
- The gut microbiota
- Your amazing pelvic floor muscles
- Intra-abdominal pressure: what it is and why it is important

For most of us, we have been living in our bodies for a little while now, and some of us might feel very in tune and connected to them; others may feel so far away from that feeling. Often as young children we are very intuitive and in touch with our physical bodies, we don't have to hold anything back. When something hurts, we cry; when we are hungry, we eat or ask for snacks; when we have energy, we run around; when we need a poo, we do it in a nappy; when we have wind, we pass it. The list goes on, and yet over time things change, and not always for the worse that's for sure – everyone in a lift is thankful when we have learnt to control our wind. But sometimes I think barriers and blind spots appear. Most of the time this is through no fault of our own, but maybe through lack of education, embarrassment, shame, or societal norms that tell us to behave a certain way. Again, the list goes on.

Our relationship with, and how we view our bodies also changes over the years and as you read (or listen to) this I am sure you will reflect on your own journey. We all come from different places, some of us will feel we have a very positive and loving relationship with our body, but for others it may be an ongoing struggle. You just come as you are and I hope that as we go through this book together, you will learn new things about your body that will show you just how amazing it is.

As we start to explore our pelvic health, what is fundamental is that you understand the key team players – what they do and how they work – to try and bring some sense to everything that is ahead. Before we start meeting 'the team', however, I wanted to begin with a little letter that I hope we can all relate to and take ownership of:

> Dear Body,
>   We've known each other for a while, thanks for keeping me going, breathing and moving throughout the years.
> Sorry at times I probably haven't looked after you as maybe you would have liked, but to be honest I am doing my best.
> There are so many things about you that I don't know about, I guess we are always learning, eh? I am determined to understand you better and give you the respect you are due.
>   Thanks for your ongoing service, you truly are amazing.
>   Love, Me x

Let's meet the **pelvic health squad** that have done us all some good service up until this point, cracking on with some pretty essential duties while we go about our everyday life.

1. **Your bladder** – The ultimate balloon
2. **Your bowels** – Your inbuilt sausage machine

3. Your **pelvic floor** – The best hammock ever

4. Your **vulva** – The external wonder

5. Your **vagina, uterus and ovaries** – The internal wonders

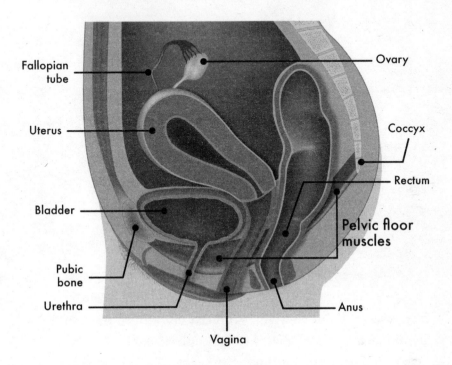

Fig. 1: Pelvic region

YOUR BLADDER – THE ULTIMATE BALLOON

In order to understand our bladder, we really need to think about the whole urinary system first. This is broken down into the upper urinary tract, your **kidneys** and **ureters**, and your lower urinary tract, your **bladder** and **urethra**. The two parts of the urinary system are like a mini relay team. The kidneys and ureters start the process, by producing urine, and pass the baton, or urine, on to the bladder and urethra to store, and get rid of and finish the

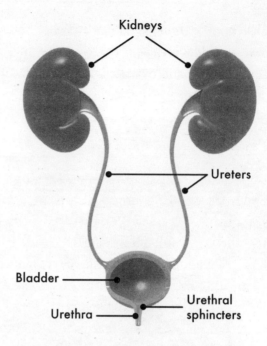

Kidneys

Ureters

Bladder

Urethral sphincters

Urethra

Fig. 2: Upper and lower urinary tracts

race when the time is right. So, what else do we need to know about this mini team in our pelvic health squad?

Your **kidneys** are the ultimate filters. They filter our blood, getting rid of what we don't need, including waste products and excess fluid in the form of urine, and keeping what we do need. They work hard, filtering on average around 200 litres of fluid in 24 hours, producing urine that travels down two tubes, the ureters, to the bladder. Here the urine stays, we hope, until we are able to find a toilet and do a wee.

Your **bladder** is an amazing little thing, a muscular organ that can stretch, like a balloon, to hold urine, and then contract to release it multiple times a day, as we go about our life. The bladder wall is made up of a number of layers, including a muscular layer, called the **detrusor**, which allows us to hold urine, as well as communicating with our brain when we need to go and then completing the task. We mustn't forget two little rings of muscle, called the **urethral sphincters**, and the vital role they play in the relay race. The external and internal urethral sphincters are hugely responsible for keeping us continent.

How do we know when we need a wee?

As urine enters the bladder it causes the walls to stretch. This stretch sends messages to the brain, via nerves, to let it know there is urine present, giving it the heads up that at some point you will need to find a toilet. This initial awareness of urine being present happens before our bladder is totally full, allowing us the time we need to find a toilet, make it home, or finish a meeting. Once we are in the toilet, sitting down and happy, the brain then sends messages back to the bladder that cause the detrusor muscle to contract, squeezing the bladder, and the urethral sphincter to relax, allowing us to wee.

If we have a happy bladder then usually we will pass urine six to eight times a day and generally not overnight. We should get a mild urge to go, which gradually increases until we decide we must go to the toilet. We should be able to hold it until we get there, and then pass around 350–500ml each time. There are a number of reasons why throughout life our bladder may get out of this routine, which we will explore as we go through the chapters. It can be helpful to track your pattern for a few days and how many times you go to get in touch with 'your normal'.

YOUR BOWELS – YOUR INBUILT SAUSAGE MACHINE

Let's face it, talking about bowels doesn't come naturally to most of us, and I totally understand that, but I want to help you realise how amazing and essential this part of our anatomy is, and hope that by the end of this book you are slightly more comfortable to talk about poo than you were at the beginning. I often say to women in clinic, this isn't glam but it is necessary. Our bowels play a key role in our pelvic health squad, and often when treating pelvic health symptoms we start with looking at the bowels because of the huge influence they have. You may have urinary symptoms but, as your bladder and bowels sit so closely together, if you are struggling with constipation or fully emptying your bowels this can put a lot of pressure on your little bladder and contribute to symptoms. I imagine this a bit like the dead arm you can get when your toddler falls asleep on you, the bladder being your arm and the bowels being your toddler!

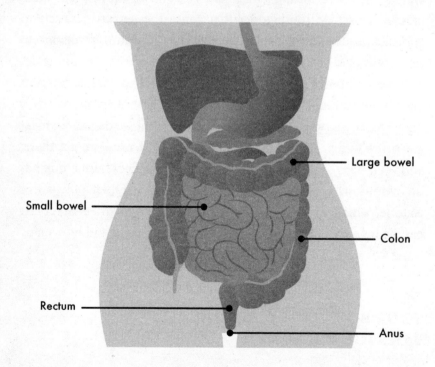

Fig. 3: The bowels

Let's start with what we mean when we are talking about our bowels. Is producing poo all they do?

Our bowels are made up of two main parts, the **small bowel** and the **large bowel**. Together they are around 7 metres long, which, I think you will agree, is pretty impressive in itself. The bowels are part of our digestive system, helping to break down the food we eat, absorbing fluid and nutrients into the blood, and processing and getting rid of anything we don't need from the body.

How does this happen?

Food from the stomach moves into the small bowel, where the majority of the nutrients from the food are absorbed as they cross the gut barrier and enter the blood stream. From here food gets pushed along by muscular contractions in the bowel wall, called peristalsis. These are muscles that are not in our conscious control, called smooth muscle, and it happens throughout the day and night without us knowing. Once the food has passed through the small bowel, it enters the large bowel where there is further absorption of water and nutrients, as well as production of vitamins. The large bowel is home to an incredible community of microbes, your **gut microbiota**, which is absolutely fascinating and so important for us to know more about. I am delighted that Kristy Coleman, my friend and an Association for Nutrition nutritionist, has shared her gut wisdom with us:

The gut microbiota is an ecosystem of different microbes, including bacteria, yeasts and other microbes. They work together to support our health and wellbeing, both physical and mental, and influence everything from our immune system to hormones. The microbes that live in your gut work on breaking down excess hormones into a form that can be removed by your body. Some of these microbes produce vitamins, such as vitamins K and B, and other beneficial compounds, such as short-chain fatty acids (anti-inflammatories) as a result of you feeding them fibre.

Your gut and your brain are intrinsically linked, with each influencing the other. They communicate back and forth all day. This is called the gut–brain axis. The gut and our mental health have also been shown to be linked. The more diverse the microbes in the gut are, the lower the risk of depression and anxiety (in some people).

HOW CAN YOU SUPPORT YOUR GUT MICROBES?

The gut microbiota is sensitive and can change for better or worse within a matter of days. To support it:

Reduce stress

Reduce caffeine and alcohol intake

Reduce consumption of ultra processed foods

Eat more plants. Expand your thoughts around plants to mean more than vegetables and fruit: they also include wholegrains, nuts, seeds, legumes, herbs and spices.

Whatever is left in the bowel after these processes of absorption and production have occurred makes up our poo, which is stored at the end of the large bowel, in the rectum, until we are ready to pass it out of the body through the anus.

How does the poo actually get out though?

This is probably not something you have ever spent much time thinking about, but it is an important process to understand as our pelvic floor muscles play a significant role. The **rectum** stretches as our poo enters and fills it, which sends a message to our brain to make us aware that there is poo present. Amazingly, the rectum can communicate with our brain as to whether it is wind or poo present so we can make a decision whether we need to head to the toilet or find a private place to pass some wind. Our clever **anus**, made up of two sphincter muscles called the **internal** and **external sphincters**, holds the poo or wind in the rectum until we are ready. We have conscious control of the external sphincter, which means we can contract it to ensure we get to the toilet in time or so we don't pass wind when we don't want to. Once we are in the bathroom and sat relaxed on the toilet, hopefully alone (for any mothers reading, I know this can be considered something of a luxury), the brain sends messages to the anal sphincters and pelvic floor muscles to relax, and out comes the poo.

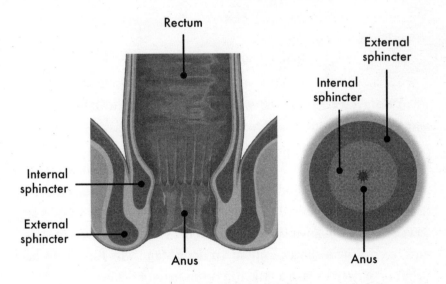

Fig. 4: The anal sphincters

There is one key muscle of the pelvic floor that I want to introduce you to, before meeting its other friends a little later, and this is **puborectalis**. As shown in Figure 5 on the following page, this muscle wraps around the large bowel, kinking the end, which helps to keep us continent as we go about our everyday life. However, in order for

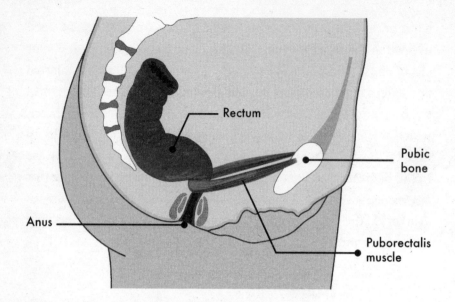

Fig. 5: Puborectalis muscle

us to do a very happy poo we need puborectalis to relax, which allows the bowel to straighten and our poo to pass out down a straightish slide, rather than round a tight corner. To help this occur there are a few things we can do. First, ensure you feel comfortable and able to relax your body on the toilet, and take some deep breaths. Secondly, you may benefit from using a stool or step to raise your feet up off the floor, which brings your knees above the levels of your hips, recreating a squat position. To understand why this might be helpful, we need to take a little trip down memory lane.

Before modern toilets were invented or widely used, humans would usually squat down low to do a poo, whether it was in the wild or using a chamber pot. In some parts of the world squat toilets are still used daily, however, more widely the modern toilet that we all use is the norm. And, I am sure you will agree, we are definitely not squatting on them. During a squat there is natural lengthening of the pelvic floor muscles and puborectalis, which,

Fig. 6: Toilet position when doing a poo

as mentioned previously, makes it easy for the poo to pass out without us needing to strain excessively. Straining to do a poo has a detrimental influence on our pelvic floor, so we want to make sure we help ourselves as much as possible.

For those of you with children you may have noticed, once they were walking but still wearing nappies, they would squat to poo. You could tell when they were doing a poo when you found them having a private moment and a squat. This is because it is an intuitive movement for us as humans, and yet as we grow up and start to use toilets this can all change. We will explore this more in Chapter 3.

Everyone is different, but most people will do a poo between three times a week and three times a day. The key is knowing your body and your rhythm so you can detect if there are any changes or problems. We also want to keep an eye on what a poo looks like... we are getting to the real glam stuff now! Figure 7 shows what's called the Bristol Stool chart: that's right, there is a whole

Type 1		Separate hard lumps, like nuts (hard to pass)
Type 2		Sausage-shaped but lumpy
Type 3		Like a sausage but with cracks on its surface
Type 4		Like a sausage or snake, smooth and soft
Type 5		Soft blobs with clear-cut edges (passed easily)
Type 6		Fluffy pieces with ragged edges, a mushy stool
Type 7		Watery, no solid pieces, entirely liquid

Fig. 7: Bristol stool chart

chart about poo and the seven types we might make, from hard pellets to water. Type 4 is the goal, the perfect poo if you will, so next time you pop to the toilet, have a quick check and see where you feel you might sit on the chart. Don't worry if you are not always a type 4, but it can be helpful to know, especially if you are struggling with your bowels or experiencing constipation.

What else can we do to help our bowels?

Our bowels love fluid, fibre and movement, as well as for us to listen to them. By this I mean, going for a poo when we get the urge and not putting it off and holding on to the poo for a while longer. Now, don't get me wrong, we are not always near a toilet when the 'call to stool' comes, but equally it can be easy to ignore our body's natural communication and rhythm for other reasons, when we don't necessarily need to. Motherhood can be one big interrupter of bowel movements, whether that be being stuck feeding a baby, unable to move in fear of waking a baby, or being repeatedly interrupted by a toddler with 'Mummy, can I have a snack?' So I say this, knowing full well I sometimes have no choice but to ignore my need for the toilet, because someone else needs me more. However, I would encourage you to just try and think about how in tune you are with your natural rhythm, and if you feel you repeatedly ignore 'the call' then see what small changes you could make.

Fibre contributes to the form of our stool, helping to make it a good size and softness so we can achieve that perfect poo (type 4). However, most of us are not consuming enough of it. Adults are recommended to consume 30g of fibre a day as part of a healthy and balanced diet,[1] which isn't always easy to achieve. Most commonly we hear about soluble and insoluble fibre, which refers to whether they can be dissolved in water or not. Soluble fibre is found in food like oats, pulses and some fruit and vegetables, including broccoli. Insoluble fibre is found in foods like wholegrain bread and pasta, some fruit and vegetables, and nuts. There is often soluble and insoluble fibre in one type of food, like lots of fruits and vegetables. The key is to get a variety of fibre in our diets to help us have happy bowels, so aim for those wholegrains, keep skin on fruit and vegetables, and try to eat 30 plant-based foods a week. Not only is fibre important for our bowels, it plays a part in our overall health and wellbeing, reducing the risk of type 2 diabetes, heart disease and colon cancer.

Soluble Fibre	Insoluble Fibre
Oats	Wholegrain pasta
Lentils	Wholegrain bread
Peas	Potatoes with skin on
Seeds	Nuts
Chickpeas	Beans
Nuts	Wheat bran
Apples	Cauliflower
Pears	Seeds
Avocadoes	Skin and seeds of fruit and vegetables
Apricots	
Flaxseed	
Psyllium	

The body needs fluid for lots of reasons, and as we've already discussed, one of the key roles of the bowels is to absorb water, from your food, into the blood and body. Therefore, if there isn't enough fluid going into our body this can make your poo harder, as our bowels will always take what our body needs to function. So, aiming for 1.5–2 litres of fluid a day helps to keep our poo soft and easy to pass.

Movement and exercise also contribute to helping our bowels move the poo along, supporting that peristaltic movement mentioned earlier. Whether it be a stroll around the block, getting out for a run, or doing a workout at home, they can all benefit our bowels. Pelvic floor symptoms can be a huge limiting factor to exercise and movement for women, which can affect other areas of our health too. This is why I am so passionate to ensure all women know how to look after and improve their pelvic health. There is often a lot of overlap. For example, if you don't want to exercise for fear of leaking, this can impact your bowels; you may then notice that you struggle with constipation more, and then strain more when trying to do a poo, which then impacts your pelvic floor further, leading to more symptoms. So, as I am sure you are starting to see, there are a lot of links and connections between the pelvic health squad. Let's head on to meet the main muscles of the moment and understand them a bit better.

YOUR PELVIC FLOOR – THE BEST HAMMOCK EVER

The pelvic floor is given this name as it makes up the floor of the pelvis. This helps us to understand their role but also their importance. Imagine your favourite handbag without there being a base – I mean, it wouldn't be very helpful with everything falling onto the floor. I am sure you will remember times when you've added lots into your bag and how much pressure that can push down on its base. Though our pelvic floor is more precious than a designer handbag, we are often not aware of the anatomy, or really understand where it is or what it is made up of. So, let's take a closer look.

The pelvis

We need to start with the pelvis, which is the bony structure that our pelvic floor muscles attach to. The pelvis is made up of a group of bones that join at the front at the **pubic symphysis**, and to the base of the spine, called the **sacrum**, at the sacroiliac joints at the back. Below the sacrum is your **coccyx**, which you may have got to know rather abruptly if you have ever fallen on it. The pelvis connects our upper body to our lower body through our spine and hips and is the bony bodyguard of our pelvic organs. The bones are surrounded by ligaments and muscles, including our beloved **pelvic floor**.

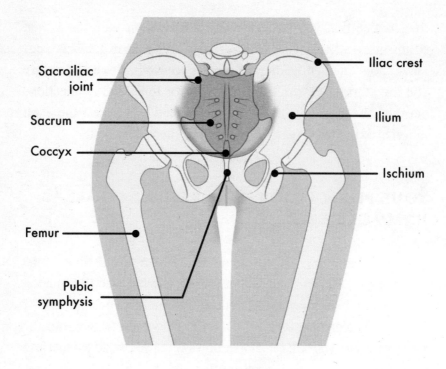

Fig. 8: The pelvis

The pelvic floor

The pelvic floor muscles attach to the pubic bone at the front, the coccyx at the back and the ischial tuberosities, otherwise known as your sitting bones, at the sides. The pelvic floor is made up of two layers – the superficial layer and the deep layer – with groups of little muscles with some great names. One we have already met, puborectalis, but there are many others, including bulbospongiosus and iliococcygeus. Along with the urethral and anal sphincters, these muscles make up the pelvic floor, which is often described as a hammock. If we look at Figure 9 we can see that the pelvic floor is also slightly diamond shaped, and this diamond really is a girl's best friend!

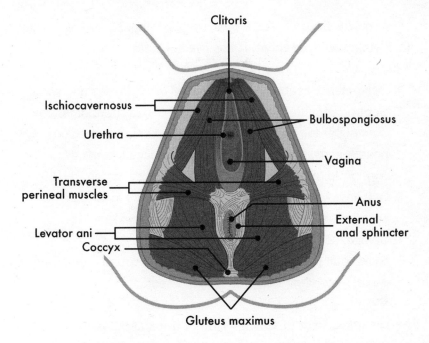

Fig. 9: The pelvic floor – external view

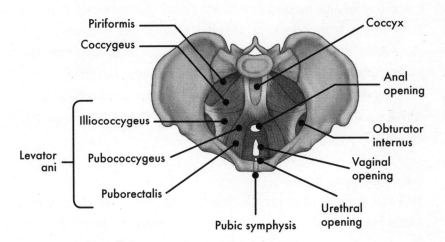

Fig. 10: The pelvic floor – internal view

Our pelvic floor is like a best friend: supportive, helpful and there when you need them. It has **five key roles**:

1. **Sphincteric:** keeping us continent of urine, faeces and wind.
2. **Support:** contributing to the support of our pelvic organs (remember the floor of the handbag holding our precious possessions, or the foundations of a house providing support to the structures above).
3. **Stability:** working with other muscles of 'the inner core', which we will meet soon, to support our spine.
4. **Sexual:** contributing to sexual pleasure.
5. **Sump pump:** helping to pump blood and lymph around the pelvic region and back towards the heart.

Five key roles, most of which we don't think about but would definitely miss if they were not fulfilled. To carry out these different roles the pelvic floor is made up of two different types of muscle fibres: slow twitch fibres (66 per cent), which provide constant support to the pelvic organs and help you to hold in a wee while trying to find a toilet, and fast twitch fibres (34 per cent) that kick in if we suddenly cough or sneeze.[2] Despite being designed for these roles, it still seems like some big jobs for these little muscles. Thankfully, like all other muscles in the body, the pelvic floor muscles don't act alone; they work with some other key players, which make up our inner core muscles. Let's meet them and find out more.

The diaphragm

This is a dome-shaped muscle found at the bottom of the ribcage, which separates our chest (thorax) from our abdomen. It is the muscle that sits above the pelvic floor, with the abdominal and

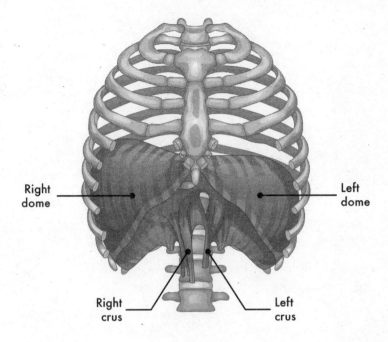

Right
dome

Left
dome

Right
crus

Left
crus

Fig. 11: The diaphragm

pelvic organs in between. It has a vital role in our breathing, moving air in and out of our lungs, but also plays a key role in our core and pelvic floor function.

Transversus abdominis
This is the deepest of the abdominal muscles and forms a natural corset for us. It wraps around from our spine to the middle of our tummy, and attaches to the ribs above, and the pelvis below, and is another close friend of the pelvic floor.

Multifidus
A small, yet important muscle that stretches along the length of our spine. It contributes to spinal stability by working with our other core muscles.

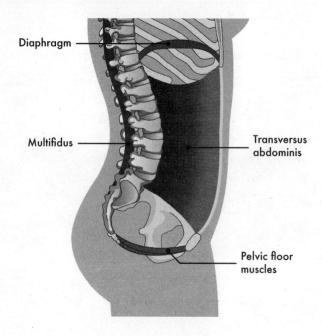

Diaphragm

Multifidus

Transversus
abdominis

Pelvic floor
muscles

Fig. 12: The inner core muscles

As the diagram above shows, together these muscles form a core cylinder within the abdomen.

How do they work together?

The relationship between these muscles and how they function is important when understanding our pelvic health, and this is why our pelvic health is so much more than just the pelvic floor. Though the latter will always remain my favourite muscle group, we need to look at and understand so much more when supporting women with their pelvic health.

When these muscles are left to their own natural rhythm, they move together in a little synchronised dance. They might not be winning *Strictly* anytime soon, but still get ten points from me. The diaphragm is essentially the driving force of the core, the Lewis Hamilton if you will, which sets the rhythm for the rest of the team. As you breathe in (inhale) your diaphragm contracts, flattens and moves down, and your transverse abdominis and pelvic floor relax and lengthen. Then, as you breathe out (exhale) your diaphragm relaxes and moves up, and the transverse abdominis recoils, along with the pelvic floor that contracts and lifts.

Together they provide spinal and pelvic stability and control before and during movement – and I don't just mean during a workout, I mean all movement throughout our day. They also contribute to changes in our **intra-abdominal pressure** as the muscles move, which is another important part of the picture we should discuss.

WHAT IS INTRA-ABDOMINAL PRESSURE (IAP) AND WHY DO WE NEED TO TALK ABOUT IT?

IAP is the level of pressure within the core cylinder at any given time. It helps to keep our body upright, as well as protecting our organs. IAP is changing all the time in response to day-to-day movements and activity. Coughing, lifting your child, jumping, running for a bus, or straining to do a poo all increase IAP. Increases in IAP can be correlated with more pelvic floor symptoms due to increased pressure on the muscles at the time. There is a natural response of the pelvic floor muscles to increases in IAP, with a reflexive contraction taking place.[3] They are therefore able to deal with and respond to IAP fluctuations, but, due to changes to the muscles throughout life, their ability to respond as well as is needed might change. Symptoms can lead us to avoiding or fearing movements where an increase in IAP occurs. However, instead of avoiding them completely, we want to train our muscles and bodies to be able to deal with pressure changes that occur. We will explore this more as we continue through the book, but please know your body has the ability to change and adapt and is probably stronger than you realise or often feel.

YOUR VULVA – THE EXTERNAL WONDER

The **vulva** is our **external genitals**, what we can see if we look in a mirror, which I know most of us have probably never done. You are not alone if you grew up calling your vulva a vagina, because, let's face it, most of us were never taught this stuff. In fact, a recent study found that only 9 per cent of women could correctly identify all parts of the vulva,[4] so you really are not alone! As the diagram below shows, our vulva is made up of a lot of structures

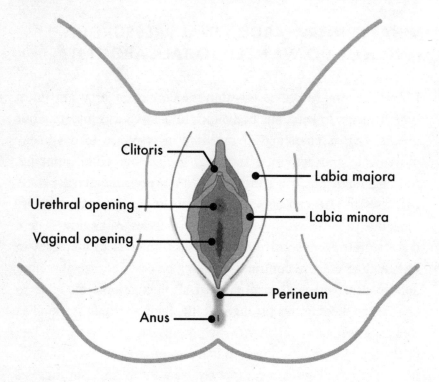

Fig. 13: The vulva

including the **clitoris**, the **labia majora** and **minora**, the **urethral** and **vaginal opening**, and the **perineum**, which is the area between the vagina and anus. I would really encourage you, if you are not sure about your own anatomy, to have a look and understand your own body better. In the next chapter we will discuss how taking a look at our vulva can actually help us to connect with our pelvic floor by looking for its movement.

Your clitoris

The **clitoral hood**, or glans clitoris, that we can see externally is just one small part of the whole clitoris. There is, quite literally, more than meets the eye. Internally the glans clitoris is connected

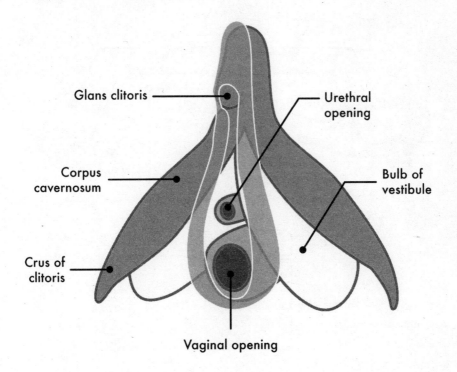

Glans clitoris

Urethral opening

Corpus cavernosum

Bulb of vestibule

Crus of clitoris

Vaginal opening

Fig. 14: The clitoris

to the clitoral body, which then splits into two crura, a bit like two legs, and vestibular bulbs. Our full understanding of clitoral anatomy only came in around 1998[5] so it is unsurprising that most of us don't know much about it.

YOUR VAGINA, UTERUS AND OVARIES – THE INTERNAL WONDERS

These are probably some of the anatomy that you are most aware of, or we hear most discussion around. At school our education around our body was predominantly around reproduction and how not to get pregnant. However, just to ensure we are all on the

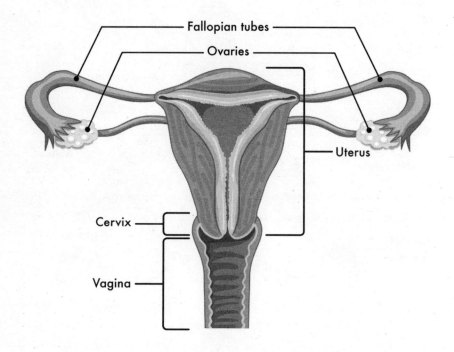

Fig. 15: The internal wonder – vagina, uterus and ovaries

same page and understand this part of our bodies, for all its glory, let's take a brief look.

The **vagina** is the muscular canal that extends internally from the vaginal opening up to the cervix. The walls of the vagina have lots of folds, called **rugae**, which mean it has the ability to be really stretchy when needed, for example, when giving birth. It is also self-cleaning, how amazing is that? So, we don't need to interfere with lots of soaps or feminine hygiene products, because it's already on it. The **cervix**, the shape of a ring doughnut, sits at the top of the vagina and is the opening to the uterus. Your **uterus** is another muscular organ, which is supported by ligaments and connective tissue called fascia, and, like the other pelvic organs, by the pelvic floor from below. It is mostly known for being the home to a baby during pregnancy, and then contracting to birth the baby when the time is right. It also contracts during our period to help remove the womb lining that builds up in the uterus during our menstrual cycle. Your **ovaries** not only house and produce your eggs but are also responsible for producing hormones. Eggs produced by the ovaries travel to the uterus via the **fallopian tubes**.

Speaking of hormones, it would be wrong to finish this chapter without a little look at our monthly hormone cycle. Another part of our health that can easily carry on without us giving it much thought, but can actually tell us so much if we tune in. There are four important hormones that are helpful to know about when looking at our **menstrual cycle**: oestrogen; progesterone; luteinizing hormone (LH); and follicle-stimulating hormone (FSH). Figure 16 shows how they rise and fall throughout a typical cycle. Our menstrual cycle is split into two parts, the **follicular phase** and the **luteal phase**, and lasts on average 28 days. However, as we are all different, a regular cycle that is anything from 21–40 days is considered normal.[6] Our period is the beginning of the follicular phase; as this comes to an end, oestrogen, FSH and LH levels

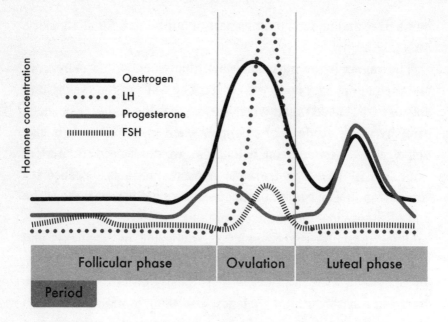

Fig. 16: Hormones of the menstrual cycle

increase building up to ovulation, which usually occurs around day 14. After ovulation we move into the luteal phase where LH and FSH levels drop back down. There is an initial drop in oestrogen before it rises again, along with progesterone which prepares the lining of the uterus for a fertilised egg, if this occurs. If it doesn't, then progesterone and oestrogen levels fall, the lining falls away and another period begins kicking off another cycle.

Don't ignore changes or challenges with your period. Please speak to a doctor if you have very irregular, heavy, or painful periods, or don't have any at all, as well as if you experience bleeding when you don't expect it, such as after sex, between periods, or after menopause. Our body has an amazing way of communicating with us, if we can slow down enough to hear it. Take it from a woman who lost her periods for a few years in her twenties and ended up on hormone replacement therapy (HRT). I had a condition called hypothalamic amenorrhea and I wish I had listened to my body better and spoken to my doctor earlier and got help. Thankfully I fell pregnant without normal cycles and, since my first pregnancy, my periods are back and I am so happy about it. I know periods can be super frustrating and horrible at times, but I tell you what - losing them changed my mindset and now I feel incredibly grateful.

* * *

I hope you end this chapter feeling amazed and confident in your body and how your pelvic health squad work. Well done for sticking with me, and now let's head on to understand more about our pelvic floor and how we can all become pelvic health pros.

CHAPTER 2

Pelvic Floor Foundations

Let's learn about:

- The pelvic floor puzzle
- Symptoms of pelvic floor dysfunction
- Diaphragmatic breathing
- How to do pelvic floor exercises
- How to know if you are doing them correctly

Now we have covered the key bits of our pelvic health anatomy together, let's think more about our beloved pelvic floor muscles: what we need them to be able to do, and how to do pelvic floor muscle exercises. Though we often hear a lot about the importance of contracting our pelvic floor muscles and doing 'our squeezes', is this the whole picture?

THE PELVIC FLOOR PUZZLE

The puzzle shows four of the key components we need to consider when thinking about our pelvic floor muscles. Our ability to contract and strengthen the muscles is just one piece that makes up the picture. We must always consider **strength, flexibility, endurance and coordination.**

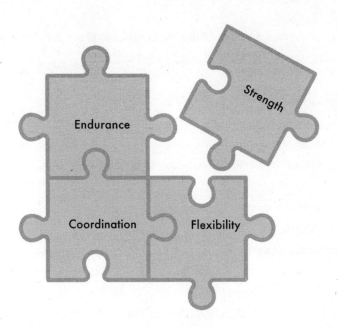

Before we dive into these individually, I do want to discuss and mention **muscle tone**. This is the tension in a muscle at rest. Pelvic floor muscles have a steady resting tone, which, as we discussed in the previous chapter, changes when we do a wee or poo to allow us to empty our bladder or bowels. The pelvic floor muscles are able to contract and relax voluntarily, (meaning we can initiate a contraction ourselves), as well as involuntarily when the muscles naturally respond to movement and day-to-day activities.[1] The resting tone of the pelvic floor muscles can change through life; it can increase or decrease from its normal tone for a whole variety of reasons, including childbirth, pain or holding patterns we get into. These changes can be linked to **pelvic floor dysfunction** and symptoms.

Pelvic floor dysfunction

Pelvic floor dysfunction is an umbrella term that includes a variety of symptoms that can occur when the function and tone of the pelvic floor muscles are impacted, and/or there are connective tissue changes. These symptoms may include:

1. **Incontinence:** This can be of urine, faeces or wind.
2. **Pelvic organ prolapse:** Where there is movement of one or more of the vaginal walls or the top of the vagina downwards, along with one or more pelvic organs, most commonly your bladder, bowel or womb. You will often experience a heaviness or dragging sensation in the vagina, or the sensation of a bulge.
3. **Difficulty opening your bowels:** Either struggling to initiate a bowel movement, pain during or after, or feeling that you are unable to empty fully.
4. **Urgency and frequency of passing urine:** When you feel your bladder dictates your day, and night. You are constantly mindful of where the next toilet is and notice you are going much more than other people.
5. **Pain with sexual intercourse:** This could be on penetration, or during, or felt deeper inside. Understandably it can be very distressing and can put a lot of pressure on a relationship.
6. **Pelvic pain:** This can be ongoing and persistent pain anywhere in the pelvic area.

It is important to note that these symptoms are often not solely due to your pelvic floor muscle function. We also need to consider the role of the connective tissue, ligaments and nerves. It is essential we always consider all factors when supporting you in your recovery. However, for now let's focus on what is in your control and what you can get started with at home.

I hear from so many women that pelvic floor exercises don't work when trying to treat their symptoms, and I honestly think that not supporting women to understand all parts of the puzzle is a key reason so many of us become disillusioned. It isn't all just about trying harder or doing more, it is about understanding the full picture. So, if you are reading this and have lost hope, stick with me and let's think about how we can bring all parts of the puzzle onto the board.

1. **Strength:** Relates to how much force we can generate with a contraction of our muscles, and strong muscles are key in many bodily functions. So yes, we must work on our pelvic floor muscle strength as a foundational part of our pelvic health, as long as it is not done in isolation.

2. **Flexibility:** All muscles need to be flexible and to lengthen and move in order to function optimally. Do we ever think much about the pelvic floor muscles lengthening or allowing the muscles to relax after contracting? A pelvic floor that is less flexible cannot easily do one of its key jobs for us, which is shock absorption, vital when it comes to any form of impact. We need the pelvic floor to move and respond to activity.

3. **Endurance:** No one runs a marathon without training, right? Our bodies can adapt so we can run a marathon, but we have to build endurance in our muscles first. We can also build endurance in our pelvic floor muscles and improve their ability to hold a contraction.

4. **Coordination:** This is the ability to use parts of the body together smoothly and efficiently. As we have discussed, our pelvic floor works with other muscles as part of a team, and not in isolation. Therefore, considering how the pelvic floor is working alongside its friends through movement is an important part of the picture as well.

Now we understand the areas we need to work on, we can start putting this all into practice.

WHERE DO WE START?

What was one of the first things we did when we were born? That's right, breathe. We take our first big breath earthside, and since then breathing has been foundational to our existence. However, do you ever think of its role in your pelvic health? As we discussed in Chapter 1, the diaphragm sits at the base of your ribcage, above your pelvic floor, and as the diaphragm moves when we breathe in and out, so does our pelvic floor. Therefore, for most of us, starting with breathing really helps our pelvic floor function. However, this isn't just any breathing in and out: we want to really focus on what we call **diaphragmatic breathing**.

How do you do diaphragmatic breathing?

- Place one hand on your lower ribs and one hand on your tummy.
- Take a deep breath in and expand your lower ribs into your hand.
- While doing this your tummy should gently expand as well.
- Visualise and think about your ribs expanding in all directions; we call this 360° breathing.
- Try this for 5–10 breaths, and take your time, there is no rush.

You can try this lying, sitting or standing and do not worry if you find this hard. Though breathing is a natural process, there are many factors that influence how we breathe, and often this style of diaphragmatic breathing is not something we do on a daily basis. Give yourself time, you'll get there. You may find it helpful to place a dressing-gown cord or scarf around your lower ribs, crossing it at the front so you feel a slight pressure. Then try breathing out into the scarf or cord. This feedback can help us to connect with where the movement should be. There should be a natural lengthening of your pelvic floor as you breathe in, however, you can also help this by working on some visualisations. A couple you can try are thinking about the vagina opening, or visualise a flower with its petals slowly opening.

IT'S PELVIC FLOOR TIME

Learning to contract our pelvic floor muscles is often not easy. Unlike other muscles, we cannot easily see them and the movement they produce, so please know you're not alone if you find it really hard, or have never tried it before. This is why we are here. I believe in keeping it simple, so let's go for it.

- Take a breath in, keeping everything relaxed.
- Then, as you breathe out, think about holding in wind or squeezing your anus,[2] which I am certain we all know how to do!
- Visualise the contraction (squeeze) coming forwards and upwards to the pubic bone at the front of the pelvis. Imagine stopping urine or squeezing around the vagina as well.
- Then let the muscles fully relax.

You should feel a gentle contraction around the anus and vaginal opening, while keeping your tummy, bottom and leg muscles all relaxed. Most of us over do it and expect a much bigger activation and give it 1,000 per cent when less effort is all that is required. We are not all the same, so if this doesn't work for you, maybe try thinking about just holding in a wee, or zipping forwards from your anus to your pubic bone at the front.

How do you know if you're doing them correctly?

You might be sitting there thinking, 'I think I've got this, but how do I really know?' Here are some top tips to help you feel really confident:

1. **Have a look:** I know it can seem a bit odd to look at your vulva with a mirror, but this is an easy way to see the movement of the pelvic floor muscles. As you breathe in you should see the perineum relax down, then, as you squeeze, you should see the perineum move inwards and the vaginal opening close slightly.

2. **Feel the movement:** You can place your finger on your perineum and feel the pelvic floor muscles tightening under your finger. You can also place your finger inside your vagina and feel muscles tightening around it.

3. **Use a device:** You might find it helps to use a biofeedback device that you place inside the vagina that detects your pelvic floor activity, which is shown on an external device like a phone. We will discuss these further in Chapter 10.

4. **See a pelvic health physio:** We can help you to learn how to contract your pelvic floor muscles through a vaginal examination, and focus on all parts of the puzzle to ensure optimum pelvic floor function.

How do we progress?

Once you feel confident that you can connect with your pelvic floor muscles, you can try two different exercise types, increase your reps and sets, as well as try them in different positions. I can sense your excitement already! The two types of pelvic floor contractions are **short** and **long**, and these work on the different types of muscle fibres we have discussed, fast twitch and slow twitch.

Short contractions

For these we contract (squeeze) and fully relax (let go) the pelvic floor muscles without any holds. Remember, the let go is just as important as the squeeze.

Long contractions

For these we contract (squeeze) and hold the contraction, while breathing in and out. Now this can feel really tricky and take a bit of time to master. It is a bit like tapping your head and rubbing your belly, but absolutely worth the effort once you've got it. Start by aiming for a 3-second hold, and then build up over time, aiming for a 10-second hold.

Try 10 short contractions and 10 long contractions, in a row, giving yourself a break between each squeeze and remembering not to rush. Quality is more important than quantity to start.

Should we all start with squeezes?

There is not a simple answer to this. Let me explain. Over time we can develop increased tone in the pelvic floor muscles, which might feel like increased tension or tightness. This can be associated with symptoms such as pain with intercourse, difficulty opening our bowels, increased frequency or urgency of needing a wee, or generalised pain around the pelvic area. If you are struggling with any of these symptoms it is often advised, instead of focusing on squeezing and contracting, to focus on improving the movement and flexibility of the muscles first. However, contracting the pelvic floor muscles can actually help to reduce the resting tone for some[3] so this is why it isn't a simple yes or no answer, but finding what works for you. Here are some top tips to get you started:

1. **Breathe:** Working on diaphragmatic breathing (see page 42), visualising the vagina opening and pelvic floor relaxing, can help. Try it now:
   - Breathe in, expanding your lower ribs and let your tummy relax and soften.
   - As you do this, visualise the vagina opening. You may find it helpful to think about a flower opening.
   - Don't push down but allow the muscles to move with your breath.
   - Then let the breath gently out.
   - Repeat 5–10 times.
2. **Relax:** Check yourself throughout the day; are you holding in your tummy and pelvic floor muscles a lot? Try to consciously let your pelvic floor relax at different points in the day.
3. **Move:** There are some gentle stretches that you can use which you might like to try:

Happy baby
   - Lying down on a mat lift both legs up one at a time into the position shown in the picture.
   - The soles of your feet should be facing up to the ceiling.
   - Spread your knees apart and hold on to the side of your feet or your ankles.
   - You may feel stretching in your inner thigh muscles.
   - Practise some diaphragmatic breathing, visualising your sitting bones widening as you breathe in.

Child's pose

- Kneeling on a mat, with your knees slightly apart, walk your hands forwards.
- Sit back onto your heels with your arms stretched out in front of you.
- As you rest in this position practise some diaphragmatic breathing.
- As you breathe in visualise your sitting bones widening and moving apart.

Deep squat

- Come down into a deep squat position as shown in the picture below.
- You can lean against a wall for some support.
- Place your elbows between your knees and gently push out.
- As you hold this position breathe deeply.
- Visual your sitting bones widening and your pelvic floor lengthening.
- Try this initially for a few minutes and build up as is comfortable and helpful.

4. **Don't fear contractions:** As mentioned, for some, contracting the muscles can actually help, so we don't want to fear contracting the pelvic floor, and certainly don't want to avoid it for ever. Determining what is right for you, and when, is ideally done under the guidance of a physiotherapist, but I hope you are feeling more aware and connected to your pelvic floor through trying these top tips.

How many exercises should I do?

If we are aiming to treat incontinence or prolapse symptoms, then building up to around 10 short and 10 long contractions 2–3 times a day is recommended. Ultimately, the best programme is what is right for *you*. Work with where you're at right now and build up from there.

All programmes should ideally follow some key principles, including overload, specificity, reversibility,[4] individualisation and variance. **Overload** means we need to gradually challenge the muscles, progressively over time, while finding the right level of challenge for each stage. Very similarly to if you started training at the gym, you wouldn't start deadlifting 70kg, but you also wouldn't want to lift 5kg dumbbells for ever if you wanted to continue challenging and building muscle. **Specificity** is training the muscles for the tasks we need them to do, for example, keeping us continent when we cough or sneeze, or when we are out walking in the park and we really need a wee. By doing pelvic floor muscle exercises and working on the two types of muscle fibres, as well as practising in different positions, we allow the pelvic floor muscles to learn how to do this. **Reversibility** means we need to keep working on them to keep the benefit, which we will discuss more in a moment. **Individualisation** is making the programme fully relevant to you, your current ability, your goals and your life. **Variance** means bringing in variety to prevent boredom setting in, which I am sure many of us can connect with when it comes to pelvic floor muscle exercises. Variety might look like doing exercises in different positions, or joining a local Pilates class where you can work on pelvic floor muscle exercises alongside others and with movement.

A vital part of the picture is to find a programme that is manageable and one that you can commit to. What I find happens too often is that we overwhelm women with an ideal that they cannot achieve with the phase of life they are in, and when this happens they disengage. Let's take a closer look at how this often happens:

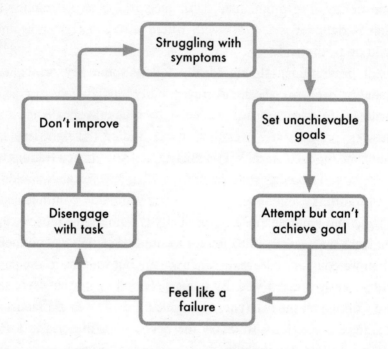

I have definitely been there, when I am set a task or a series of exercises I need to do, but life is busy, and when I can't meet the target I just disengage. I know I am not alone, so neither are you.

When you are ready, progression should not only focus on reps and sets, but on the position that we do pelvic floor exercises in as well. Often the focus is on doing them lying or sitting, but like all other muscles, training in functional positions, such as standing, is important. They often feel a lot harder to do standing when you start, with gravity more at play. However, this is another way to challenge your pelvic floor and train it to meet the demands of everyday life. We don't often have symptoms of incontinence when lying or sitting down; it is often when that big sneeze comes as we are walking down the street, or when running for the bus or after the kids on their scooters. So, when you are ready, move to a standing position to increase the challenge. Take the pressure off, you don't have to have a perfect contraction to start with. It is a process, one step at a time, and you will get there. It is important to note that exercise isn't a quick fix for most conditions. It is about gradually building up muscle strength, flexibility and coordination that brings about change.

When it comes to our pelvic floor, we need to give it time to respond. Though sometimes frustrating, slow and steady really does win the race, and realistic expectations can help keep us motivated. Generally pelvic floor muscle strengthening takes months, so don't get disheartened if it takes a while to notice a change, not only in how the contraction feels but also your symptoms. For some, it can take a year or more to notice a full change in symptoms, and it is often a very gradual journey. You may then reach the stage where you think 'how long do I have to do these exercises for?' and the honest answer is, for ever. Don't shut the book on me though, bear with me. I am absolutely not asking you to be pumping out 60 reps a day for the rest of your life, but I want to just suggest that our pelvic health is like any other part of our health and needs ongoing attention.

It is easier to focus on something when we know it is treating symptoms, but also being preventative and proactive about our health is only a good thing. I don't just brush my teeth if I have pain or need a filling; I brush my teeth daily to prevent these things. So, just like our dental health, our pelvic health needs to be taken regular care of. Try and find a little routine that works for you – maybe it is doing a few when you brush your teeth, or a few before you sleep at night. Stay connected, keep looking after those foundations and, I promise, you won't regret it.

I hope this chapter helps you to start connecting with your pelvic floor muscles better. If you are struggling with any of the symptoms mentioned the good news is that there is help and treatment. Pelvic health physiotherapists support women day in, day out with these symptoms, so you are *not* alone. As we move through the book we will address all of these in a lot more detail, and there will be opportunities for you to work out how to respond to help your own personal journey.

Your Floor Foundations

- Pelvic health is lifelong, with lots of different contributing factors.
- Pelvic floor exercises are more than just strength; remember to work on flexibility, endurance and coordination as well.
- Don't forgot the power of your breath.
- Try different cues to find what works for you, but thinking about holding in wind and squeezing upwards and forwards to the pubic bone is a good place to start.
- There are a variety of symptoms that can relate to our pelvic floor.

PART II

Where Did Our Story Begin?

CHAPTER 3

Where Did It All Begin?

Does it surprise you that there is a whole chapter about childhood and the teenage years in a pelvic health book? You're not alone if it does. The conversation around pelvic health is still quite new for women, let alone for children or men. However, we all have a pelvic floor and, just like our dental health, if we take care of it from a young age it lays great foundations for what is ahead.

Pelvic health, like other aspects of our health, starts from birth, on our journey to continence. This is usually long before we realise our daily experiences are connected to our pelvic health, probably before we have real memories, and certainly way before pregnancy. I often discuss this with women in clinic, and it is amazing how sometimes when we discuss symptoms that someone is experiencing as an adult, we can track it back to childhood. 'I've always had a weak bladder,' 'I've always struggled opening my bowels,' or 'We always laughed that I was the one constantly going for a wee.' Any of these sound familiar?

The reason I wanted to write this chapter isn't only to help you understand your own journey, but to help you, if you are a parent, hopefully understand your kids better and how you can support them with their pelvic health. I want to be clear at the beginning that this chapter isn't a 'how to treat childhood pelvic health problems', or a step-by-step guide on 'how to potty train your child'. It is purely to raise awareness, help understanding and, hopefully, help you as an individual and as a parent. However, I want you to know that if you are concerned about any of these symptoms for your child then please do speak to your doctor. There are pelvic health physiotherapists who treat children and can really help you and your child to work towards improving symptoms. They don't have to wait until they are older to get help.

POTTY TRAINING

Potty training is the most widespread term used to talk about learning how to control our bladder and bowels at a young age. What we are truly talking about is a child's ability to become continent, whether this be using a potty or a toilet, so I quite like the term 'gaining continence'.

However, I am going to mainly use the term potty training as that is the most commonly used term that I think we all understand and identify with. It is essential to acknowledge that there are many different approaches to supporting our children to gain continence, and I am not here to be a potty-training guru and tell you what you did, or are doing, is right or wrong. However, I do want to challenge the pressure or expectation that can often be there 'to crack it in 3 days'. Potty training is like most other physical skills or developmental stages, and children don't achieve those in 3 days, do they? If we think about rolling, crawling or walking, we watch our children for ages practising, nearly getting there, getting up but falling over, on repeat for days and often weeks in the process. I'd love us to view potty training in the same way. It is a new skill that takes time, and we are all different. This is why I don't believe there is one age when potty training is 'ideal', and it isn't a tick-box exercise. It is another stage of childhood that is individual and needs support at the right time. However, there can be a lot of pressure on us as parents to do it at the right time and we can often feel judged or embarrassed if our friends' kids are potty trained before our own. I want you to know that your child's age when they potty train is not a reflection on your ability as a parent, in the same way that your child's ability to walk is also not a reflection on your ability as a parent. Children are individuals who are all different. I learnt this through my own kids. Both of my children walked at 9 months, it felt so early and, compared to some of their peers, it was 9 months earlier than they walked. Did I have them on a strict walking training programme to achieve this? Of course not. Was it due to anything different I did compared to others? No, this was simply when they were ready. So, I would love to encourage us that this can be the same for potty training as well, allowing our children to learn over time so they really get to know their body better. Yes, we are there to guide and support, but in *their* right time.

There are many different approaches to supporting our children. Some will use a potty with their children from when they are very small babies, not leaving them to sit individually on the potty as a toddler would, but using it as part of their journey to gaining continence. For others, they may wait until their child is older, maybe 2 or 3. Whenever you start this process, the key part is that we are led by the child. I love this quote from Dr Lea Feghali, a paediatric pelvic health physiotherapist:

> This is your child, this is their process and we are here to facilitate it.

We are helping them to learn about many skills that contribute to gaining continence, including how to use and connect with their pelvic floor.

I am going to guess the majority of us were never told or educated about our pelvic floor as a child. This isn't our parents' fault – they were not told either – but I really think we have the power to support the next generation. I believe our own journey of understanding our bodies can have such a positive impact on our children.

How can we help children to have a positive introduction to their pelvic health?

Kids love to understand their bodies, they are naturally inquisitive, especially when it comes to their genitals, and as parents we can support them in this understanding. Don't be afraid to use the real names for their anatomy. I know saying 'that's your vulva' or 'that's your penis' doesn't flow as easily or feel as comfortable to say as 'that's your arm', and won't be part of the classic 'Head, Shoulders, Knees and Toes' song anytime soon, but that doesn't mean we should shy away from their use. Kids will also often ask where poo comes from or what wee is, so having the knowledge ourselves and being ready for these sorts of questions is key.

When it comes to potty training, thinking about the environment and what they are going to sit on is foundational to their comfort. Let's be honest, toilets are not very kid friendly: the hole is too big and they are high up off the ground, so kids end up having to hold themselves on the toilet using their arms with their feet dangling down. Put yourself in their shoes. Imagine sitting on a well that you could fall down, holding on tightly with your arms with your legs dangling, and then try to relax your tummy and pelvic floor. Pretty impossible, right? Well, that is exactly what it is like for kids trying to use adult western toilets. So, for us to help them relax their pelvic floor to let a poo and wee out, as we explored in Chapter 1, they need to feel supported and positioned where their body can relax. This is why using a potty on the floor is often a popular choice (although I would check the height of some of them, as a lot are like a chair and don't allow children to be in that natural squatting position). The other popular choice is adding a child's seat and some steps to the toilet that they can use to climb up and also place their feet on. Whatever is used, the key is your child is comfortable, supported and able to relax their body and pelvic floor.

Children, like adults, need water and fibre to help them to poo and the Bristol Stool chart (see page 22) applies to them as well; we want that soft type 4 poo. It can be such a battle getting fruit and vegetables into children at times – trust me, I've been there. What I have found helpful as my children are growing up is talking about all the reasons they are good for our bodies, including, that's right, how they help our poo to be soft and easy to get out. Not always dinner-table conversation I admit, but having these conversations with our children deepens their understanding and knowledge.

When it comes to their bladder control and learning where to do a wee, we don't want to be repeatedly taking them to the bathroom 'just in case' because we want them to learn what it feels like to get the urge to wee. If we recap page 15, where we learnt about how we know when to wee, we know that the bladder stretching sends the message to the brain to make us aware of the urine present. Therefore, we want our children's bladders to fill and stretch, so the signals go to the brain, raising awareness of the bladder-filling feeling and allowing our children to learn how to control this sensation. It is that learnt control of the pelvic floor and external urethral sphincter that keeps them continent.

It is a fine line trying to find the right amount of prompting and encouragement to use the potty that a child needs, without over-prompting or taking them 'just in case'. As parents we want to prevent accidents and the clean-up that comes with them, but we need to let our kids get in tune with their body's natural communication. The way I like to view it is, short-term mess for long-term pelvic health gain! I do think there are certain situations where it is very understandable to encourage our children to go for a wee, like before a 3-hour car journey, but I do suggest trying not to encourage them to do this on a daily basis. Many of you may remember being encouraged to go to the toilet before every time you left the house. I know lots of women tell me this in clinic. We often learn patterns from our parents, so if they always went before going out, so will we.

Issues with our bladder and bowels can be highly emotive and hold a lot of embarrassment and shame, which I am sure lots of you may identify with. I meet women in clinic who can still remember being told off when they had an accident as a child, so it can stick with us. Now, before any of you panic, do not beat yourself up if you've ever got angry with your child about having an accident; it is very natural and probably how you were responded to as a child. We are not going to be perfect – that I learnt pretty quickly on my parenting journey. This is just about trying to think about how we can reduce embarrassment, fear and shame for our kids around their toileting. Toilets can feel scary, whether that be the sound of the flush, or the size, feeling like you are going to fall down the hole, or just a new experience. Providing as much reassurance and validation of our kids' emotions as we can in those moments is a powerful support for them.

What might children start to struggle with?

Challenges around going to the toilet can start at any point in childhood. Sometimes they start at potty training, sometimes they start later on. My focus is going to be on behaviours and symptoms that have a common knock-on effect on the pelvic floor going forwards, so this is not an exhaustive explanation of all possible symptoms or reasons that children may struggle.

Constipation is very common in children and can affect one in three,[1] including babies. It can happen for a variety of reasons, including lack of fluid or fibre in their diet, being unwell and getting dehydrated, or the child withholding and not wanting to do a poo. When poo remains in the bowel it becomes bigger as more food is digested and moves through the intestines, and harder as more water is reabsorbed. This then has a knock-on effect of making it harder to pass, which can be painful and lead to further withholding. A child may hold in a poo for a variety of reasons, including if they have had a previous painful experience of doing a poo and want to prevent this happening again. To protect themselves from pain they hold in the poo and decide not to go. When potty training a child may withhold from doing a poo as they are afraid of doing it on the toilet, or feel like they don't have enough privacy. It is quite a shift from doing a poo in a nappy wherever you want, to being stuck in one place on a potty or toilet. The most important thing is to keep poo moving out of the bowel, the same for us adults, and so for some children, when potty training, this means they may only poo in a nappy, for example, when it is put on at night. And though we don't want this in the long term, it is an important short-term solution to prevent further withholding. It is natural if a child is struggling to open their bowels that they start to strain to pass a stool, and this habit when learnt young can be something that continues through life. As mentioned in Chapter 1, straining can impact and weaken the pelvic floor, so this can, for some, play into their pelvic health journey.

Constipation has a knock-on effect on bladder control, because an enlarged bowel with lots of poo in it puts a lot of pressure on the bladder, which can lead to symptoms in children and adults that we will explore a little later on. As mentioned, constipation and habits around opening our bowels can start really young and can continue into adulthood, with studies suggesting 25–30 per cent of children with constipation had symptoms past puberty into adulthood.[2,3] This doesn't mean that it is ever too late to get help, because I believe it is never too late. This is also not to say that everyone who struggles with constipation as a child will have longer-term struggles with their pelvic floor; however, it can be one part of the picture.

Bedwetting can be another common symptom that children struggle with and that can continue into the teenage years. The emotional impact of this can be huge for a child, while also being very challenging for parents as well. You might have experienced this and remember not wanting to go to a sleepover with friends for fear of wetting the bed. Learning to control our bladder during the day is different to night-time, and they often do not occur together. Children will often gain continence during the day, on average around 10 months before gaining continence at night.[4] For this reason children will often still need to wear nappies at night-time even when they are not needed during the day. This time lag between gaining continence during daytime and night is due to a few factors, including secretion of antidiuretic hormone (ADH), which causes reabsorption of water and therefore decreases urine production, and increased bladder capacity. Most children are dry at night by 5 years of age, but for others bedwetting may be an ongoing problem for them. Like many symptoms, it is not always fully understood; however, potential contributors include overactivity of the bladder muscle, lower levels of ADH, and constipation.[5] As mentioned previously, when there is poo sitting in the bowel, this puts pressure on the bladder meaning it cannot fill as much, and it also means the child, or adult, may feel they need to pass urine more frequently. Therefore, bedwetting and constipation can come hand in hand.[6]

Starting school is a huge shift for any child, and this transition and change to routine can also influence their bladder and bowel habits. Moving from the freedom of being at home or nursery, and going as needed, to a more structured setting where you need to ask to go and leave the class environment to find the toilet. It is not uncommon for children to be encouraged to wait to use the

---

TOP TIPS FOR HELPING YOUR KIDS WITH THEIR PELVIC HEALTH

- Help them to understand their bodies, let them be curious.
- Don't be afraid to use the real names for their genitals.
- Help them to trust their bodies.
- Think about their position on the toilet or potty.
- Ensure they feel safe and relaxed.
- Remove shame and fear.
- Reassure them it is OK to have accidents.
- Open conversations about how our bodies work.
- Control our own emotions.

---

toilet until break-time, which often encourages them to ignore their own bodies' communication as well as potentially getting into holding patterns that were not there before. I get it, teachers can't have children constantly popping off to the toilet, but I often wonder whether for some children this impacts their normal rhythm and pelvic health.

THE TEENAGE YEARS

The teenage years are a time in life that I am sure we all look back on with different feelings and emotions. It is often a time of great exploration, pushing boundaries and finding our place in the world. It is also a time when we become more self-conscious and aware of our changing body during puberty. For those where bedwetting is an ongoing problem this can really impact self-esteem and lead to anxiety and stress around bladder and bowel habits. It is often a time in life when we go from freely passing wind as a child, to holding on for dear life in order not to pass wind in front of friends and risk getting teased. I don't know about you, but I clearly remember being self-conscious of using the toilet at school if there was anyone else in there. The thought of someone hearing you do a wee or poo just felt so embarrassing. Holding in wind and poo, contracting our pelvic floor in order to do this, can lead to us getting into holding patterns. This can lead to constipation and further bowel struggles, as well as developing increased tone in the pelvic floor as we explored in Chapter 2. Understanding whether we used to do this, or still do this, can help our understanding of our overall pelvic health. If you identify with this, why not try the tips on page 46 to work on fully letting the pelvic floor relax.

Teenage girls can experience urinary incontinence, especially stress urinary incontinence (head to page 201 for definition), while playing sport. For example, during activities such as gymnastics, dance, trampolining or other high impact sports. You might remember this yourself and some of the embarrassment that came with it. Supporting younger girls to take care of their pelvic health and not just put up with these symptoms should be a priority for us all. Another symptom some of you might have experienced is giggle incontinence; though rare it can have a big impact on a girl's confidence. Having the time of your life with friends, laughing your head off but also leaking urine; I think all of us have probably experienced this at some point as a one off, but for some girls this is a frequent symptom. Can you imagine being afraid to laugh in case you wet yourself? Many suffer in silence due to embarrassment, but there is treatment. It will vary depending on the child or adolescent, but may include addressing bladder and bowel habits, pelvic floor muscle rehabilitation (including biofeedback) and medication.[7]

Our periods starting is another momentous occasion. Though the average age is 12, before those teenage years officially begin, we spend our teenage years getting used to how to manage our periods and what works for us. There are so many period product options these days, with lots of women wanting to move away from the use of plastic. Now we can use Mooncups, period pants, organic tampons and reusable pads, but when I was a teenager it was pretty simple – pad or tampon. Starting to use tampons can be a daunting thing; probably the most common issue is not being sure where to aim it, especially if you are not even sure about your anatomy and where it should even go. I mean, how many teenagers are grabbing a mirror and having a look at their vulva? I'd say not many in my day. Awareness has increased, which is brilliant, and we can all be part of that. For some of us, we may remember tampons causing us pain when we started to use them; for some this may have improved over time, while for others this may have continued, leading you to not using them anymore. I meet women in clinic where this has become an ongoing decision as they always have pain with their use. If that is you, why not head back to Chapter 2 and start practising that diaphragmatic breathing (see page 42). Sometimes using this breathing while trying to insert a tampon or Mooncup can really help the pelvic floor relax and reduce pain.

For some the later teenage years might be when they become sexually active and although often we are educated around how not to get pregnant, which, don't get me wrong, is very helpful, I don't feel teenage girls really get taught about their bodies, anatomy and role of the pelvic floor as part of their sexual well-being. We will explore this more in Chapter 11, but I want to acknowledge at this stage that everyone's journey to becoming sexually active – their views, religious background and parental influence – is different. I fully respect everyone's background, journey, sexuality and views. My mission and passion are to ensure that whatever decision women make, they are empowered to understand their body so they can enjoy sex, and not live with any pain or embarrassment associated with it.

Our early experiences of sex, whenever this might be, can be hugely influential in many ways. However, before we discuss this any further, we need to establish what we are talking about when we use the word 'sex'. So often when we use the word sex, we mean penetrative sex. However, sex is actually 'any physical or psychological act that uses your body or mind for sexual pleasure or expression', as defined by Dr Karen Gurney in her wonderful book *Mind the Gap: The Truth About Desire and How to Futureproof Your Sex Life*. 'Sex' does not equal intercourse. Intercourse involves vaginal penetration. Therefore, my focus in this book is predominantly going to be on intercourse as this is what most women report pain with when they seek support from a pelvic health physiotherapist. I will also explore other conditions in Chapter 5 where pain is not only experienced during penetration.

Many women report the first time they experience intercourse as being uncomfortable, but this doesn't continue and they go on to have a very positive sex life. However, for some, their first experiences of intercourse were painful, very hard to tolerate and maybe impossible to continue. Naturally when we have a painful experience, we don't want to repeat it and our body wants to protect us from it. The pelvic floor muscles can get very protective, and contract, aiming to prevent penetration. This is called vaginismus. This contraction can then lead to more pain, and the cycle continues. Over time we can get into patterns of anticipating pain and contracting our pelvic floor subconsciously in order to protect ourselves. This can be another reason women get into holding patterns in their pelvic floor from a younger age, and it might be something that feels relevant for you as you read this. There are many factors that can influence the development of vaginismus, but the wonderful news is that it is treatable, and I will share more about this in Chapters 5 and 11. I want to be crystal clear at this stage though: sex and intercourse should not be painful. You don't have to put up with it or accept it as normal. Please seek help, and let's support younger generations to do the same.

* * *

As you can see from this chapter alone, there are many factors at play through our childhood and teenage years that can influence our pelvic health and pelvic floor muscles. I encourage you to take a moment to reflect and jot down anything that has popped into your mind about your own experience in the Foundation Reflections section on page 69.

MYTH BUSTING

'Potty training needs to happen in 3 days'

Absolutely not! It can take time over weeks and months, as a gradual process. Yes, when we finally remove the nappy and a child lives without one this can lead to a few days when we want to be at home and we can expect some accidents. However, we can introduce our children very gradually to gaining continence over time.

'If a child continues to struggle with bedwetting it is all about the bladder'

It is natural to think that any leakage a child or adult has is just about their bladder, but as we have explored, the bowels have a huge influence on bladder symptoms. So, treating constipation and supporting our children to have regular bowel motions is essential in improving bladder symptoms.

Foundation Reflections

Take a moment to reflect on what you have read. Jot down anything that has stood out to you about your own journey, as well as anything you want to chat to your kids about.

....

....

....

....

....

....

....

....

....

....

CHAPTER 4

A Defining Season

Let's learn about:
- Different contributing factors that can influence our pelvic health throughout life
- More about the role our bowels play
- Our inbuilt bodyguard (AKA the pelvic floor) a bit more
- Smear tests and the struggles some of us have
- More about our bladders, including urinary tract infections, overactive bladder and bladder pain syndrome

---

As we move forwards together, we enter our twenties, another hugely influential time in our lives. For many, this decade often holds a lot of change: starting careers, developing careers, leaving university, falling pregnant, having children, travelling the world, settling down or spreading your wings. Whether you are in this season or are looking back, I am sure we all feel differently about this time. Personally, I look back with mainly fond memories and, at times, I felt pretty invincible – the joy of youth. It was an exciting time when I really worked out what I wanted to do within the world of physiotherapy, fell in love with pelvic health, travelled the world, re-met my now husband (that's a long story but we first met when we were teenagers), got married, fell pregnant and had my first child. This decade was also hugely defining for my own pelvic health. Let me tell you a story.

At the age of 24 I noticed that my periods were not regular anymore. I'd never been one to track them, but I realised there were months when I had no period at all. This led to a visit to the GP, where the doctor recommended some blood tests, but also suggested I could be in premature menopause. I was devastated, as I am sure you can imagine. I was single at the time and longed to have children, so this potential diagnosis felt life shattering. After more tests and investigations by the amazing team I worked with in the NHS, I was diagnosed with hypothalamic amenorrhea, which is where women stop having periods due to stress, poor diet or too much exercise. I probably fell into all these categories. There had been a number of quite big life changes, I was exercising a lot, including training for a half marathon, because I loved it, and though I definitely didn't not eat, I wouldn't say I was great at having a balanced diet. I also had a lifestyle where there was little rest, and this is something I have had to work hard at. (I am still not great at resting, but I really want to teach my kids the power of resting and the act of self-love and self-respect that it is.)

As my oestrogen levels were undetectable on blood tests, I needed to have my hormones replaced. I tried various means, different contraceptive pills, as well as hormone replacement therapy (HRT) that is given to women who are perimenopausal and postmenopausal. To say it was a rollercoaster is an understatement and it has given me such empathy and a slight insight into what women feel during menopause. This went on for 3 years, going on and off medication to see if my body would kick back in. Just before I got married at 27, I decided to take another break from the medication, and though my oestrogen levels were still saying 'undetectable' on blood tests I just felt I needed my body to have a break. Little did I know that in a month my body was going to give me the surprise of my life. I fell pregnant and honestly couldn't believe my eyes when I turned over that pregnancy test. Since having my gorgeous daughter my periods are back to normal and I will never take them for granted again.

So, why is any of this relevant to my pelvic health or to anyone else in a similar position? Changes in hormones can have a variety of influences on the body, some of which we will explore in more detail in Chapter 12. Hormonal changes can have an influence on the bowel, contributing to symptoms such as constipation. I definitely noticed increased constipation during this time and struggled to open my bowels, getting into habits of straining – which I always teach women not to do, but at times I felt like I had no option. I don't think this was only down to hormones but also an influence of stress as well. If I knew then what I know now, I would have gone about things very differently. But unfortunately we can't go back in time. As I shared earlier on in the book, after the birth of my first child, I was diagnosed with a prolapse. Though I can see how parts of the birth process contributed to me having a prolapse, I also look back and identify this time in my life as being a potential contributor as well.

I share this story because I know so many of us face struggles with our pelvic health postpartum, but often don't recognise that the period of our life before can have a huge influence on our bodies and how they are in the future. Pelvic floor dysfunction symptoms are not exclusive to postpartum women, and therefore we cannot treat birth as the only driver for these symptoms. I want to acknowledge that some of us might have had babies as teenagers, during our twenties, thirties or forties, and some of us don't have children at all. For those of you that have had children, then you can just treat this section as your life BC (as my parents would say) – aka Before Children! I want to explore some of the symptoms we might experience and patterns we might have got into. They won't all be or feel relevant to you, or be exclusive to life before pregnancy, but let's take a deeper look at some of the factors at play.

YOUR BOWELS

You're probably starting to see a theme here, and noticing I chat a lot about bowels. Constipation is incredibly common, and more common in women than men,[1] but really not easy to talk about, right? Back in Chapter 1 we discussed how our bowels are meant to work, and how it is normal to go anywhere between three times a day and three times a week. So if we are going less than this, and persistently struggle to open our bowels with hard stools as well, then this would be classified as constipation.

There are a variety of factors that can contribute to constipation, two key ones are: slow or delayed transit of the poo moving along the bowel, or our pelvic floor muscles struggling to relax or coordinate what they need to do to let the poo out. If we are finding it difficult to empty our bowels we can often find ourselves straining to help force the poo out. Now, every so often this isn't a big issue, but repeatedly straining can weaken our pelvic floor muscles and connective tissues, increasing our risk of pelvic floor dysfunction, including pelvic organ prolapse.

Other factors that may play a part include:

1. **Diet:** as we discussed in Chapter 1, what we eat and drink hugely impacts our bowel function and the poo that we produce. Not eating enough fibre or drinking enough fluid can lead to constipation.
2. **Reduced movement:** our bowels, like the rest of our bodies, love us to move. Physical activity increases

peristalsis, so when we move less this can cause us to have a more sluggish bowel and be a contributing factor to constipation.

3. **Stress:** this can be a huge driver of bowel symptoms. When we are stressed, hormones are released which influence many organs, including the bowels. They deregulate how the bowel functions, and this can contribute to symptoms such a bloating and constipation.[2]

4. **Lifestyle factors:** this might include struggling to find time to open your bowels as you rush to get out to work or do the school run, never finding time to be alone and have some peace and quiet, or the fear of being heard or someone knowing you are doing a poo. These can all lead to us withholding and the poo getting bigger and harder, which can lead to constipation.

IRRITABLE BOWEL SYNDROME

Irritable bowel syndrome (IBS) is a common condition, impacting around 10 per cent of the world's population. It is most commonly associated with symptoms of abdominal pain, bloating, diarrhoea, constipation, wind, or a combination of these. IBS is diagnosed when there is recurrent abdominal pain on average at least 1 day a week over the previous 3 months with two or more of the following symptoms: pain with defecation, changes in frequency of doing a poo, or change in the appearance of the poo.[3] There are four subtypes: IBS constipation (IBS-C), where abnormal bowel movements are usually constipation; IBS diarrhoea (IBS-D), where abnormal bowel movements are usually diarrhoea; IBS mixed bowel habits (IBS-M), where abnormal bowel movements are a mixture of constipation and diarrhoea; and IBS unclassified (IBS-U), where someone does not meet the criteria for the other three subtypes. IBS is more common in women than men, especially when it relates to constipation.[4]

There can be a variety of factors that can contribute to IBS symptoms, but it is understood to be a disorder of the gut–brain axis, which we discussed on page 18. I am sure many of you might have been given a diagnosis of IBS at some point, or can identify with the term in some way.

If you have been diagnosed and do struggle with constipation, like so many other women, you're not alone. Seeking support and personalised guidance is key, as there are so many contributing factors. Pelvic floor physiotherapists are well placed to support you and help to ensure your pelvic floor function is optimised so you can poo happily. I asked my colleague and friend Lucy Allen, a clinical specialist physiotherapist, to share some top tips to help with constipation:

- **Have a look a your diet:** Focus on fibre, and when life gets busy try to add a heaped dessertspoon of flaxseed on your breakfast cereal, in a yoghurt or smoothie. If you're on the go I recommend Ortis cubes, which are chewable fibre supplements.
- **Poo position:** The most important thing is that you relax and rest forward on your forearms, don't hold your breath and if you need to give a little push to start the motion make sure you think of directing that into your bottom, not your vagina.
- **Speak to a medical professional:** If you're getting the urge to poo less than three times a week, or have lost that urge

sensation, speak to a medical professional. There are other reasons aside from your typical constipation that can cause this so the sooner it's checked the quicker we can get you pooing better.

- **Reduce stress:** As stress can influence our bowels and how they function, reducing stress can help improve symptoms of constipation and IBS. This is often easier said than done and won't look the same for everyone. Considering our work–life balance, doing hobbies that help you to de-stress, using breath work, meditation or yoga can all help too.
- **Think about your activity levels:** Being more active and exercising not only helps peristalsis and moving poo along the bowel but has been shown to have a positive influence on emotional wellbeing as well.

* * *

Our bodies and bowels need to feel relaxed and safe to poo, they often don't love change of routine or location. Ever noticed when you go on holiday that you struggle to go for a few days? Well imagine travelling the world and staying in lots of different places, which I did for a month in my early twenties. My bowels didn't know whether they were coming or going! My point is that sometimes our lifestyle in our younger days – working hard, partying hard, staying at friends' houses, eating at weird times, drinking alcohol, travelling, and generally leading busy, high-stress lives – is not the most bowel friendly. Saying that, even as parents we are often still working hard, partying hard (at night in a different way), busy attending kids' events and functions, forgetting to eat, living on snacks for energy and not getting enough sleep, which is also not the most bowel-friendly lifestyle. However, being aware of potential contributing factors that can influence our bowel habits, seeking support if these habits change, keeping an eye for any blood in our poo, and not straining on the toilet should be our absolute bowel-loving priorities.

STRESS

Stress is a funny thing. We wouldn't always say we feel stressed, but our bodies can definitely show signs of it, especially if our stress levels are higher for long periods of time. Stress will mean and feel different for all of us, and different seasons will bring different challenges and stresses. I know for me and lots of my friends in our twenties, we were forging career paths, working long hours, socialising lots, in new relationships, dealing with break-ups and everything else that comes with being young. Though for most this is a lot of fun, at times it can bring with it a high level of stress. I wanted to touch here on how stress can impact our pelvic floor muscles and how over time high levels of stress may influence their function. As with all things, this is not one-dimensional, and I am not saying that stress is the main cause of pelvic floor dysfunction, but it can be a significant part of the puzzle. In certain situations, stress can be helpful, life-saving in fact; however, it can also have some detrimental effects.

I like to think of our pelvic floor as a bit like a bodyguard, there to protect us, and it has been shown to have this response. One particularly interesting study looked at women's pelvic floor activity when they were shown different film clips. During threatening film clips there was a significant increase in involuntary pelvic floor activity, meaning there was contraction of the pelvic floor muscles automatically as a response to what the women were seeing.[5] This shows that our pelvic floor is responding to our everyday life without us consciously telling it to contract. Therefore, if our body feels under threat quite a lot, through day-to-day stresses (this doesn't always need to be significant danger), we can conclude that our pelvic floor is feeling the need to be on high alert a lot as well. We often associate muscle tension in our neck and jaw with stress, but I'm guessing most of us never thought about the pelvic floor–stress connection.

(BTW, jaw tension is another fascinating element to explore and its possible connection to the pelvic floor. We do often find they can present together, though the exact reason isn't clear. Working on consciously relaxing your jaw, releasing muscles around the jaw and addressing this in light of stress in your life may also help your pelvic floor. It isn't a miracle cure, more just becoming aware of other parts of our life and body that can play into what is happening at our pelvic floor.)

YOUR TUMMY

Do you ever notice that you hold your tummy in? The pressure on women to look slim is still very present in society, and though I am delighted to see this being challenged I still feel the pressure, through social media and societal norms, is quite significant. Look at the constant conversation about celebrities and if they have 'bounced back' or not after having a baby. However body-confident we feel, it is hard to ignore these conversations and subliminal messages that are everywhere. This can lead women to repeatedly hold in their tummy muscles, to make themselves look or feel slimmer. This pressure isn't just present for younger women, but throughout life.

If we think back to Chapter 1 where we discussed all the inner core muscles, they all need to be able to move freely to do their jobs and manage intra-abdominal pressure. Therefore, repeatedly holding in any of the core muscles can have an impact on other members of the team. This is why in clinic I often find women who are holding in their tummy muscles are also gripping through their pelvic floor muscles, which can lead to increased tone in the muscles and, over time, be a contributing factor to other symptoms. They may also be struggling to manage their intra-abdominal pressure, which can contribute to incontinence and prolapse symptoms. Increasing our body awareness can be a helpful part of treatment.

Body scanning – try this with me

It can be fascinating to do some body scanning, drawing attention to different parts of your body and where you are holding tension. You can do this in any position, but you may find it easiest or most relaxing lying down.

- Draw your attention to your jaw. Are you clenching your jaw or grinding your teeth?
- Draw your attention to your shoulders. Are they drawn up towards your ears? Can you relax them down again?
- Draw your attention to your breathing. Are you breathing into your upper chest? Are you breathing quickly? Can you slow your breath down? Can you try to widen your lower ribcage and try diaphragmatic breathing?
- Draw your attention to your tummy muscles. Are you holding your tummy in? Can you give your body permission to let go?
- Draw your attention to your pelvic floor. Are you squeezing your pelvic floor when at rest? Can you let the muscles relax and the pelvic floor drop?

You might be surprised about what you found doing this little exercise. If you start to notice you are holding quite a lot of tension throughout your body, try doing this regularly and help your body to re-learn to relax, and drop some of the habits we develop over our lives.

LET'S TALK ABOUT SEX... AGAIN!

As we discussed in the previous chapter, we all start to have sex at different ages. For those who had different partners through your twenties, you may have had different experiences with intercourse. There may have been times when you experienced pain: did this change your ongoing experience? Or was this short-lived? I appreciate you may not want to think about the past too much, but I'd like to just encourage you to think about how your body felt. Do you remember any themes of discomfort or any problems you experienced? If anything comes to mind, jot it down in the Foundation Reflections section on page 86.

We can't talk about sex and fail to talk about smear tests. Oh, the smear test! So vital, and yet another one of those things as a woman that can lead us to thinking 'do I have to?' All women in the UK aged 25 to 64 are invited for a smear test where they are checked for types of human papillomavirus (HPV). HPV is transmitted through sexual contact and certain types can lead to changes in the cells of the cervix, which could develop into cervical cancer. In theory it is a quick check, usually done at your doctor's surgery, and you can be in and out in a few minutes, but it isn't that simple for everyone. When we have our first smear tests it is often the first time that we have experienced the use of a speculum, which is needed to open the vagina and support the vaginal walls so that the cervix can be reached. I am yet to find a woman who finds the experience comfortable. I would say most of us find it uncomfortable, but tolerable. However, what about if you find it incredibly painful?

Painful smear tests can be the cause of a woman starting to experience increased pelvic floor tone as a natural protective response to the experience. The pelvic floor stepping up to be our bodyguard again, experienced as vaginismus. A smear test can also be a huge source of anxiety if you already struggle with vaginismus. Whatever your age, I want to give you some top tips if you struggle with smear tests and I asked Dr Stephanie Ooi, whom I have the joy of working with, to share some tips from a GP perspective as well:

TOP TIPS FOR HELPING REDUCE DISCOMFORT DURING A SMEAR TEST

- Take someone with you that you trust and can support you if you are feeling anxious or worried.
- Tell your nurse or doctor about how you are feeling.
- Ask if it is possible to use a smaller speculum.
- Before your appointment practise diaphragmatic breathing with pelvic floor relaxation visualisations, for example the vagina opening like a flower (see page 42-3).
- During the appointment use this breathing to help relax the pelvic floor.
- Ask if you can insert the speculum yourself.
- Try not to anticipate pain, if at all possible, although this is hard if you have had a painful experience before.

YOUR BLADDER

Though our bladder habits start as children, they continue to change throughout our lives. One of the common habits we can easily fall into is hovering over the toilet, when we are out and about. Now I get why we do this, and I've definitely done it, but let's for a moment consider why this might not be best for our beloved pelvic floor. When we hover over the toilet it is more challenging for our pelvic floor muscles to fully relax, and allow our bladder and bowels to empty completely. It is often quite hard to sustain the position and it can lead to us rushing and straining to pass urine. Now I am not asking you to sit down on visibly dirty toilet seats, but be aware how frequently you are doing this. Is it each time you do a wee at the office, or anytime you are in a public place? When you start to add it up, you may start to realise that you hover for more wees than you don't.

Urinary tract infections (UTIs) are something that most of us have probably experienced at some point in our lives, and I'm sure we all remember the symptoms well. Pain or burning when you wee, needing to go more frequently or urgently, noticing the urine is cloudy, has blood in it or has a strong smell. Women are more likely to get UTIs (oh goodie!) as we have a shorter urethra, so it is easier for bacteria to track up to the bladder. A couple of simple things we can do to try and prevent UTIs that I still find women are not told about are: wiping from front to back after going to the toilet and going for a wee after having sex. During sex bacteria from around the anus can move up towards the urethra – remember, everything is very close together. Going for a wee after sex is thought to flush out the bacteria before it travels up to the bladder.[6] I know this can feel really annoying if you are all snuggled up and warm, but it can make a big difference for your bladder. Some women experience recurrent UTIs, which are defined as two or more UTIs in the last 6 months, or three or more in the last 12 months.[7] This can impact our quality of life and be stressful, with ongoing pain and symptoms. Clinically we can find that women who experience recurrent UTIs have pelvic floor muscles that are in protect mode, more 'switched on', with increased tone.

You may have noticed that you go to the toilet more frequently than your friends. Maybe you've always been like that since you can remember, and have been labelled as the one in the family with a 'weak bladder', but does this bother you? Does the number of times you are going for a wee during the day or night, or how urgently you need to go, bother you? You're not alone if it does. There can be several different reasons for these symptoms and there is help. Some women are diagnosed with an overactive bladder (OAB), which is where women have symptoms of needing a wee very urgently. This urgency may also be associated with leaking, and they may also feel they go frequently during the day as well as at night.[8] Speaking to a doctor or seeing a pelvic health physiotherapist can help you to understand why you have these bothersome symptoms, as there can be a variety of different reasons. They can help to make a plan for the right treatment for you. Treatment may include bladder training, pelvic floor rehabilitation, medication and lifestyle changes, which we will explore more in Chapter 10. Equally, sometimes we need to step away from the pelvic floor and look at other muscles around the hip and pelvis as well.[9] As I say, treatment is not one-dimensional and we need to look from all angles to ensure that women get better. I want you to know that even if you have lived with these symptoms for years, it is not too late to get help.

The reason assessment is so important is that there are a variety of conditions that can present with similar symptoms. We need to work out the correct diagnosis to ensure best treatment. Another condition I want you to be aware of is Bladder Pain Syndrome (BPS), which is persistent or recurrent pelvic pain, pressure, or discomfort in the bladder region, alongside at least one other urinary symptom, such as urgency or frequency to pass urine, however, there is no urine infection present. It used to be called interstitial cystitis, but this term is no longer used. BPS symptoms can be really debilitating and, again, I want you to know that pelvic health physiotherapists are primed and ready to support you if you are struggling now or at any point in the future. There is help.

If you are anything like me, you may have started your adult life feeling pretty invincible, but slowly realised that our bodies are far from that and need some TLC and understanding. If this chapter has caused you to look back with frustration, or has brought up any self-blame that you should have 'done things differently', please know that not knowing about your pelvic health at this stage was *not* your fault. I knew a lot of things about pelvic health and still struggled to take care of mine, so we are all in this together. Take a moment to reflect, jot down any thoughts or feelings in the Foundation Reflections section on page 86, and definitely talk to someone about how you feel. I am aware that sometimes thinking back on past relationships can be hard. Sometimes we become aware that we didn't always feel safe or fully consenting during a sexual interaction with someone. It is not too late to talk or explore this with someone, and I encourage you to seek support if you feel you can. Speak to your doctor or a trusted friend, and consider some talking therapy to create a safe space to explore these thoughts, feelings and emotions.

MYTH BUSTING

'If you go for a wee more frequently than your friends, that is just who you are'
Thankfully you don't have to accept this as normal if it is bothersome for you. We can all get into patterns of going more, at different times of our lives, but this doesn't have to be lifelong. You need to think about your bowels, bladder habits and what is going into your bladder, which we will explore more in Chapter 10. A pelvic health physiotherapist can help you with pelvic floor awareness, understanding your bladder, and with bladder training if you want to bring about some changes.

'If you find smears painful there is nothing that you can do'
FALSE! For too long women have grinned and borne the pain of a smear test or avoided them due to the pain they have experienced before. We need to open up the conversation about this and support women more. Yes, they are not comfortable and none of us like going for them, but if you are actively avoiding them or too scared of the pain you might experience then please, please, please reach out for some support. Remind yourself of the top tips on page 81.

Foundation Reflections

Jot down any thoughts, feelings or reflections from this chapter. We've covered a lot, so maybe make a note of three main things you want to think about further, or tips you want to try.

....

....

....

....

....

....

....

....

....

....

CHAPTER 5

Some Key Pelvic Health Players

Let's learn about:
- Some very important conditions, including:
  - Vaginismus
  - Vulvodynia
  - Vulval skin conditions
  - Endometriosis
  - Adenomyosis
  - Chronic pelvic pain

There are so many things that I wish women were told earlier in life. I don't think we need great details of absolutely everything, but we need some awareness of the important things at the very least. As we've discussed, knowing our anatomy is definitely the first step, but then I believe understanding some of the conditions that we might experience is also vital. Being able to advocate for yourself when it comes to your health is important. I truly believe you know your body best and are the best detective to help us, as healthcare professionals, work out what is going on. You can't go far without meeting a woman who has felt not listened to, been told her symptoms are 'normal' or explained away by reasons such as 'age', or that they are in some way her fault, and who has lived with pain and discomfort for years. You might be one of them, and if you have ever felt dismissed I am so sorry. Your symptoms and feelings are valid, and sadly sometimes as healthcare professionals we fail women and don't listen well. I really want to educate and empower you, so you can go forward, armed with the information you need to advocate for yourself, if you ever need to. So, without further ado let's take a look at some important, but less well-known players.

VAGINISMUS

Vaginismus occurs when we try to insert something into the vagina, but the pelvic floor muscles tighten up involuntarily. This can be as a result of pain but can also lead to pain or a feeling like there just isn't space in the vagina. Let's explore this a bit more.

Vaginismus can develop at any point in life. For some it might occur on their first experience of penetration if they were worried, fearful, or felt maybe they were doing something wrong. For others it may occur after this, if they have had a number of experiences of painful intercourse, a traumatic sexual experience, a painful smear test experience, or after birth due to scar tissue or vaginal dryness. It is possible to have had years of intercourse without any problems and then to develop vaginismus. There are so many reasons, but it is our inbuilt bodyguard trying to keep us safe and protect us. Over time the pelvic floor muscles may struggle to stand down from their protective role and to fully relax. This can then increase pain during penetration even further, which then can lead to more protection, and the cycle continues. Just to be clear, vaginismus is not the pain, but the muscular response and tightening. Pain that occurs during intercourse is medically called **dyspareunia**. Dyspareunia can be superficial (where it occurs during touch to the vulva or on initial penetration) or deep inside. Understanding where and when the pain occurs can help us to work out the cause.

Vaginismus can be really upsetting and cause issues in relationships. Thankfully there is help and it can improve, and pelvic health physiotherapists love to support anyone who is struggling. I am going to explore more about what treatment would involve and what you can do to help in Chapter 11, so head there now if you want to read more on this. So many women feel alone in their struggles, but I can reassure you, you most certainly are not, as I meet lots of women in clinic with the same experience. It can be a hard road, but reach out and ask for help – it can be life-changing.

VULVODYNIA

Vulvodynia is diagnosed when there is ongoing pain in the vulva for over 3 months without a clear identifiable cause, and is broken down into **unprovoked vulvodynia** and **provoked vulvodynia**. Pain can be quite widespread across the vulva or in a more specific area. Women report the pain as burning, itching, feeling raw, or stinging. Unprovoked vulvodynia is where these symptoms are present without touch or stimulus to the vulva. Provoked vulvodynia is where pain occurs in response to touch, either by a finger, tampon or during intercourse, and is also referred to as provoked vestibulodynia. It is thought to impact between 8 and 28 per cent of premenopausal women[1] but many don't get help or get diagnosed, and I have met a number of women with this story. Sadly, our understanding and knowledge of vulval pain is still behind where it should be, and women often see several professionals before getting the help that they need. All I can say is don't give up. If you have pain in your vulva and are struggling with day-to-day life, or with intercourse, keep seeking help. Ask to see another doctor and keep pushing for answers.

We are still learning about why some women develop vulvodynia, which is frustrating for those who experience it as we don't always have answers; however, a variety of contributing factors can often be identified. Like with vaginismus, often the pelvic floor muscles are on high alert and can feel tighter, partly due to the body trying to protect us from the pain.[2] However, this is not the only factor when it comes to the pelvic floor; the muscles can be weaker as well, so treatment is about finding a balance between improving tone, flexibility and strength. Thankfully there is help, and pelvic health physiotherapy treatment can really help women live with reduced pain and increased confidence. Treatment may include pelvic floor rehabilitation, use of vaginal dilators and education around pain so you understand what is happening in your body. We will explore these more in Chapter 11.

VULVAL SKIN CONDITIONS

Eczema and psoriasis

It is easy to view the skin of the vulva as different to other parts of our body, however, it is still skin that can be affected by common conditions that lots of us will be aware of. Two of these are eczema and psoriasis. Women often report symptoms of itching, soreness during intercourse or during wiping after the toilet, and may even notice splits in the skin. This is understandably very uncomfortable; however, such conditions can easily be misdiagnosed as thrush, which also causes itching. Therefore, if you have itching and soreness, this needs examination and possibly a swab to check for infection to confirm what the cause is. Don't just assume it is thrush if you have tried over-the-counter medicine and are still experiencing symptoms. A vulval itch that is ongoing is commonly related to a skin problem and there are dermatologists who specialise in vulval skin, if you need further support after seeing your doctor. Treatment will depend on diagnosis, but my experience of supporting women in clinic is that treating any underlying skin concerns is an essential first part of treatment to reduce pain and discomfort. Then we can help to rehabilitate the pelvic floor that may have responded to the ongoing pain that you have been experiencing, reassuring your natural bodyguard that it can relax and you are safe.

Lichens sclerosis

This is another skin condition that can impact the vulval skin, as well as other parts of the body. It is chronic inflammation that can lead to scarring. The most common symptoms women report are, once again, itching, soreness and pain during intercourse. The similarity of symptoms across a variety of problems is why certain skin conditions can be picked up quite late, as they can often be misdiagnosed as thrush. Women may also notice whitening of the skin of the vulva, reduced size of the labia, changes in texture of the skin and restriction of the clitoral hood. It can impact women of any age but is more common after 50. We don't know what causes it or why some women get it while others don't, but the evolving picture is that it is an autoimmune condition, with a contribution from genetics as well.[3] There isn't a cure for lichens sclerosis, but treatment can help reduce and manage symptoms. First-line medical management is the use of steroid creams, with a review to determine further support. Understandably, women with lichens sclerosis often develop vaginismus and so physiotherapy treatment can be a helpful adjunct to improve their quality of life.

Lichens planus

This is a skin condition that can affect the vulva as well as the vagina and the mouth. There is inflammation of the skin and mucous cells and often presents as red areas, with symptoms of burning, pain on urination, soreness, pain with intercourse and sometimes itching. It is more common in postmenopausal women and symptoms can often be misdiagnosed as just 'normal' for a postmenopausal woman. We should never be normalising vulval pain or discomfort: it needs investigation. The causes of lichens planus are not fully understood, but it is thought to be an autoimmune condition. Medical assessment and treatment are needed, with physiotherapy being a helpful adjunct once the skin is treated.

Vulval cancer

I wanted to talk about vulval cancer as, though a very rare form of cancer, as women we need to know what to look out for. Symptoms can include a persistent itch, pain, as well as small lumps, sore areas, a mole that changes shape or colour, or changes to the vulval skin, for example, becoming thickened and raised. These changes will appear on the vulva, so should be visible if you look with a mirror. A lot of the symptoms are similar to the other conditions we have discussed, therefore it can be really hard to know what you might be experiencing. All I can say is if you have any symptoms that align with any that we have discussed and don't improve with certain treatments you might have tried, please see your doctor. This is why we need to know our anatomy and should get to know our vulvas. If we don't know what is normal, how can we detect changes?

ENDOMETRIOSIS

This is a condition where tissue similar to the lining of the uterus (womb), called the endometrium, grows outside it. It can be on the uterus itself, or the ovaries and fallopian tubes. This tissue behaves the same as the endometrium during the menstrual cycle and thickens and then bleeds. Over time this can lead to scarring and adhesions forming. The bleeding that occurs, along with these adhesions, can lead to a variety of symptoms that women report. Commonly, women experience significant pain in their lower tummy or back, which is worse during their period, as well as having heavy periods. The levels of pain they experience are so high that it stops them going about their normal life, for example, needing to take days off work. Women can also experience pain at other times in their cycle, or during and after intercourse, which is often felt more deeply than in other conditions such as vulvodynia. Endometriosis can also affect a woman's fertility and many can struggle to fall pregnant. They may need surgery to remove endometriosis to support their fertility journey. Treatment for endometriosis varies depending on the individual and the severity of the disease, but may include pain medication, medication to reduce bleeding, hormonal treatment including the contraceptive pill or Mirena coil, or surgery as mentioned.

Endometriosis mainly impacts women during their reproductive years when they are having periods. Women often report delays in diagnosis – on average between 7 and 10 years[4] – or of not feeling listened to about the levels of their pain. If you are reading this and have any of these symptoms and are still struggling without support, please do go to your doctor for review and see if you can get any more answers. Pelvic health physiotherapists support women with endometriosis, and though we are not directly changing the cause we can really help you to manage your symptoms. Living with significant levels of pain for years can alter how we breathe, and how our tummy muscles and pelvic floor move and function. Experiencing pain with intercourse can also lead to increased pelvic floor tone and decreased confidence and libido. Through listening to your story and concerns, and helping you to understand your body and pain better, physiotherapists can really improve your quality of life. For women who have needed surgery to investigate or remove endometriosis, physiotherapists can also support with scar-release work and muscle retraining after surgery.

ADENOMYOSIS

This is an even lesser-known condition than endometriosis – many women have never heard of it. It is similar to endometriosis in that it involves the growth of tissue like the womb lining (endometrium) where we don't want it, but this time it is in the muscle layer of the womb. Similarly to endometriosis, during the menstrual cycle the tissue thickens and then bleeds, but the blood can't escape and this irritates the muscle, which makes periods really painful. Over time this process of bleeding and inflammation leads to scarring of the uterus, and this can make it more stiff and enlarged. This can also lead to heavier periods, as well as pain or discomfort at other times of the month apart from during the period. Women can also report bladder symptoms, such as needing a wee more frequently due to more pressure on the bladder from an enlarged uterus.

Adenomyosis is more common in those over 30 and those who have been pregnant, however, it can occur at any point in the reproductive years. It also seems to be more common in women who have fibroids, which are muscular growths in the wall of the uterus that can also cause heavy and painful periods. This shows again the importance of correct assessment to determine what is the cause for you as an individual. Medical management is key and may include, in a similar way to endometriosis, pain management, medication to reduce bleeding and hormonal treatment, including the Mirena coil.[5] This isn't a condition that pelvic health physiotherapists commonly see women with, however, as we discussed when talking about endometriosis, there can be lots of benefits from physiotherapy. I hope awareness increases and less women suffer in silence so we can help more women with these conditions improve their quality of life.

CHRONIC PELVIC PAIN

It is important to discuss chronic pelvic pain (CPP) as it impacts around one in six women[6] and can significantly affect a woman's quality of life. CPP is pain that is felt in the lower tummy or pelvic area for over 6 months. The reason women experience CPP is often multifactorial, with lots of contributing elements including physical and psychological factors. This is absolutely *not* saying that this is something that is in a woman's head. However, the brain is fundamental in our experience of pain, and mental health conditions, such as depression, are commonly experienced alongside CPP. Other conditions that could also contribute to the development of chronic pelvic pain are endometriosis, adenomyosis, bladder pain syndrome and IBS. As you can see from this list any of the pelvic organs can be involved, or be part of the initiation of symptoms, even if symptoms do change over time and become more widespread.

Physiotherapy often plays a vital role in helping those with chronic pain, and CPP is no different. Pelvic health physiotherapists are able to assess, treat and help women learn ways to manage their pain. Changes to the pelvic floor, more commonly increased tone that can feel like tightness, can contribute to symptoms, as well as being a consequence of living with CPP, as ongoing pain often results in changes to the pelvic floor and abdominal muscles. Therefore, helping women to learn how to connect with and relax their pelvic floor can improve pain and symptoms. However, it is just one part of the picture. The best outcomes come when a multidisciplinary approach is taken, which means when different professionals work together to support a woman, for example, physiotherapists and psychologists.[7] Physiotherapy support may include pelvic floor muscle rehabilitation, exercises focused on the mobility of the muscles around the pelvis and hips, and advice and education around pain. Though CPP can be really debilitating, there is help to support you, so if you are struggling and haven't managed to access support please do reach out. To get you started, if you are struggling with symptoms of CPP, why not head back to page 46 to try the breathing and exercises outlined there.

MYTH BUSTING

'It is normal to not be able to get out of bed due to period pain!'
*Absolutely not! If you are experiencing such high levels of pain
during your period that you cannot get out of bed to go to school,
university or work, then you need to speak to your doctor. We need to
understand why this is happening and support you so you can go
about your everyday life. We need to keep challenging the narrative
that this is just 'part of being a woman' and ensure we listen to
women and move towards a solution.*

'Sex is just painful for some women'
*Sex and intercourse should not be painful for anyone, whatever their
gender. I think it can sometimes still be normalised as just what
some women experience and it is their lot in life, but this is wrong. As
we have explored in this chapter, there are a number of reasons why
intercourse can be painful, so seeking assessment is the first step for
anyone struggling. Medical professionals talk about sex and these
conditions all the time, so, although I know it can feel really
embarrassing and hard to talk about, we are here and want to help.*

Foundation Reflections

As we draw this chapter to a close, take a moment to jot down any thoughts or reflections about any of the conditions we have discussed. If you feel that any of these conditions could be relevant for you, make a note and head to your doctor to get support.

....

....

....

....

....

....

....

....

....

PART III

Bump, Birth and Beyond

CHAPTER 6

Bump – An Introduction

Let's learn about:
- The changes that occur in our body during pregnancy
- Top tips to help navigate these changes
- Aches and pains of pregnancy, including:
  - Pelvic girdle pain
  - Back pain
  - Rib pain
  - Hand and wrist pain
- Top tips, movement and exercises that might help these aches and pains

I think we can all agree that the body is amazing – how it works to do so many important functions without us needing to tell it, *and* having the ability to do things we ask it to do. With the right training it can adapt to doing crazy challenges like climbing mountains, running through deserts, rowing over oceans and jumping over high poles just holding on to a stick – pole vaulting will never cease to amaze me. However, one task that many of us go through, and which demands a huge amount of the human body, is the ability to create and grow another little human during pregnancy. Having been pregnant twice, and now having two little people that grew in my body, still blows my mind.

Pregnancy is often a very powerful time in a woman's life when they gain a new-found respect and admiration for their body; I know I did. Now that doesn't mean we float around for months with total admiration without any struggles – I certainly have not met any pregnant women who feel like that. It is a time of great change for us physically, mentally and emotionally. Understanding these changes can really help at the time, but also afterwards when we are no longer pregnant. Sometimes, in order to make sense of our pelvic health, we need to understand what our body went through to bring context to where we are now. I think that pregnancy can often be portrayed as a season we all crack on with, without really understanding the fundamental changes. Therefore, I want to explore with you the changes our bodies go through and some of the not-so-positive symptoms we can experience, in order to help anyone struggling at the moment. Lots of changes occur to allow our babies to develop, as well as to prepare our bodies for labour and delivery, and it can feel like a hard road, one that seems to impact some of us more than others. I'm sure we will all know women who glow through their pregnancies, without any sickness, who seem to eat well and exercise throughout, and others who struggle to get out of bed for weeks, who can only eat anything beige and for whom the thought of going for a walk around the block feels like a marathon. We are all so different, so we just have to meet ourselves where we are and work with what we can do.

THE ULTIMATE ROLLERCOASTER – HORMONAL CHANGES

Oh hormones, a girl's best friend, or something like that! Usually by the time we fall pregnant we are all familiar with the hormonal changes we feel during our menstrual cycle, which we explored briefly in Chapter 1. The ebb and flow, the rollercoaster if you will, of hormones that occurs during the month. During pregnancy, there is less ebb and flow, more just a steady increase of the hormones we are more familiar with, **oestrogen** and **progesterone**. But there is another key hormone we need to discuss, and this is **human chorionic gonadotropin** (hCG) – doesn't that just roll off the tongue! It is a hormone produced by the placenta that helps to stimulate the production of progesterone, and is the hormone that pregnancy tests detect to confirm pregnancy (see Figure 17 overleaf). An even less familiar hormone is **human placental lactogen** (hPL), which helps to ensure the foetus gets enough nutrients and energy, as well as supporting the development of milk ducts in the breasts in preparation for breastfeeding. The hormones work together to support your body to provide the right environment to allow your baby to grow, as well as support its development. All of this is amazing, but it can have a knock-on effect on how we feel emotionally, so if you find yourself crying at adverts that before you would have barely noticed, or find your tolerance for certain things lessened, you are not alone. I was heavily pregnant with both of my babies at Christmas time and, honestly, the John Lewis advert would bring me to tears – and even singing Christmas carols got me. To be honest, I feel as a mum I am just more emotional overall, and easily cry at adverts, just as my mum did when I was growing up and I never got it, and yet here I am.

If you are pregnant and find yourself struggling emotionally and mentally, whether you feel this is primarily down to hormones or other contributing factors, please do speak to your midwife or doctor. Mental health support during pregnancy is so important. We often hear about postnatal depression and support during motherhood, but there isn't as much conversation around mental health during pregnancy. There can be pressure to feel that you should only be happy and grateful for being able to fall pregnant and grow a baby; however, all emotions are valid. There is no shame in saying you are struggling, so don't hide away; speak to your midwife or doctor.

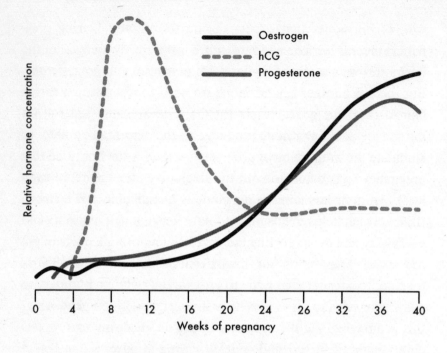

Fig. 17: Hormones during pregnancy

TEAM HEART – YOUR CARDIOVASCULAR SYSTEM

Significant changes also occur in our cardiovascular system during pregnancy, which includes the heart and blood vessels that move blood around the body. These changes start in the early weeks and last throughout the pregnancy. Our blood vessels dilate and expand during pregnancy, which can influence our blood pressure and make us feel more faint, especially in the first trimester. I remember the first time I wondered if I was pregnant with my daughter was when I nearly fainted in a Pilates class. The teacher thought I was just dehydrated; turns out it was because my body was busy making changes to help grow the baby I didn't know about yet. Our clever body adapts and meets an increased demand by raising the amount of blood pumped out of the heart with every heartbeat. Amazingly, this can increase by 45 per cent during pregnancy.[1]

BREATHING SQUAD – YOUR RESPIRATORY SYSTEM

Our bodies need more oxygen when we are pregnant, so the depth or rate of your breathing may change to compensate for these changes. As your bump grows and there is less space in the abdomen, we can find ourselves a bit short of breath and taking a deep breath becomes more of a challenge. I remember this feeling so well when trying to speak to someone on the phone while walking up the stairs and being so out of breath by the time I got to the top. These are all normal and necessary changes, but they can feel a bit unnerving at times.

YOUR MOVERS AND SHAKERS – YOUR MUSCLES

When we think about muscles in pregnancy, I think the common message is that they are just getting weaker. Your bottom, your legs, your core and your pelvic floor – everything is just weakening. Although I understand this narrative, I would love to challenge it and argue that it just isn't helpful for pregnant women for a few reasons. Number one, I think it makes us feel fragile in our bodies, when they're actually doing an incredible and strong thing! And number two, it makes you feel like there is nothing you can do about it. Neither of these things are true! Yes, there are changes to our muscles, however, we can use our muscles during pregnancy and stay strong – it isn't all doom and gloom.

Generally, in pregnancy a lot of us feel we can't exercise as we used to, especially because of sickness or fatigue in the first trimester, and then we don't always know what is safe to do for the rest of pregnancy. Thankfully there is more support now for women keeping active, which we will discuss in the next chapter in more detail. Our pelvic floor is put under a lot of strain during pregnancy, carrying the extra weight of a baby or babies, and this can weaken and stretch the muscles. However, this doesn't mean there is nothing we can do to support them. The abdominal muscles also go through some big changes, and gradually stretch apart to allow our babies to grow. This is called **diastasis rectus abdominis**.

Diastasis rectus abdominis (DRA)

This is the separation of the rectus abdominis muscles (the six pack) and stretching of the linea alba, the connective tissue between the muscles, during pregnancy. It is a totally natural process that occurs in 100 per cent of women, by 35 weeks of pregnancy, to allow your baby to grow.[2] You may see a bulging up or doming of the tissues down the centre of the tummy during certain movements, such as getting in and out of bed or the bath. Don't panic if you see this; however, try to adapt your movement to reduce this doming. Here are some top tips to help you:

- Roll onto your side to get up and out of bed as your bump grows.
- Avoid straining on the toilet when doing a poo. This reduces pressure not only on the pelvic floor but the abdominal muscles and tissues as well.
- Don't fear all core exercises, but as your bump grows move away from exercises such as sit-ups. Pilates-based exercises that are pregnancy specific can be a great form of exercise.
- Work on diaphragmatic breathing as outlined on page 42.[3]

WHAT'S THE DEAL WITH POSTURE?

When people find out I am a physio they often sit up tall and say, 'Oh I must have my best posture.' From my perspective, this couldn't be further from the truth. I don't want you to be in a perfect posture all the time, but just in different postures throughout the day. Our bodies love movement, they don't love one position all the time, and this is also true in pregnancy. However, our day-to-day lives often don't allow for this in the way that historically maybe they did. There are some postural changes that occur during pregnancy as our tummy and breasts grow in size. Being aware of these changes can be helpful but without the pressure to find a 'perfect' posture, instead focusing on your comfort.

Pressure to have a constantly perfect posture at any point in life is not helpful.[4] Instead try these general principles:

- Move often throughout the day.
- Focus on a variety of positions throughout the day.
- Don't force yourself into postures because you believe they seem better.
- Find comfortable positions and postures that work for you. This won't be the same for everyone.
- You might find it helpful to sit back fully in your chair, with your feet flat on the floor, when sitting working at a desk.

HOW IS *THAT* MY BRA SIZE?! – BREAST CHANGES

If you are pregnant at the moment or have been pregnant you will be very aware of how much breasts change throughout this time.

This can impact our comfort, how we hold ourselves and how we feel. Siobhan O'Donovan, a physiotherapist passionate about breast health and posture, and founder of Posture Fitting, has kindly shared with us her thoughts:

> There are many changes that happen to our breasts through different life stages, from puberty up to older age, with pregnancy being a key time for change. The breasts lie on top of the chest and can act as a weight pulling the torso forward and down. Breast weight can be supported via an optimal bra fit. Pregnancy and postpartum are often when our breasts are the largest we have known them to be. While this is due to the temporary hormonal effects of preparation for or actual milk production, that doesn't mean you should just wait for this time to be over to find your optimal fit bra. Seeking a correctly fitting bra is essential at this stage of life. You might be surprised that the size you have been wearing isn't right for you.

THE INBUILT SAUSAGE MACHINE – YOUR BOWELS

One of the most challenging parts of the first trimester I found was the bloating and discomfort that it brought. It is pretty impossible to fall pregnant and not discuss our bowels in some way. Most commonly, women report struggling more with constipation and opening their bowels, however, for some they can experience things going the other way. Often to blame are our hormones, and diet changes, especially during any pregnancy sickness when – let's face it – reaching for any green vegetables is often not top of our list. Fibre-rich food often gets replaced with processed foods that help us get through the day. They definitely did for me, and often our bowels tell us they are not a fan.

As we have discussed, ongoing constipation and straining can cause symptoms of pelvic floor dysfunction, so working on ways to prevent this is key. Additionally, being on iron tablets, which some women require during pregnancy, can often make us constipated, adding another layer of challenge. Despite trying our best, it can be very hard to resolve constipation during pregnancy, and if you do struggle please flag this to your doctor. It is easy to see how repetitive straining during pregnancy, at a time when our pelvic floor is already experiencing extra challenges, could contribute to further weakening and stretching of the muscles and ligaments. Straining and constipation can also lead to **haemorrhoids**, which I am sure many of us are unfortunately familiar with.

Haemorrhoids

Haemorrhoids, or piles as they are often called, are a normal part of our anatomy. They are like little cushions in the anus. At different times in life they can become inflamed and irritated, making us very aware of them. During pregnancy and after birth are common times to experience this due to the increased pressure in the pelvic area, straining to open our bowels and during vaginal delivery.

Symptoms may include:

- Fresh blood on wiping, on the stool or in the toilet.
- Pain around the anus.
- Itching around or in the anus.
- Something popping out of your anus when you open your bowels.
- Feeling that you haven't emptied your bowels fully.
- More mucus when wiping after a bowel movement.

To help at any stage of life you can try:

- Increasing your fluid and fibre intake to help with stool consistency, keeping it softer.
- Don't strain. If you can't poo without straining then please speak to your doctor, as you may need some laxatives in the short term to help you.
- When cleaning after opening your bowels use wet tissue or wipes to help reduce discomfort and help you to clean better.
- Try using a step to place your feet on, lean forwards and work on relaxing as much as you can (refer to Figure 6 on page 21). When we fear a bowel motion, often we are more tense and this makes stools even harder to pass.
- Gentle pelvic floor exercises, including contracting and relaxing, can help with blood flow and reduce swelling and discomfort.
- Ice packs can help reduce pain and discomfort. Always wrap an ice pack in a towel or flannel before placing it over the anus. Leave for a maximum of 10 minutes at a time.
- Speak to your doctor as there are specific ointments and creams that can help to reduce pain, itching and swelling.

UNDER PRESSURE – YOUR BLADDER

Most commonly, women report needing to wee more frequently during pregnancy, which starts due to changes in hormones and blood flow to the kidneys that cause us to produce and pass more urine. As pregnancy progresses and there is a growing baby sitting on the bladder, there is really no surprise that this increased frequency continues. Especially when it feels like they start to use your bladder as a mini trampoline day and night! But keeping hydrated should be a priority during pregnancy, and watching out for any symptoms of urine infections, which are more common during pregnancy.

THE INTERNAL WONDER – YOUR VAGINA

During pregnancy we don't often think too much about our vagina until we start to consider our birth preferences and how we would like to deliver our babies. We will explore this in more depth in the next chapter, but I want you to know that the vagina is designed so that it can birth a baby. As we learnt in Chapter 1, the vagina has folds, called **rugae**, which allow for the vagina to stretch as a baby passes through. Think about the rugae as being like the folds on an accordion: they expand and come back together to make the music happen. In this case, the music is giving birth!

Discharge is another topic that often we don't talk much about and some of you might even shudder a bit at the word. Essentially, discharge is totally normal and cleverly keeps the vagina clean and lubricated, as well as helping to prevent infections. This is why we don't need to excessively clean our vagina with lots of soap as we always have an inbuilt cleaning mechanism, and the more we interfere the more problems we can actually cause. Over-cleaning, using scented products or specific feminine-hygiene products can actually wash away and affect good vaginal bacteria, which are important for preventing certain infections. The vagina has its own microbiome, in the same way as the gut does as we explored in Chapter 1. We want to support the vaginal microbiome and not wash away or impact the good bacteria that live there. During pregnancy women report more discharge and this is totally normal. However, if you notice other changes, such as itching or a foul smell, then please speak to your doctor or midwife, as it could be the sign of an infection that needs treatment.

Thrush

Thrush is a yeast infection caused when there is overgrowth of a fungus called candida. The growth of candida is usually kept under control by normal vaginal bacteria, however, if these bacteria are interfered with or changed this can affect the candida growth. Common times when this occurs are during pregnancy, if we wash with lots of soap around the vulva and anus, and when we are taking antibiotics. Most common symptoms are a white discharge that looks a bit like cottage cheese, which doesn't smell, and itching and soreness around the vulva and vaginal opening. There is medication that we can get over the counter from your local pharmacy, however, during pregnancy you should always speak to your doctor or midwife before taking or applying any medicines.

Bacterial vaginosis

Bacterial vaginosis (BV) occurs when an imbalance of the bacteria in the vagina occurs. The most common symptoms are an off-white or grey discharge that has a particular 'fishy odour'. Having BV in pregnancy does have some associated risks, including premature labour and birth, therefore, seeking treatment as soon as possible is important.

THE EXTERNAL WONDER – YOUR VULVA

We often don't realise that there can be quite significant changes to the vulva during pregnancy, both visually and to how it feels. There is increased blood flow to the pelvic area and so the tissues of the vulva are often more swollen. This isn't a bad thing, but I know it is something that women notice but are often too embarrassed to ask about. For some women they will start to experience discomfort or soreness as well, and this can indicate **vulvar varicosities**, which most of us have never heard of.

Vulvar varicosities

These are varicose veins that occur in the vulva, caused by hormones which relax the walls of the blood vessels, increased blood flow and increased pressure from a growing baby. Symptoms often include heaviness, soreness or a feeling of pressure, which are usually felt after having been upright or more active. They cause no harm but can be really uncomfortable and affect how you feel day to day. To help, you can try:

- Gentle pelvic floor exercises, see page 43.
- Wearing a maternity pad between two pairs of knickers to give some external pressure and support to the vulva and in turn reduce discomfort.
- Don't strain to open your bowels.
- Take time to lie down and avoid long periods of standing.
- Use some ice. The best way to do this is to wet a sanitary or maternity pad with water and pop it in the freezer. Once frozen, wrap completely in a flannel and pop over the vulva for 5–10 minutes.

DON'T TALK ABOUT FENNEL! – PREGNANCY SICKNESS

If you are anything like me, you may still feel sick at the thought of certain foods you either had or had aversions to during pregnancy.

Fennel is something that I am not sure I will ever be able to eat or look at normally again. I know, rather niche, but I remember so vividly the day my nausea kicked in badly in my first pregnancy. I had fennel as part of a meal, and since that day it has never been the same. Even the word makes me feel a bit nauseous! Thankfully, I can live without fennel, but I know lots of women are deeply affected by nausea and sickness during pregnancy, which can play out even after our babies arrive.

Nausea and sickness impacts around 80 per cent of women during pregnancy, and it can be the hardest part of the first trimester – and, for some, can last the entire pregnancy. Turning up to work and trying to lead a normal life when all you really want to do is lie in a dark room and not be sick, is really challenging, and I think we are all superheroes for getting through it. For some, what is labelled as 'morning sickness' and assumed to last only for the first trimester, will be all day, extreme and last a lot longer. **Hyperemesis gravidarum** impacts 1–3 per cent of women, and is extreme nausea and sickness that occurs during pregnancy. Many women will need medical support in hospital to prevent dehydration or more extreme illness.

Women can start to notice that they develop pelvic floor symptoms during periods of ongoing vomiting, more commonly incontinence. It can feel very distressing to be leaking urine when you are also vomiting and know there is nothing you can do to stop it. Leakage occurs due to the significant increase in intra-abdominal pressure (see page 31) that occurs when we vomit, and with repetitive pressure over weeks the pelvic floor muscles can weaken and struggle to maintain continence. Our body is amazing at recovering and adapting, so though at the time it can feel impossible to improve symptoms, it doesn't mean that you won't be able to later in pregnancy or in the future through pelvic floor muscle rehabilitation.

* * *

Now that we understand some of the wonderful and significant changes that occur in the body during pregnancy, let's consider some of the more challenging symptoms that women can experience.

OUCH! – PELVIC GIRDLE PAIN

Pelvic girdle pain (PGP) is the term used to describe pain in the pelvic girdle, and when it occurs during pregnancy it is called **pregnancy-related pelvic girdle pain**. Women's symptoms and stories are often very different, but may include pain around the front or back of the pelvis near the pubic bone and sacroiliac joints, which may also go down into the bottom and legs. This is often experienced during movement such as when walking, climbing the stairs, rolling in bed and getting in and out of the car. It impacts around half of women during pregnancy, which I think you will agree is a high percentage. So, what causes it?

A key hormone that is discussed during pregnancy is relaxin. This isn't a hormone exclusive to pregnancy, as it is often presented, but actually one that is always present in our bodies. During pregnancy, as we have discussed, there are hormone changes and levels of relaxin, oestrogen and progesterone increase. These changes help there to be a little bit more movement at the pelvic joints to allow a baby to pass through the pelvis during a vaginal delivery – very clever, I think you will agree. This was thought to lead to a lack of stability in the pelvis and pelvic girdle pain. However, we now know this isn't the case. If relaxin was the prime cause, then every pregnant woman would experience PGP, and yet they don't.[5] The pelvis is incredibly stable, even with slight increased movement. So, if it isn't relaxin or an unstable pelvis, what is it? The honest answer is the reason will be different for everyone, but potential contributing factors may be:

- Previous injury to the area or trauma. This can be a physical injury or emotional trauma, including birth trauma.
- Subsequent pregnancies, i.e., second or third pregnancies.
- Previous history of lower back pain.
- Being overweight.
- Not believing that we can improve, which is understandable if we blame it on relaxin and inevitable changes that occur in pregnancy that we can't do anything about.
- Work dissatisfaction, as this can lead to high levels of stress, which in turn impacts our nervous system and our experience of pain.[6]
- Depression and anxiety.[7]

Whatever the cause, women with PGP need support as it negatively impacts day-to-day life and can really affect a woman's mental health.[8] If you struggle with PGP, I want you to know that your body is not broken, your pelvis is stable, and there is help out there. Seeing a clinician who is experienced at treating PGP, and who can assess and understand why you are experiencing pain, is ideal.

Treatment may include:

- Exercises to help you improve your everyday movement and function, supporting you to feel confident to move while working with where your body is at.
- Pelvic floor rehabilitation and diaphragmatic breathing. Our muscles around the pelvis can become more protective if we experience PGP, including our pelvic floor (our bodyguard kicking in again to take care of us).[9] Addressing these changes, and helping the muscles to relax, as well as strengthen, is important.
- Manual therapy and hands-on treatment can be effective at providing pain relief.

- Supporting you to not fear movement and to know that your pelvis isn't unstable.

Alongside treatment, try the following at home to see if they help:

- Pregnancy yoga or Pilates.[10] Movement that is little and often, frequently helps women to manage their symptoms.
- Trying not to be in one position or posture for too long; variety is the spice of life.
- A support belt or supportive leggings around the pelvis can help you feel more comfortable and confident to move.
- Work on your sleep hygiene, e.g. reducing screen time before going to bed and getting to bed before 10pm, as well as finding a comfortable position. Women often find a pillow between their legs, and one under their bump and waist, can really help.
- Wear comfortable and sensible footwear; it is probably time to say goodbye to the high heels for a while.
- Reducing stress where possible in a way that is effective for you. Finding activities which bring you joy and a sense of wellbeing will have a positive impact on your pain.

My experience

I want to briefly share my own personal experience of PGP as I had it in both pregnancies. It started in my first pregnancy after a fall in the gym, a rather clumsy moment! I was so worried about how I would cope, and definitely found myself catastrophising about how I would continue my physically active job and give birth![11] I generally had a lot of fear around birth as well, which I will share more about in the next chapter, and I can now see, looking back, how both contributed to my experience of pain. This isn't saying that it was all in my head, but these fears and thoughts played a part, alongside the physical injury that I had. I received treatment and was able to remain active, working and with low levels of discomfort through both pregnancies. I just wanted to share this, because I know it can be hard to hear sometimes that our brain, mental health and thoughts can influence our pain. It doesn't mean that we are making it up – our physical experience is real and there are physical contributors – but we have to look at all the factors at play to help us make the best recovery.

IS THIS NORMAL? – BACK PAIN

Most of us will have some aches and pains during pregnancy at some point and we may find some gentle exercise, a heat pack, or a massage help to relieve any discomfort. If you have significant back pain that is impacting your everyday life, then this needs assessment. Again, please don't let someone tell you that back pain is just another part of pregnancy that you have to accept and get on with. However, if you have back pain, alongside new numbness down your legs, numbness of the vulva area, or changes to your bladder and bowel control, then please flag this to a doctor urgently. In very rare cases one of the discs in the spine compresses the nerves in the lower spine, causing these symptoms, and this needs urgent medical review.

There are a few basics that I want you to focus on if you are struggling with your back:

- Try little movement 'snacks'. Pick a movement like a pelvic tilt (see page 119) that you can do little and often throughout your day. Remember, our bodies love to move.
- Find comfortable positions and postures that work for you.
- You might find it helpful to sit back fully in your chair, with your feet flat on the floor, when sitting working at a desk.

- Rest as your body needs, but don't avoid all movement due to pain.
- Place a hot-water bottle or heat pack on your lower back for 10–15 minutes at regular intervals.

How to do a pelvic tilt

- Sit on the edge of a chair or gym ball.
- Tilt your pelvis back, as shown in the picture below.
- Then grow tall.
- Repeat this 10 times, slowly and steadily.
- You may feel a gentle stretching in the lower back.

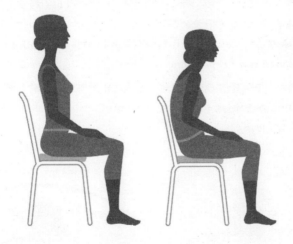

A PAIN IN THE SIDE – RIB PAIN

This is another pesky symptom that lots of women can get during pregnancy. Your growing baby and tummy mean that the ribs move slightly to create more space. This, alongside the position of our baby, can lead to pain. To help reduce this pain, think about how you are sitting; make sure you are not in a slumped position as this will increase pressure on the ribs. Supporting the lower back with a rolled-up towel can help you too, as well as ensuring you are wearing the correct bra for your changing breasts to optimise support. Assessment and treatment by a physiotherapist can help, alongside gentle mobility exercises for the upper back like the arm openings exercise shown below.

How to do arm openings

- Lie on your side with your head supported on a pillow.
- Place your arms out in front of you at shoulder height.
- Your hands should be together like they are clapping.
- Take the upper arm up and over the body as far as you can, keeping your pelvis in position.
- The movement should come from the upper body and not from your whole body rolling.
- You should feel this opens up the front of the chest and may feel a stretch across the chest and ribs.
- Try this 10 times each side.

WHAT HAS HAPPENED TO MY HANDS? – HAND AND WRIST PAIN

Carpal tunnel syndrome is common during pregnancy and often presents as pain, numbness, or tingling in the hand and fingers. It is caused by compression of a nerve, called the median nerve, as it passes through the wrist to the hand. It is more common in pregnancy due to increased swelling that women often get in their wrists and hands, which can contribute to the compression. It is often worse overnight and first thing in the morning, due to the position of our hands and lack of movement when we are asleep. So, wearing hand splints overnight or during tasks such as working at a computer, which aggravate our symptoms, can help relieve discomfort. Additionally, gentle movement of the hands and wrists regularly, alongside physiotherapy support, can help.

WHEN THE BEST HAMMOCK STARTS TO STRUGGLE – PELVIC FLOOR SYMPTOMS

For many of us pregnancy is the first time we start to experience pelvic floor symptoms. Whether this be urinary incontinence when being sick, during exercise, or when we have a horrible cough. We are going to explore more about caring for our pelvic floor during pregnancy in the next chapter, but I wanted to state that incontinence is not just a normal part of pregnancy, and neither is ongoing pain or discomfort. If you have a heavy or dragging feeling in the vagina, don't ignore it, but also please don't start googling prolapse as it will send you off on a very negative journey. Over the next few chapters we will be exploring how to help and improve pelvic floor symptoms, so I hope if you are struggling at the moment the pages ahead will provide comfort and solutions.

*   *   *

Our body is amazing in how it adapts and changes during pregnancy without us even realising, and I hope this chapter helps you to recognise what a wonder it is that most of these changes go on without us knowing. Our journeys are all different, and I hope you now know that if you are struggling now, or in the future, there is help.

MYTH BUSTING

'Pelvic and back pain is just part of pregnancy'
Absolutely not! Challenge anyone who says this and know that treatment is available and effective at treating both PGP and back pain. You don't just have to suffer or spend your pregnancy under the expectation that pain will just continue to get worse.

'You can prevent diastasis recti with certain exercises'
You won't have to look far on a Google search before seeing something pop up like 'Five exercises to prevent or heal diastasis recti.' However, diastasis recti isn't something we can prevent in pregnancy. As we have discussed, it is necessary to allow our babies to grow. Some women, if they have premature babies, won't have a diastasis as their babies were smaller when born. However, past 35 weeks we understand that all women will have a degree of separation, and this will be larger for some. So don't fear the change; follow the tips I have shared and know that your body is doing exactly what it needs to do.

Foundation Reflections

Take a moment to jot down any symptoms you might be experiencing. You can use this as a prompt or to help as you seek support. You might also find it useful to refer back to as you read on through the other chapters.

....

....

....

....

....

....

....

....

....

CHAPTER 7

Bump – To Care and Prepare

Let's learn about:

- Why pelvic floor exercises are important in pregnancy
- How many pelvic floor exercises to aim for
- Supporting your pelvic health through pregnancy
- Exercising during pregnancy
- Perineal tears
- Preparing for birth with perineal massage
- Fear of birth and how to seek support
- Hypnobirthing
- The role of a doula

Caring for our body during pregnancy is important, but what does this look like? Is it a massage or spa day? Hopefully, yes, but I think there are some foundational things alongside these treats that we can focus on during pregnancy, to help us thrive and prepare for birth. Pregnancy is often the time when we hear about our pelvic floor muscles for the first time, or definitely the concept of doing pelvic floor exercises. More often than not we are asked, 'Are you doing your pelvic floor exercises?' and are given a leaflet that explains what they are, and we smile and nod thinking, 'I guess I am, but I'm not really sure what I am meant to do!' So, if you have ever felt like that, or currently feel like that, you are not alone. I hope by now you have been able to connect to your pelvic floor more, but is caring for our pelvic health just about pelvic floor exercises during pregnancy? Thankfully not. So, whether you are pregnant right now or not, let's chat it through. This information could help you support a friend, a daughter or a granddaughter on her journey. Remember, together we are stronger!

WHY ARE PELVIC FLOOR EXERCISES RECOMMENDED IN PREGNANCY?

Let's face it, we all have far too much to do, especially when pregnant. Whether that be trying to navigate wrapping up work, prepping a nursery or moving house, as many of us do when pregnant. We moved into our house just a month before our daughter arrived, and to say it was manic and there wasn't a lot of head space is an understatement. Therefore, if we are going to have to commit time to doing something like pelvic floor exercises, we need to understand why we are doing them and what the benefit is.

As we have discussed, during pregnancy our growing babies increase the weight and stretch on our pelvic floor muscles, which can lead to the weakening of the muscles and experience of new symptoms, such as incontinence or prolapse. This is why pelvic floor muscle exercises are recommended, as doing them keeps the muscles functioning as well as they can in the new situation they find themselves in. **Pelvic floor exercises reduce the risk of experiencing incontinence during pregnancy and postpartum.**[1,2] The focus here is on prevention and this is why starting exercises early on in pregnancy, rather than once symptoms have started to occur, is important.

This idea of prevention goes beyond us as an individual, as we now have guidelines suggesting that pregnant women who have a mother or sister with pelvic floor dysfunction should be given support with supervised pelvic floor muscle training from 20 weeks of pregnancy for 3 months. This means sessions and guidance with a pelvic health physiotherapist to help them with their pelvic floor exercises and overall pelvic health.[3] **Prevention is always best**, and by being open with our family, which I appreciate isn't always easy to do, it could encourage our children to gain more support. I genuinely feel excited for the next generation, that we can support them in a way and help them to gain knowledge that for generations until now just hasn't been there. Doing pelvic floor exercises during pregnancy isn't only about preventing incontinence though. They may also reduce the length of the second stage of labour, which is the stage where the baby passes down the birth canal and is born, and reduce the severity of perineal tears.[4] I think you will agree they are certainly worth the time and effort, and this is why we need to tell our friends, our daughters and, well, anyone who will listen!

PELVIC FLOOR PREGNANCY PROGRAMME

Getting started can be the hardest part, and doing something is better than nothing. Below is a phased way of getting started, whatever stage of pregnancy you are at:

Phase 1

Begin by having a recap of the technique and cues to try on page 43 to remind yourself of what works best for you.
Start with 5–10 diaphragmatic breaths (see page 42), sitting or lying.

Now combine breathing and pelvic floor contractions by doing the
following:
- Breathe in gently and keep the pelvic floor relaxed.
- Breathe out and contract the pelvic floor.
- Then let it fully relax as you continue to breathe normally,
  then repeat this 10 times.

Phase 2

Once you feel completely happy with this connection with the pelvic
floor and breathing, you can try doing regular repetitions
throughout the day.
Start with 10 repetitions, simply contracting and relaxing the pelvic
floor. Ensure that you feel a relax between each contraction.
These are called **short** contractions.
Try and build up to doing this 3 times a day in a lying or sitting
position.

Phase 3

Now we want to work on endurance, so let's introduce working on
holding the pelvic floor contraction.
Keep the contraction and cue the same as for phases 1 and 2, but
this time, when you contract the pelvic floor, hold for 5 seconds
while breathing normally. It is tempting to hold your breath but
make sure you are able to gently breathe while the pelvic floor
holds. These are called **long** contractions.
After each hold allow the pelvic floor to relax fully, and work on
repeating this 10 times.
Over time, build up to holding for 10 seconds and continue to do
this 10 times.

Phase 4

Try doing 10 short contractions and 10 long contractions in a
sitting position 3 times a day.
Also start to try doing them standing. It will feel harder but it's really
good to practise this.

Trying to remember to do pelvic floor exercises is another big challenge. I recommend setting a reminder alarm on your phone, or pop a sticky dot on your laptop if you use it for work, or on the kettle or kitchen cupboard if you are at home, to be a visual prompt. You can also download the NHS Squeezy App that sends you reminders.

WHAT ELSE CAN YOU DO TO SUPPORT YOUR PELVIC HEALTH DURING PREGNANCY?

As we have spoken about a few times now, preventing constipation is vital for our pelvic health – especially during pregnancy when we are more likely to suffer from it. Always come back to the foundations of fluid, fibre and movement. This might be a time in your life when you find using a step for your feet while sitting on the toilet really helpful, when at other times in your life you haven't felt it was necessary. If you continuously struggle with your bowels then please speak to your doctor, to prevent extra strain on your pelvic floor and connective tissues.

We all know there are benefits of movement and exercise, however, it remains quite a controversial topic during pregnancy, and many women are still confused as to what they can and can't do. The fact is, our body, brain and pelvic floor all love it when we exercise, and there are lots of benefits for both mum and baby (see box below). However, what do we need to change during pregnancy and how do we navigate this season if we are feeling really unwell?

First and foremost, I want you to know that exercise is safe during pregnancy and has not been found to increase risk of miscarriage.[5] We will need to adapt to meet our body where it is at. I loved exercising during my pregnancies, but definitely struggled in my first trimesters when I felt sick all day. In my first pregnancy I was delighted to meet Charlie Launder, founder of Bumps and Burpees, and trained with her to keep active, and it made so much difference to how I felt both physically and mentally – our sessions were an absolute highlight of my weeks. During both pregnancies I had to learn what my body needed and there is absolutely not a one-size-fits-all programme. However, we do need to reduce fear around exercising during pregnancy and support women to be active.

BENEFITS OF EXERCISING DURING PREGNANCY

Exercising during pregnancy has been shown to decrease the risk of:

- Pre-eclampsia
- High blood pressure in pregnancy
- Gestational diabetes
- Depression
- Severity of back and pelvic pain
- Weight gain

The UK Chief Medical Officer encourages pregnant women to aim for 150 minutes of moderate-intensity activity spread across at least 3 days of the week. They encourage us that every activity counts, so doing what we enjoy is key. The important word we need to focus on here is *activity*. Activity can include all movement that we do – walking, taking the stairs, or having a dance with our kids – and removes the pressure to feel like we always have to be completing comprehensive exercise programmes. This doesn't mean you have to stop the exercise you have done before pregnancy if you feel comfortable doing it and don't have a high-risk pregnancy, or any of the contraindications outlined in the box below. Women who have not been physically active before are encouraged to start during pregnancy, gradually introducing more activity over time so they can lap up all the benefits.[6]

CONTRAINDICATIONS TO EXERCISE IN PREGNANCY[7]

Please always speak to your own medical team to seek advice; these are just here for some general guidance.

Absolute contraindications:
- Ruptured membranes (waters broken)
- Premature labour
- Unexplained persistent vaginal bleeding
- Placenta praevia (the placenta is attached to the lower part of the uterus and can completely cover the cervix) after 28 weeks' gestation
- Pre-eclampsia
- Incompetent cervix
- Intrauterine growth restriction

- High-order multiple pregnancy (for example, triplets)
- Uncontrolled type I diabetes
- Uncontrolled hypertension
- Uncontrolled thyroid disease
- Other serious cardiovascular, respiratory or systemic disorders

Relative contraindications:
- Recurrent pregnancy loss
- Gestational high blood pressure
- A history of spontaneous preterm birth
- Mild/moderate cardiovascular or respiratory disease
- Symptomatic anaemia (low iron in the blood)
- Malnutrition
- Eating disorder
- Twin pregnancy after the 28th week
- Other significant medical conditions

There has always been a lot of fear about lifting weights and whether this is safe during pregnancy and for the pelvic floor, which I totally understand. However, we are seeing evolving research supporting the benefits of exercise and lifting weights during pregnancy, without detrimental impact on the pelvic floor.[8] Now, this doesn't mean that it is safe for everyone and should be done without consideration. However, for low-risk women, continuing to lift weights if they have been doing it prior to pregnancy, and with modifications as needed, has benefits. I mean, most of motherhood feels like a weight-lifting programme! If you are unsure what is right for you, or you have any medical conditions that make you high risk, then please always seek medical advice before exercising during pregnancy.

To help you navigate this season if you are pregnant at the moment, I have asked Charlie Launder to give us her top tips:

1. Do something you LIKE to do. There are no 'shoulds' when it comes to exercise in pregnancy, there are loads of ways to move your body and if you don't enjoy it then you're unlikely to stick at it.

2. Make it a social thing. Exercising is great for mental health but why not enhance that by adding a social aspect to it and doing it with a friend, or signing up to a class to meet other mums-to-be?

3. Get outside. Plenty of exercise options can be done outside and this can really help lift our moods; it can be something as small as walking the longer way to the shop, walking the dog, or going for a walk in the woods with a friend.

4. Listen to your body. Your body will tell you quicker than any gadget or watch will whether something is right or not, but it's up to us to listen and respond, so don't ignore signs that your body is giving you.

5. Talk test. This is the best way to measure intensity when exercising in pregnancy. Can you hold a relatively normal conversation during your workout? If so you can be reassured that the intensity is at a good level for you.

6. Lying on your back. Many women are very fearful of spending even a second on their back, and while we do need to be careful in the later months of spending too much time lying flat on our back this doesn't mean that you can't do any exercise lying on your back for the whole pregnancy, for example, glute bridges. There are ways you can adapt them as needed through pregnancy, like resting your upper back and shoulders on a box or a sofa as your bump gets bigger. If you feel dizzy, light-headed or breathless lying on your back, then roll onto

your side, and take it as a sign to adapt the exercise going forwards.

7. Don't bump the bump. We want to minimise the risk of you falling over or having your bump knocked and while you will obviously be very mindful of it, others may be less so. So, team sports where you're likely to get knocked, such as netball, are probably best paused for now.

8. Rest is just as important as exercise. This goes for every stage in our lives but even more so in pregnancy. Our body is doing something super important that takes up a lot of energy, so make sure to give yourself the time to fully recover from workouts rather than pushing it to its limits. Factor in those rest days.

9. Don't feel guilty if you have days or weeks where you can't do your normal exercise routine. Pregnancy throws us many a curve ball, whether it's sickness, exhaustion or anything else, so we don't need guilt on top of it all. Focus on general activity and know that every activity counts.

WHAT CAN YOU DO TO PREPARE FOR BIRTH?

As we move through pregnancy, our mind moves towards birth, and how we can prepare. You may have done, or are doing, antenatal classes, which help to highlight some of the key things you need to consider: how to care for a baby and how you can prepare for birth. However, I meet so many women who didn't feel fully informed or prepared. Women don't come into my clinic room angry that they were over-informed; they are angry for being under-informed. Birth can be a really overwhelming and scary thing to think about, especially when everyone loves to tell us the horror stories. Educating women about what can occur during birth can be tricky, as we don't want to be labelled as scaremongers. My main hope is to ensure that no one feels under-informed, that you are aware of what your body might go through, and to inform you about how to prepare and reduce risk. Through doing this I do believe we can reduce distress and shock for women during the days and weeks after delivery.[9] As well as help them to make truly informed decisions.[10] So let's start with understanding what may happen during a vaginal delivery.

Perineal injuries

During a vaginal delivery the vulval and vaginal tissues have to stretch to allow your baby to pass through. These tissues are designed to stretch, however, sometimes despite this brilliant design the stretch is too great, and tears occur. Additionally, sometimes the medical team will advise a cut to the vaginal opening, called an episiotomy. Most of the time women are not clear on what type of tear they had – let's face it, there is a lot going on after a birth when this information is given to us. Let's chat through the different types of perineal injuries:

- **First-degree tears:** a small graze or tear to the tissues that often doesn't require stitching or further treatment. Despite being small they can still be very sore, so don't underestimate these.
- **Second-degree tears:** a tear that involves the skin and muscles and often requires stitching to aid healing.
- **Episiotomy:** a cut completed by the medical team if needed to allow for an instrumental delivery to be completed, or if they feel there is high risk for a more significant tear. This is repaired by a midwife or doctor after birth.

Tears that progress from the vaginal tissues to the anal sphincters are called obstetric anal sphincter injuries (OASI) and can be broken down into:

- **Third-degree tears:** include injury to the anal sphincters, which can be to the external or internal sphincter. There are three sub-categories, 3a, 3b and 3c, which outline how much of the sphincters are involved in the tear.
- **Fourth-degree tears:** include a tear of the anal sphincters, as well as the bowel lining.

OASIs occur in around 6 per cent of first-time mothers, and in 2 per cent of women who have had a previous vaginal delivery.[11] Repair is completed by a doctor in theatre as soon after birth as possible, to help the sphincter and muscles repair and heal.

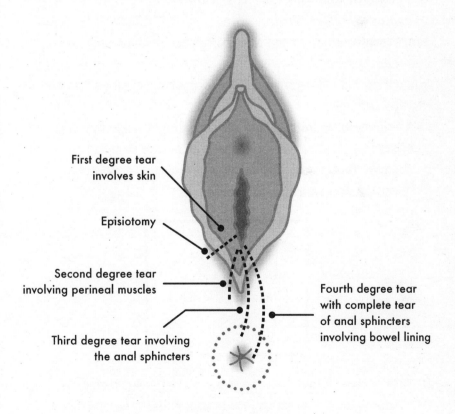

First degree tear involves skin

Episiotomy

Second degree tear involving perineal muscles

Third degree tear involving the anal sphincters

Fourth degree tear with complete tear of anal sphincters involving bowel lining

Fig. 18: Perineal injuries

Around 90 per cent of first-time mothers will have some degree of perineal trauma, which can get us all squeezing our pelvic floor in fear. This is something I really struggled to think about when pregnant, so you are not alone. However, there are things you can do to help reduce the risk and severity of a tear.

Perineal massage

This is a technique used to help stretch the perineal and vaginal tissues in the weeks running up to birth to help reduce the risk of having a tear, need for episiotomy, or the severity of any tear sustained.[12] It can be started around 34 weeks of pregnancy and completed by following the steps below:

1. Wash your hands and make sure your nails are short and not sharp.
2. Use a natural oil or lubricant and apply this to the vulva and your thumb.
3. Place your thumb a couple of centimetres inside the vagina.
4. Start by sweeping along the perineum side to side 10 times. This should feel slightly stretchy and allow your vaginal tissues to get used to touch.

5. Then think about the vulva like a clock. Twelve o'clock at your pubic bone, six o'clock at your anus, three and nine o'clock towards each of your legs.

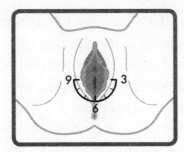

6. Hold and stretch towards your anus (six o'clock) for 30 seconds. It should feel like an intense stretch but not painful. Then complete this stretch in each direction from three to nine o'clock, holding in each direction for 30 seconds.

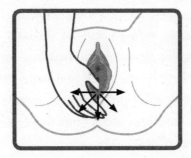

7. As the weeks go on you may feel able to use both thumbs inside the vagina to increase the stretch that you feel.
8. Try to relax your body and pelvic floor muscles while doing this, which can be easier said than done.

PLEASE NOTE: If you have any vaginal bleeding, if concerns have been raised about your cervix or placenta during pregnancy, your waters have broken or you have a vaginal infection, please don't complete perineal massage. Seek advice from your medical team.

Perineal massage is a technique that I find divides women. We are either willing to try anything to help reduce the risk of tears, or we just can't get our head around it and can't face doing it. It can also be a logistical nightmare trying to reach around a growing bump, so try different positions, like sitting up supported in bed, in the bath, standing with one foot on a small stool, or ask your partner to help. The research doesn't only show us that perineal massage reduces the severity of tearing, but it can also help to decrease the length of the second stage of vaginal delivery, and decrease postpartum perineal pain and faecal incontinence.[13] So I think you will agree – lots of potential benefits if you can get your head around it.

Preparing for birth will look different for everyone, and we will all have different wishes and desires. It is about finding out the information and making an informed decision that is best for you and your baby. Some women will be advised or will ask for a Caesarean section, for a variety of reasons, and I am delighted women are now being heard more and supported in seeking out the right birth choice for them. The priority is that it is an informed decision based on facts, considering the risks and benefits, and not just out of fear.

The fear of birth

I want to be totally honest with you: I really struggled in my first pregnancy with the idea of having a vaginal delivery. I knew deep down this is what I wanted, but being a pelvic health physiotherapist means you are very exposed to the more severe complications that can occur. Yes, the percentages are small, but for me that was my whole exposure and experience of birth, and understandably I was deeply scared. I was on the hunt for an obstetrician who would agree to give me a Caesarean, and I found one! However, it was through my conversation with him that I started to realise I was making this decision solely from a place of fear and not through considering all my options. I hadn't realised how much my fear was impacting me until I started having very vivid dreams, which felt like nightmares, of giving birth and my worst-case scenario occurring. I started to accept this wasn't normal and reached out to Tessa van der Vord, a specialist mental health midwife, who was based at the hospital I was giving birth in. We had met many years before during our first weeks of work and have stayed friends ever since. Tessa booked me an appointment with her and allowed me space to explore my fears and seek support.

I know I am not the only one who fears birth, it is very common and severe fear of birth is called tokophobia. Tessa has kindly shared with us some thoughts and tips on what to do if you are afraid of birth and how to seek help if you feel you need it:

> When it comes to being fearful of birth, you are not alone. Most people of our generation have been subjected to outdated, traumatic clips of childbirth in our sex education sessions at school, which is then compounded by dramatised images and scenes we see in the media. It's no wonder our outlook on childbirth is a little skewed. Who wants to put themselves through that? The fact is, birth is not like that in the majority of cases but it's very hard to think about it in a different way when that's our only point of reference. I would suggest you start to explore some positive stories, images and evidence-based research around birth and see how that feels for you. This can be extremely powerful, but is by no means a quick solution. Secondly, speak to your midwife or responsible clinician about how you feel and what you are worried about. They may be able to placate some of this anxiety themselves or perhaps signpost you to local services that can help. As I

mentioned, this is a common thing so there are services out there to help parents-to-be. Lastly, you are in charge. This is an important and pivotal time in your life and you deserve to have a happy, memorable experience bringing your child into the world. It's not for healthcare professionals to dictate how you should do that. They can certainly provide you with all the risks and benefits of different modes of birth, with as much evidence-based information as possible in order for you to make informed decisions. But ultimately, it's your body and your baby. You deserve to have this information and guidance to help you towards making decisions.

One idea that Tessa mentioned to me was hypnobirthing, and, to be honest, like so many I was very dubious about it. It all sounded a bit wacky to me and as a medical professional I wasn't sure. However, determined to find out more I got in touch with Crystal Miles, a hypnobirthing teacher and founder of Connected Babies, and signed up to her course. I can honestly say that it was the most helpful thing I did in my pregnancy to help me prepare for birth. It goes beyond the technique of hypnobirthing; it really helped me to understand my body and birth, and left me feeling empowered to know what to expect and with tools to use to help me navigate birth. I wanted to share Crystal's wisdom with all of you, so below you will find her explanation of what hypnobirthing is and how it can help you prepare for and during birth.

Let's start with the word Hypnobirthing. In honesty, it can make people hesitate. The 'hypno' refers to hypnosis, a state of deep relaxation 'characterised by heightened susceptibility to suggestion'. The concept of Hypnobirthing is that if the body and mind are in a deeply relaxed state, you can work with, rather than against, the birth process. Practice during pregnancy can also help to change preconceptions and release fears that may have developed around birth. Studies show that the use of Hypnobirthing may help to manage pain, shorten labour, reduce the need for intervention, increase confidence and help parents to feel informed and in control.

Hypnobirthing prepares expectant parents for all birth choices. Participants have reported that the powerful relaxation techniques and supporting theory have enabled them to progress with a drug-free vaginal birth, others have found them invaluable for supporting them alongside various pain-relief methods, for vaginal, assisted or abdominal birth. In all situations, Hypnobirthing can help keep the parent and birth partner calm, relaxed and in control. Our main goal is for parents to achieve the best birth for them, and to come out of the experience feeling that it was a positive birth, that they made informed choices and that those choices were respected. We know that birth can be unpredictable and that's why we ensure you have in-depth information about the birth process and your birth choices to be fully informed, whichever road it takes.

We have been programmed to believe that birth is an emergency, that it is painful, and that fear is part of it. Understandably, the idea that you can be calm during labour may seem foreign and unfortunately these preconceptions can actually make a big difference to how comfortable you are during your labour. Hypnobirthing courses work on changing that perception through relaxation scripts, positive birth stories and, most importantly, education. Our bodies can do wonderful things, it's often our minds we need to convince.

Hypnobirthing allows you to experience and practise self-hypnosis relaxation and provides you with tools such as massage, mindfulness and breathing techniques in order to get your oxytocin and endorphins flowing when you most need them to. Oxytocin is a powerful hormone during birth, it keeps labour progressing, it keeps you calm, relaxed and comfortable.

Hypnobirthing, done comprehensively, is full antenatal education. Most clients, especially the more sceptical, tend to be really impressed with the logic and science involved in the theory sessions. We delve into the physiology of birth, the intricacies of the muscles and hormones involved, we help prepare parents to make informed choices about their care, and, of course, we provide the tools to benefit from relaxation and think positively about birth.

HOW MIGHT A DOULA HELP?

A doula supports women during pregnancy, birth and in the postnatal period with information and education to empower them, and to act as an advocate for a woman during this time. The support a doula can provide is so powerful. During my first birth I had a doula present as they worked at the birth centre that I gave birth in, so it wasn't something I had planned or sought out, but I could not believe the central role she played in my delivery. I totally gravitated to her support, and she guided me through my breathing and trying to stay calm when I started to panic. Since that moment I have totally understood how a doula can be paramount in a woman's experience. Many of us still haven't heard of doulas or really understand the difference between what a doula provides compared to a midwife, so I am delighted that Emma Armstrong, founder of The Naked Birth Coach, has answered some FAQs.

Q: How can a doula support a woman during pregnancy to prepare for birth?
During pregnancy a doula will support women to find the information they need to make informed choices in the birth room, as well as helping them when they're choosing their birth preferences.

Some doulas also have additional skills like teaching hypnobirthing. During the pregnancy the doula and client have the chance to create a trusting relationship, which is so important during their labour and birth.

Q: How can a doula support a woman during birth?
They are not medically trained, however, they can support by using massage, or assistance with breathing, as well as offering emotional support and comfort. The doula does not replace the birth partner but provides support to the whole family. They are able to provide continuity of care and ensure that women feel safe and heard.

Q: How can a doula support a woman after birth?
After birth a doula will usually visit the mother and baby as and when they need. They offer emotional support, creating space to talk about the birth or any struggles the mother is having. They also offer help with a newborn baby, as well as allowing the mother to take a break or that much-needed shower. They also offer help around the house, cooking food or maybe making that hot cup of tea. A doula really is there to care for the mother and baby however it is needed.

Knowing how to care and prepare for birth can make a big difference to our experience, however, we don't all get the information when we need it. If you are reading this chapter after pregnancy and beating yourself up or blaming yourself that you didn't do enough pelvic floor exercises, please don't. Just remember that pelvic floor exercises are just one part of the picture, and it isn't your fault that your education around pelvic health wasn't better. There are many things out of our control, and it isn't too late to make changes. I did plenty of pelvic floor exercises during pregnancy, and though I didn't struggle with incontinence, it hasn't meant that I have not struggled with other aspects of pelvic floor dysfunction. Reflecting on this time can make us feel angry about the information we should have received, so take a moment just to think things through and jot down any thoughts or feelings in the Foundation Reflections section opposite. You may feel that there are still unprocessed feelings or emotions, and I encourage you to speak to your friends, family, or a medical professional about this.

MYTH BUSTING

'Doing pelvic floor exercises will make my pelvic floor too tight and increase my risk of having a tear'

This is a common concern and also a myth that continues to spread. I totally understand where this thought process comes from, however, women who do pelvic floor exercises during pregnancy are not more likely to have perineal tears. You can be confident that doing pelvic floor exercises is not putting you more at risk, so you can reap the benefits without fear. I would always encourage you to ensure you relax between every squeeze so you continue to work on the flexibility of the muscles and not just on strength.[14,15]

'Incontinence is just part of pregnancy, just wear a pad and crack on!'

Absolutely not! We must stop telling women there is nothing they can do to help. There are definitely times when we need pads to support us to manage symptoms, however, that does not mean we can't do anything to work on improving them.

Foundation Reflections

Jot down any thoughts or feelings that this chapter has brought up, or make a note of anything you want to remember to do or explore more.

....

....

....

....

....

....

....

....

....

CHAPTER 8

Birth Recovery

Let's learn about:
- What happens during vaginal and Caesarean births
- Top tips for recovery after vaginal birth
- Top tips for recovery after Caesarean birth
- Restarting pelvic floor exercises after birth
- Common postnatal FAQs
- Postnatal checks, including a checklist to help you prepare

---

We often spend a lot of time focusing on preparing for birth, understanding our options and working out our birth preferences, but, overall, I would say that the majority of us don't spend lots of time thinking about recovery. You *might* have a friend who takes you through their recovery blow by blow, but chances are you've probably heard very little about it. I honestly find that the immediate postnatal recovery period can be one of the biggest shocks for a woman, often because she wasn't educated or informed about what to expect. I want to highlight at the beginning of this chapter that though we are hearing more about birth trauma, which is so important, for some the early postnatal period is actually what they find traumatic. So, if you are reading this, however far along the journey you are, and you still feel traumatised by your postnatal experience, please know it is not too late to seek support. Birth is a big shock to the system, and in the space of a few days there are huge physical, hormonal, emotional and psychological shifts that occur.

As we discussed in the last chapter, a lot of challenges come when we are not informed or don't understand what is going on, so I want to give you an overview of a vaginal and Caesarean birth so you understand some of what your body has been through, whatever stage you are at.

YOUR AMAZING BODY

Vaginal birth

During a vaginal delivery the uterus contracts causing the cervix to dilate and thin, before pushing the baby down the vagina and out into the world. The baby passes through the pelvic floor on its journey, it is not the pelvic floor pushing the baby out. The pelvic floor is like the gate that needs to fully open (stretching) to grant our babies full access to the outside. It has been shown that for some women certain parts of the pelvic floor stretch up to around 2.5 times their original length during vaginal delivery, which I think you will agree is pretty impressive.[1,2] Alongside the stretch of the pelvic floor, there can also be damage to nerves, especially one called the pudendal nerve, which occurs through significant compression. It is therefore understandable, when we think of the stretch our muscles, nerves and connective tissue have experienced, as well as perineal tears that many of us sustain, that our pelvic floor can struggle a bit in the weeks and months after vaginal birth.

What to expect from the early days

I remember these days vividly. I had vaginal births for both of my children, and though I knew all the information in theory, nothing quite prepares you for the actual reality of what you feel. Sitting down was really sore, I struggled to hold in a wee on the way to the toilet and to be honest I felt a bit like a beaten-up rag doll. Saying that, knowing some of what to expect definitely helped me mentally to not panic and remember that my body needed time to heal. So, if you are heading into the postnatal period, or are in it now, I want to outline what to expect to reassure you. If you are past this stage, take a picture of these sections and ping it to a friend or family member who might need it.

1. Your vagina, vulva and perineum will feel and look swollen, and feel painful and tender.

2. You may notice you struggle to hold in a wee on the way to the bathroom. This can vary from a few drops to feeling like you have lost all control. If you have no awareness or sensation of needing a wee and have absolutely no bladder control, please flag this to your medical team.

3. You may notice you cannot control your bowels as well, either experiencing urgency or incontinence of faeces or wind. For many this is temporary and can especially be the case if you had a tear involving the anus (a third- or fourth-degree tear). If symptoms of faecal urgency or incontinence do not improve over the initial postnatal weeks please do speak to your medical team for review, to ensure you have all the support you need.

4. You will have vaginal bleeding, which is called lochia. The heaviness does vary from person to person. If you are concerned or unsure if what you are experiencing is normal, or notice an offensive smell, then please flag this to your medical team.

5. You may feel a heaviness or dragging sensation in the vagina. Don't panic, this is a common feeling in the early days and weeks after giving birth. If this feeling persists after 6 weeks, then please do speak to your doctor for review.

TOP TIPS FOR THE EARLY DAYS

- *Take it slow* – You have just birthed a baby and your body needs lots of TLC and rest where you can.
- *Sitting* – Roll up two towels and place them on a chair or sofa under your thighs so your perineum isn't in contact with the chair. This will take pressure off any areas of stitches, grazes or swelling.
- *Ice* – Use a clean sanitary pad, wet it with water and freeze it. Wrap in an old flannel and pop over the perineum for 5–10 minutes max at a time. Try this every few hours to help reduce swelling and discomfort.
- *Movement* – Little and often really is the best way. This may mean just pottering around your home in the early days, a stroll around the block for some fresh air, and progressively increasing your distance as the weeks go on.
- *Painkillers* – Take these as long as you need. It is normal to not want to take painkillers for too long but it really makes all the difference and it is better to stay on top of pain.
- *Bowels* – Hold a clean maternity pad over your perineum to support any stitches while you open your bowels. Make sure you don't strain. Raise your feet and lean forwards when sitting on the toilet.

Caesarean birth

I want to start here by saying I will be talking about Caesarean birth, or abdominal birth as some prefer to call it, instead of Caesarean section. I want to acknowledge that for too long, women who have delivered their babies via a Caesarean section feel that they have not 'birthed' their babies as it was not a vaginal delivery. Our language really matters and too often you will hear 'vaginal birth' or 'natural birth' for those that had a vaginal delivery and 'Caesarean section' for those who had a Caesarean delivery. We must ensure that all women feel supported and empowered in their birth experience, even if it wasn't necessarily what they hoped for. I am delighted that Emiliana Hall, founder of The Mindful Birth Group®, an award-winning antenatal and postnatal course provider, has agreed to share some thoughts with us on this:

> A motherhood journey comes with many expectations and social norms. Birth is a chapter that is not excluded and people's 'views' can have a long-lasting damaging effect on how someone perceives their own birth experience.
>
> This approach to birth is outdated and needs to be addressed. The most important factor of a birth experience is that you feel supported, understood and listened to and you do not feel out of control or even abused in any shape or form. If the former things are true, you can be sure that your birth will happen in the best and safest way for you and baby, whether vaginally with or without assistance, or abdominally by Caesarean.
>
> If you are reading this and you have already given birth and not felt those things, it is not your fault. You have been let down by a care provider or system and it is important that you seek support to help with any feelings that you may be struggling with. You deserved to be supported then and you more than deserve to be supported now.

An important part of recovery and knowing how to approach the early days is understanding what occurs during a Caesarean birth, without too much detail! To bring our babies into the world, the doctors need to go through six layers to find them. They go through the skin, fat and fascia (connective tissue) layers, between the abdominal muscles, through the peritoneum (the tissue that lines the abdominal wall and pelvis and covers our organs) and uterus to find your baby. A key part of this to note is that they are not cutting your abdominal muscles. They go through the connective tissue between them. So though on the outside there is a horizontal scar, this is not the same through all the layers. Most women find this helpful to know when navigating getting out of bed in the early days.

What to expect from the early days

1. Your tummy will feel sore, tender and painful. You will be given regular pain relief to help you stay on top of the pain.
2. You will have a dressing over the wound, which will be removed as appropriate.
3. Your scar may look red, swollen and bruised and can feel numb.
4. You will have vaginal bleeding, called lochia. The heaviness does vary from person to person, and if you feel it is more than you were expecting please flag this for review.
5. You may notice you are more constipated and struggle to open your bowels, and you may also have trapped wind.

TOP TIPS FOR THE EARLY DAYS

- *Take it slow* – You have just birthed a baby and had major surgery so give your body lots of TLC and rest where you can.
- *Pain relief* – Keep taking the pain relief for as long as you need; this can be for a few weeks.

- *Early mobilisation* – This is usually recommended, so if you have your baby in the morning try and get out of bed that day (with guidance from your medical team). Gentle movement can actually help manage swelling and pain.
- *Bed transfers* – To get out of bed, roll onto your side and push up with your arms as you would have done towards the end of pregnancy, as this reduces strain through your tummy. To get back in, just do the opposite, lie down on your side, bring your legs up and then roll onto your back. If you have someone around to help, ask them to help support the weight of your legs as they come off and onto the bed.
- *Scar support* – If you need to cough, sneeze and laugh then have a blanket or towel at the ready to put over your scar and apply pressure to support your wound. Your stitches won't open but the support helps to reduce discomfort.
- *Sleeping* – Pop a pillow under your knees if you are lying on your back, or under your tummy if lying on your side, to prevent any pulling or dragging on the scar in the early days.
- *Bowels* – Trapped wind can be more painful than the scar, so movement can help this, as well as peppermint tea. Make sure when you feel the urge to do a poo you don't put it off to help prevent constipation.

Also remember that the reason you don't open your bowels for a few hours or days after giving birth is not because you haven't eaten for a while. It is actually because your bowels have gone to 'sleep' due to being touched during surgery. Don't eat big heavy meals until your bowels have 'woken up' and you are passing wind again.

When can I start pelvic floor exercises after birth?

You can start pelvic floor exercises once you have done your first wee. This will vary depending on whether you have had a catheter inserted or not. A priority after birth is to ensure your bladder is emptying properly, which can be impacted by birth or when we have a catheter. So, your medical team will want to ensure that you have done a wee within 6 hours of giving birth or the catheter being removed. They will often ask to measure this first wee, and will provide you with a container to wee into, to make sure you are passing good volumes. If all is well then you can gently get started on some pelvic floor contractions, always making sure you let go as well. Don't be alarmed if after a vaginal birth you struggle to feel much contraction. This is very normal, especially if you have a tear, as pain and swelling can make it harder to contract. View this time as just reconnection. I know pelvic floor exercises are not top of anyone's list and there are so many things to do and get used to in the early days and weeks. My top tip is, once feeding is established, try to do a few every time you feed your baby. There is no rush or pressure, just slowly work up to the exercises explained on page 43.

Guidelines do state that all women should be encouraged to do pelvic floor exercises postnatally. Supervised pelvic floor training with a pelvic health physiotherapist should be considered for women who have had assisted vaginal birth, which includes forceps or ventouse deliveries (see the box overleaf for more information), a back-to-back delivery or a third- or fourth-degree tear where there has been injury to the anal sphincter.[3] Pelvic floor exercises are for all women after birth, however you give birth to your baby. Pregnancy puts a lot of pressure on the pelvic floor, as we have discussed, so though it can seem that if you have had a Caesarean birth you don't need to do pelvic floor exercises, this isn't true. There is natural recovery of the pelvic floor muscles after birth during the first year, which is great news,[4] however, we can all benefit from working on our pelvic floor postpartum to aid recovery, treat incontinence[5] and prevent symptoms.

ASSISTED VAGINAL BIRTH

An assisted vaginal birth is when a medical professional uses specialist equipment to aid the delivery of your baby. This can be needed if your baby is distressed, is in a difficult position, there is a long second stage of labour and you have been pushing for a long time, there are any concerns about your health, or you are exhausted and need some extra help. Around one in eight vaginal births are assisted and this is more common for women having their first baby.[6] The two types of assisted vaginal birth are:

1. Ventouse birth: A vacuum cup is applied to the baby's head and as you have a contraction and push, the medical professional will pull to help and support your baby to be birthed.
2. Forceps birth: Forceps are smooth, curved metal instruments that fit around the baby's head. As you have a contraction and push the medical professional will pull to help and support your baby to be birthed.

When should I be worried?

It can be really hard to know what symptoms we should be worried about after birth, and what is just par for the course and our body needing time to recover. My advice is that if you are worried, there is no harm in speaking to a medical professional and seeking assessment. A few things I encourage you to look out for are:

- **High levels of pain** that are not being helped by regular painkillers such as paracetamol and ibuprofen. This, alongside a wound looking red, angry and with a bad smell, could be a sign of infection. Whether this is a vaginal or abdominal wound this needs immediate medical attention. So please make sure you flag it as soon as possible.
- **Loss of bowel control.** If you are really struggling to control your bowels, experiencing ongoing faecal incontinence, please speak to your medical team. There are rare occasions when the grade of perineal tear is misdiagnosed, and a third- or fourth-degree tear is missed. Early support can help physically and emotionally.
- **Reduced bladder sensation and control.** If you lose all feeling of needing to do a wee or have absolutely no bladder control, speak to your medical team. They will help you to understand why this is happening, how to manage symptoms and provide ongoing help.

RETURNING TO PHYSICAL ACTIVITY

As we have discussed, being physically active has so many benefits in pregnancy, and this continues into the postpartum period. However, this time can be as hard to navigate as pregnancy in terms of feeling unsure of what to do and when. There is no one-size-fits-all way to becoming more physically active, which I am sure is no surprise considering how different our birth experiences can be. Whenever we are ready and able, slow and steady with gradual and graded activity is best.

During the early days and weeks, stepping outside for a walk up and down your road may be enough, alongside pottering around the house and 24/7 care of a newborn. As a new mother, you are not inactive. Being led by pain and any symptoms is wise, and gradually increasing the length of the walks that you do. I advise to not wait until you feel much better and then head out for a really long walk. Instead, whenever you feel ready, start small and build up steadily. This might be up and down your road, then round the block, then a 20-minute walk, then slowly and steadily building up to an hour. Little bits of movement that we can do throughout the day often feels really good, especially when we can find ourselves in funny positions supporting a baby while feeding, sleeping or burping.

A few ideas of what you can do alongside walking in the early days and weeks are:

1. **Diaphragmatic breathing** – Working on some diaphragmatic breathing (see page 42) is a lovely place to start in your postnatal recovery. You can try this in a lying position as it can help you to relax before naps or as you prepare for an interrupted night of sleep. Try 5–10 breaths and allow your tummy and pelvic floor to relax as your rib cage expands.

2. **Pelvic tilts** – Lie on your back on the floor or your bed and gently tilt the pelvis back, like you are squashing your lower back into the floor or bed. Then move back into your starting position. This is not a big movement but can feel really lovely to get your lower back moving more. Don't push through discomfort, but if you feel comfortable enough try around 10 repetitions.

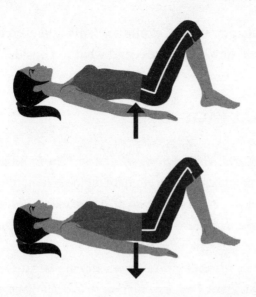

3. **Arm openings** – Lie on your side with your arms out in front of you, at shoulder height, with your hands together. Take your top arm over the top of you, like you are drawing a rainbow, opening up your chest. Take your arm as far as is comfortable. You should feel a pull in your chest. Don't push through discomfort, but if you feel comfortable enough try around 10 repetitions on each side.

In the next chapter we will explore activity and exercise after birth in more detail, how to progress and what to consider.

POSTNATAL FAQS

Q: It really hurts when I poo, what can I do to help?

It is very common for women to experience haemorrhoids and anal fissures postpartum, both of which can cause pain when doing a poo. For more information on how to help haemorrhoids head to page 109.

Anal fissures are little splits or tears in the lining of the anus that can be really painful. Pain can be due to the tear itself or the muscle spasm that can occur alongside it, which can make it harder to open your bowels. They can occur during birth or can be as a result of constipation and harder poo. Symptoms include pain and bleeding when doing a poo or on wiping.

Top tips to help:

- Focus on ensuring you are getting enough fluid and fibre.
- Try to relax on the toilet, which is easier said than done. Use deep breathing and raise your feet on a step as this can help.
- Speak to your doctor for advice on laxatives or creams that might help reduce pain, and keep your stools softer and easier to pass.

Q: Should I use an abdominal support or binder to help my tummy recover?

There is no clear cut yes or no answer on this. They can be helpful for certain women, especially if they have a larger diastasis recti postpartum. They can provide a lot of comfort, support and reduce distress, especially after a Caesarean birth.[7] So if women want to try one then I am not against it, but they should not be prioritised over exercises and rehabilitation of the abdominal muscles.

Q: I still have PGP, what should I do?

For some, PGP seems to disappear like magic after birth. However, unfortunately for approximately 17 per cent of women it persists postpartum and is still present 3 months after birth.[8] Thorough assessment and individualised treatment is always best, looking at the pelvis itself, as well as the muscles around the pelvis including the pelvic floor. Women often ask if they should give up breastfeeding to help their PGP get better as some women report this helps. I don't encourage this as I think a woman should be supported to breastfeed her baby for as long as she wishes. It is also possible that breastfeeding is protective, as higher levels of prolactin and oxytocin can help reduce inflammation in the body and therefore reduce discomfort felt. As with all things, there is no one clear-cut plan, but there is help. So please don't suffer in silence, seek support.

Q: I've got pain in my thumb – what is going on?

This is quite common postpartum, and for many is due to a condition called De Quervain's tenosynovitis. Pain is caused by swelling of the tendons, and of the sheath around them, of the muscles that move the thumb. Looking after a baby involves using our hands a lot: picking them up, holding them in place to get the perfect latch when breastfeeding, burping, and carrying them around. This repetitive use can lead to developing De Quervain's and it can make day-to-day mum life painful and tricky.

Treatment often involves:

- Immobilising and resting the wrist, which is pretty hard for a mum. Wrist and thumb spica splints can be worn for as much of the day and night as possible to aid rest.

- Use of ice over the wrist. An ice pack should be wrapped in a towel and placed on the area for 10–15 minutes at a time, every few hours.
- A physiotherapist or hand therapist can assess and give you exercises, and in some cases make a personalised bespoke splint.
- Some women require steroid injections.

POSTNATAL CHECKS

Depending on where you live around the world will determine what your experience is of postnatal checks with medical professionals. Review is pretty standardised in the early days and weeks, for you and your baby. However, past the first few weeks there is a lot of variety. Within the UK, where I am based, there is a huge disparity in women's experiences, first of all whether they even see a doctor at around 6 to 8 weeks after giving birth and, if they do, what this check involves. I want to make sure that this conversation never becomes a GP-bashing experience, as I am married to a GP so am naturally protective, as well as working alongside amazing GPs. The reality we have within the UK is that GPs generally have between 10 and 20 minutes to cover some very large topics, such as physical recovery, feeding, maternal mental health and contraception. To put this into context, when I see women after birth, I have an hour to focus purely on physical assessment and recovery. The other challenge we face is that in order to attend a lot of postnatal exercise classes, women need to have been checked by a doctor, for insurance reasons. Therefore, the postnatal check is often viewed by women as an extensive check to clear them for exercise, when, unfortunately, this could never be the case.

There is a call for more support for women after birth, and I am fully behind this as I see first-hand, and have personally experienced, the benefits of comprehensive physical postnatal assessment. Most importantly I think women need help in identifying issues they need to raise. So, I have developed a checklist for anyone heading to their postnatal check. You can use it to make notes and take it with you to your appointment.

CHECKLIST FOR POSTNATAL CHECK

Do you still have any pain in your body? If you do, jot down where it is.
Are you leaking urine if you cough, sneeze, laugh or walk?
Are you leaking urine when you get the urge to do a wee, but can't get to the bathroom in time?
Are you experiencing urgency to do a wee?
Are you finding you very frequently need to do a wee, over 8 times a day?
Are you experiencing urgency when needing a poo?
Are you struggling to control your bowels and experiencing faecal incontinence?

Are you struggling to control wind?

Do you have any pain in a vaginal tear/scar?

Do you have any pain in your Caesarean scar?

Are you experiencing a dragging feeling or heaviness within the vagina?

Are you noticing a bulging up or dropping down of the tissues down the middle of your tummy?

Have you experienced any pain during intercourse since giving birth?

If you have answered 'yes' to any of these, please flag this to your doctor and seek advice. It might be appropriate for you to be referred to a pelvic health physiotherapist for further review and support. The earlier we support you, the better you will feel physically and mentally.

Please remember that a postnatal check isn't a final sign-off for you to seek help with symptoms. It is so hard to know at times how we feel at 6 to 8 weeks after birth, everything can feel a bit like a survival blur. So if you just go through the motions and later on realise that there are symptoms you would like support with, please make sure you seek assessment. We will be delving into this more in the chapters ahead, so come with me and let's keep exploring and understanding more about this amazing but often quite challenging time in our lives.

Foundation Reflections

Take a moment to jot down any thoughts after reading this chapter, or any reminders that you can refer back to in the days, weeks and months ahead. You may want to expand on some of the topics from the postnatal checklist and write down any questions that you have for your doctor.

....

....

....

....

....

....

....

....

....

CHAPTER 9

Beyond

Let's learn about:

- Moving beyond the early postpartum weeks
- How to return safely to the exercise you love
- Movements to get you started
- Some of the barriers to being active again and how to navigate these
- Taking care of scars, including vaginal and Caesarean scars
- How to navigate the transition to motherhood mentally and emotionally
- Birth trauma and support available
- Recovery FAQs

Moving beyond those first 6 weeks feels like a huge milestone. I remember being told 'just get to 6 weeks and it will get easier', and yet I found myself at 6 weeks and wasn't sure if I found it much easier! This was the first moment of me learning quite how different motherhood experiences, postnatal recoveries and children are. I felt the timescale of the fourth trimester, which is the first 12 weeks after birth, was more realistic for feeling a bit more together and physically comfortable. I do think by so much focus being put on the first 6 weeks, we set women up with unrealistic expectations of how they will feel at this point.

Many of us are very keen to return to physical activity and exercise that we may have done before or during pregnancy but are unsure how to do this safely and correctly. I therefore find that we either just crack on at 6 weeks with what we did before, for example, running or HIIT, or we struggle to find our way, not sure where to start and can take months to get started. I truly believe we need to support women to become physically active after birth, to support their physical recovery, build strength to handle the demands of motherhood, support their mental health and create space for themselves as they navigate their new role. It is one of my biggest passions that women feel educated and supported whenever they would like to return to the kind of physical activity they enjoyed before pregnancy and birth – whether this be going for an hour's family walk, entering a triathlon, dancing with their kids at home, or running a marathon. The UK Chief Medical Officer encourages postnatal women to aim for 150 minutes of moderate-intensity activity per week, the same advice as during pregnancy. This is helpful guidance, but the question still remains: *how* do we get back to this?

The 6-week postnatal recovery timescale is talked about for a number of reasons. From a physical perspective it is because the average soft tissue (i.e., muscles and skin) healing time is 6 weeks. However, this doesn't mean that at 6 weeks everything is miraculously recovered, it is just the initial part of the story. The way I like to view the postnatal recovery and transition is with 3Rs.

Recovery ←——→ Rehabilitation ←————→ Reintroduction

There are not rigid timescales for each stage, but just general ranges and at times we may need to move between the phases quite freely. This is why I use arrows going in both directions as I see postnatal recovery as much more fluid than is often presented and communicated. To be totally honest, the way I think it should be presented is in a Venn diagram (as shown below), acknowledging the different stages but also knowing they overlap and each of our realities are a mix of them all. I definitely know mine has been. Let's take a look at each phase together and understand a bit more about them.

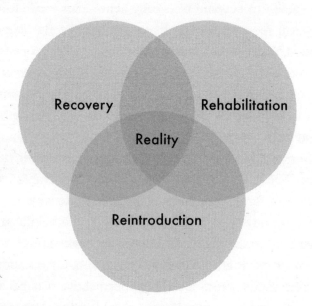

RECOVERY

This is that immediate period after birth that we discussed in the previous chapter. It mixes with rehabilitation as this can easily begin in the early days and weeks postpartum, even though it won't feel like we are extensively active. Working on being gradually more physically active through walking, as well as working on diaphragmatic breathing, pelvic floor and abdominal exercises, are all part of the recovery and rehabilitation process.[1]

REHABILITATION

I encourage women to view the time from 6 to 12 weeks postpartum as rehabilitation. Now, this doesn't mean just lying on a mat doing boring exercises that you don't enjoy. It means acknowledging that there have been muscle, nerve and connective tissue changes that we need to consider in our return to being more physically active, which means sometimes we have to scale back or modify our favourite form of activity initially. If we have specific goals in mind, this phase needs to be planned so it is related to the tasks we want to get back to. For example, if the goal is running, then working on exercises that will prepare us for this is important. I am a personal believer, alongside many other physiotherapists and trainers, that we need to make rehabilitation functional, which means representing everyday movements that we carry out. This phase honestly looks different for everyone, but some general principles that we can all follow are:

1. Continue with your pelvic floor exercises. Work on progressing to doing these whilst standing, which is a functional position most mothers find themselves in a lot of the time. There are not many mothers I meet who complain about sitting down too much!
2. Aim for activities that you enjoy.
3. Finding a specific postnatal class local to you can be a lovely way to rehabilitate, meet others and be part of a community.
4. Postnatal Pilates or postnatal yoga classes can be a very supportive and graded way to return to more physical activity.
5. Know that you are incredibly active as a mother and that *all* activity counts.

6. Focus on functional movements that you need for everyday life and motherhood, such as squats, lunges and deadlifts.

REINTRODUCTION

This focuses on your return to the activities and exercise you love and make you feel like you. For some this might be HIIT classes, running, spinning, climbing or CrossFit. For others it will be a long walk in the woods, chasing your kids in the park or going on a bike ride. The priority should always be supporting your body to be ready for the tasks you need or want it to perform without symptoms or pain. Sadly, I can't provide a specific programme for every type of activity, as that would make a rather long book, but I want to share with you some advice and general guidance.

1. Graded return to impact activities is advised for all women, however you birthed your baby.
2. During running, jumping or lifting weights there will be a rise in intra-abdominal pressure (IAP) and forces transmitted through the pelvic floor. Our recovering pelvic floor muscles, especially if you have had a perineal tear or episiotomy, need time to get used to these higher levels of IAP again, especially when repeated during a run or high impact exercise programme. We will discuss this in more detail in a moment.
3. Impact exercise and lifting weights can be beneficial for a variety of reasons, but the pelvic floor needs to be ready for the task. I think of this a bit like my first days back at work after maternity leave. I was trying to catch up and

make sure I was up to speed with changes and new programmes, etc., while also not getting much sleep. I just needed some time, patience and understanding that I wasn't quite back to full speed. This is how I imagine our pelvic floor feels when we return to running and lifting weights. It is keen, and wants to perform, but needs our understanding that it has been through a lot and so needs a gradual and graded return.

4. Recent return-to-running guidelines suggest that the earliest most women should return to running is 12 weeks postpartum. They also recommend using a graded running programme, such as Couch to 5K, using walking and running to help your body get used to running again.[2]

5. Working with our breath can help our pelvic floor function. A simple way to remember this is to exhale on the effort of a movement. For example, as you stand up from a squat, breathe out. What is most important for all exercise is that we just remember to breathe.

6. It isn't all about the pelvic floor! Never thought you would hear me say that, right? But honestly, so many of our muscles go through changes in pregnancy. The abdominal, leg, bottom and back muscles should also be considered when contemplating postnatal return to exercise.

7. It is good to get back to weight and impact training for our bone density, which, though something we don't often think of at this stage, we will be thankful for when we are older.

8. The UK Department of Health encourages us to build back up to muscle strengthening activities twice a week, so considering how we can do this is important.

9. Continue with pelvic floor exercises through this period and through life, as long-term training is important to prevent symptoms.[3]

Though I can't give you a specific programme tailored to you, I wanted to give you a general idea of what rehabilitation and returning to functional movements could look like, with our mindset and goals focused on reintroduction. I am delighted that Lulu Adams, my wonderful friend and pre- and postnatal coach, has joined me to share her thoughts and guidance on how to navigate this time.

As Clare says, it's important that you find activities that you enjoy, as you're more likely to do it more often if it's something you actually like. A full body functional strength programme is a pretty good place for new mums to start, whatever their goals or passions, to help the body get back to a place where it can function as well as it's designed to.

When we talk about a 'functional' strength programme, we are really thinking about focusing on the movement patterns that we use day in and day out through our daily tasks. There are many arguments out there for how many categories of functional movement there are, but for the purposes of postnatal training I like to focus in on:

Pull – this includes movements that require us to contract our muscles to 'pull' a weight towards our body, which, if you think about how often you're lifting a baby to you in the early weeks, is a movement we do a lot of!

Push – the reverse of 'pull', this is where we contract our muscles to 'push' a weight away from us – so you can think about pushing a buggy as a good example of 'pushing' that we do regularly as mums.

Squat – a very common and well-known movement pattern, where you bend your knees to lower yourself down, then stand back up. It's a pattern all of us are probably already doing, if you think about how you stand up out of a chair.

Hinge – in contrast to the squat, the hinge is dominated by the movement happening at the hips and a good way to tell if you're squatting or hinging is to see which way the hips are moving. Hips down = squat, hips back = hinge. If you think about unloading a dishwasher or picking a car seat up from the floor, these are hinge movements.

Lunge – there are technically quite a few 'lunge' variations – but essentially these are single leg movements that are similar to a squat, as your front (and working) leg bends at the knee. They can be done statically, with both feet staying on the ground, and progress to being more dynamic as you 'step' one leg back. Lunges are an important exercise to help work our coordination and balance, and to ensure we're able to load one side of the body at a time (we do that all the time when we're walking anyway).

Rotation – rotation is key when it comes to fundamental human movement and is something that can become quite restricted during pregnancy. It's particularly important to ensure we have the ability to rotate well postnatally because if we can't, it's likely that we're going to feel stuck in certain positions and this can affect our body's ability to manage pressure.

Now in reality, the movements we perform as mothers tend not to fall directly into any one of these – they are usually a bit of a combination of two or three of them (picking up a car seat to get it into the car = hip hinge and a push with maybe a sprinkling of rotation in there). Generally, finding a programme that covers all of these patterns will mean you're working multiple muscle groups at the same time through patterns that the body needs to be strong in order to function well.

Our bodies are incredibly clever, and adaptable, and they will find a way to do a movement however they need to, even if there are limitations at play. We don't always need to be laser sharp and precise with every movement pattern and I am certainly an advocate for moving for movement's sake (and for our mental health), but at this stage, when we're looking to maximise our recovery and get our body functioning and moving well, it really does pay off to spend a bit of time on each movement pattern. This way we are setting ourselves up to play the long game.

Getting started

The focus in this stage is being able to move and breathe freely in each movement. A helpful way to try this and get started is to breathe in as you start the movement, and exhale on the more effortful part. For example, breathe in as you go down into a squat position, and exhale as you stand back up. Using your breath like this helps the pelvic floor to move naturally with the breath and our core to manage intra-abdominal pressure well. You might then like to try gently engaging the pelvic floor as you exhale as well. Working on body and breath awareness and 'connection' to the pelvic floor helps us bridge the gap between isolated rehabilitation of the pelvic floor and integrated training.

Squat – sit to stand
- Stand in front of a chair or sofa.
- Sit back by bending your knees to tap your bottom onto the chair or sofa. Let your knees go out in front of you: it's a myth that you shouldn't let your knees go over your toes in a squat. This should let you stay a little more upright.
- Think about widening your sit bones as you lower down, and breath in as you lower.
- As you come back up, exhale and drive your feet down into the floor.

Once this feels good and you feel confident, try doing the same without the chair or sofa behind you, which moves you into a free squat.

You could also try:

- Adding a weight – Having a weight out in front helps you shift back because you're counterbalanced with that weight. When holding the weight lift your elbows up slightly rather than just hugging into your chest. I usually recommend finding a weight similar to that of your little one – because that's the weight you're already lifting and pushing and pulling and carrying every day. However, if there is any concern around movement, if you feel vulnerable in certain movement patterns due to pelvic floor symptoms or previous injuries, etc., it is definitely worth starting with just your bodyweight and focusing on getting a good range of movement first.

Hinge – shoulder bridge

- Lie on your back on a mat on the floor.
- As a general rule, your feet should be just far enough away from your bottom that you can tickle your heel with your middle fingers.
- Initiate the movement with a gentle tuck of the pelvis backwards: think about tipping your pubic bone up towards your ribs or squashing your back onto the mat.
- Then lift the hips up, with a gentle exhale, maintaining the tuck of the pelvis as this will help prevent you over-extending into your back.
- Aim to get the hips up so they are level with your lower ribs and knees in a straight line.
- Inhale at the top, then exhale as you lower down.

NOTE: If you feel the movement too much in the muscles at the front of the legs, called the quadriceps, move your feet further away from your bottom. We want to feel the hamstrings, at the back of the legs, and the bottom muscles, in this movement.

Lunge – split stance squat

- Stand with one foot in front of the other, about shoulder-width apart.
- Try not to have your feet too far apart when you set up (think about having your feet on train tracks, not a tightrope), but make sure you have about 80 per cent of your weight in your front foot, through the middle of the foot.
- It can help to try this movement with the heel of the back foot against a wall.
- Keep your body upright without slouching over. It might help to reach the arms forward while thinking about your ribs being stacked over your pelvis.
- Push the back heel into the wall as you lower down with an inhale, allowing the front knee to move forward so you can stay fairly upright.
- Exhale as you push back up.
- You should feel this working in the thigh of the front leg, but also the bottom muscles as you drive up. When doing this movement with one foot against a wall, you may also feel it in the back leg, and this isn't a bad thing.

Pull – three-point bent over row

- Stand in front of a chair and hinge forward from the hips.
- Place one hand on the edge of the chair, with your wrist under your shoulder.
- Push into the chair with that hand, and hold a dumbbell or water bottle in the other hand.
- Inhale as you reach down with the dumbbell, allowing the shoulder blade to glide forwards over the ribs towards the floor.
- Keeping the wrist relaxed (don't grip too hard on the weight) exhale and draw the weight up to your waist, by bending your elbow.
- Think about leading the movement with your shoulder blade and wrapping it back around the rib cage towards the spine.

NOTE: A common problem I see mums having with 'pulling' movements, like bent over rows, is that they feel it in their neck or the front of their shoulder, rather than their back – which is where we want to be feeling it. Make sure as you are doing it that, as your elbow comes back, your shoulder doesn't fall forward.

TOP TIP: look slightly ahead of you, keep the hand and elbow soft and focus your attention instead on what's happening around the shoulder blade. Start with a small range of motion to begin with while you get used to feeling this around the shoulder blade instead of your neck.

Push – 90/90 floor press

- Lie on the floor with your heels on a sofa or chair that allows you to find a 90/90 position (90° at hip and 90° at knee).
- Have two light weights, for example, water bottles or tins of beans in your hands, with elbows out at 45°.
- Dig your heels into the chair slightly.
- Inhale into your ribcage to prepare.
- As you exhale, press the weights away from you, finishing the movement with a reach towards the sky with your arm, keeping your upper back on the floor.
- Start your inhale at the top as you're reaching, and then slowly lower the arms back down to the start position.

Rotation – thread the needle

- Start by coming into a four-point kneeling position on a mat.
- Your hips should be above your knees and your wrists under your shoulders.
- Take one arm and reach it through the gap created between the opposite arm and leg. The free arm is the thread, and the gap is the eye of the needle you are threading it through.
- Reach the free arm all the way through. You can rest it on the floor and hold a stretch before bringing it back through and reaching up towards the ceiling. Allow your head and neck to move round with the free arm.

NOTE: Keep your hips still as much as possible and focus the movement through the upper back and ribs.

RETURNING TO ABDOMINAL EXERCISES

Remember that your tummy muscles and core will be working through all of the movements we have discussed so far, however there is also benefit to completing exercises focused on the abdominal muscles. Here are a couple of exercises to try:

Curl up

- Lie comfortably on a mat on the floor with your knees bent.
- Place your hands behind your head and tuck your chin slightly to your chest.
- Gently lift your head and shoulders up off the mat, curling up, like the beginning of a full sit-up, as you exhale.
- Curl up high enough that you feel your tummy muscles working.
- Slowly lower back down to the mat.

NOTE: As you do this movement, if you see a bulging up of the tissues down the middle of the tummy, or a dropping down of the tissues, this could indicate that there is ongoing diastasis recti. Head to page 229 to read more.

Supermans (or, as I prefer, Supermums)

- Start by coming into a four-point kneeling position on a mat.
- Your hips should be above your knees and your wrists under your shoulders.
- Start by lifting one arm up, reaching it away from the body as you exhale.
- Keep your back totally flat: imagine there is a tray of your favourite drinks on there that you don't want to spill.
- You should feel your tummy muscles gently engage as you lift one arm up.

- Then try sliding one leg away as you exhale, keeping both arms on the mat. Follow the same principle of keeping your back totally flat.
- Then try lifting the leg slightly. Make sure that as you lift the leg your back doesn't drop down.

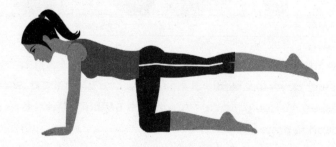

- Once you feel confident with lifting the arms and legs separately, you can try lifting the opposite arm and leg together. Keep focused on not allowing the back to drop down or your body to rotate.

INTRODUCING IMPACT

There are ways we can introduce impact into our exercise routines before we head out for a run or to a HIIT class to help our pelvic floor to be ready.[4] By gradually introducing impact we are allowing our pelvic floor time to get used to, adapt and flag any struggles it is having. Practising isolated movements while making sure we breathe helps our body to prepare for what's ahead. Before we talk about some options you could try, however, I wanted to briefly talk about what the pelvic floor does during activity.

The pelvic floor muscles during activity

The pelvic floor muscles have been found in research to activate in an anticipatory and reflexive manner during high impact exercises such as running and jumping.[5] This means there is a natural and subconscious response of the muscles in response to impact. It is this reflexive nature that we are trying to support and train through graded impact. This is why we don't want to be contracting our pelvic floor muscles consciously when being active, but allow the muscles to respond naturally.

Why not try the following?

Hopping

- Try hopping on each leg for 10–15 repetitions.
- Make sure you don't hold your breath or contract your pelvic floor.
- Gradually increase the number of repetitions if you are symptom free and comfortable.

Jumping

- Try jumping on the spot, making sure you land with soft knees.
- Again, make sure you are not holding your breath or contracting your pelvic floor.
- Try 10–15 repetitions and increase the number if you are symptom free and feel comfortable.

Running on the spot

- Trying running on the spot for 1 minute.
- You can use this as a little warm-up to other activities or exercise you are doing.

* * *

Throughout all these movements you should remain symptom free. If you notice any urinary or faecal leakage, a heaviness or dragging sensation in the vagina, or any pain, don't push through. This can be a helpful prompt to book an appointment with your doctor or to find a physio to support you. In the meantime, you can try doing fewer repetitions or less time running on the spot to try and find a symptom-free zone to work in.

REALITY

Most of us have all the best intentions postpartum to return to our previous exercise routine or activity level, and many do. However, I want to acknowledge that for many of us it just isn't that simple. Before kids I could pick and choose when I wanted to go to a class or for a run, fitting around work and my social life. Being a parent is very different. There are so many factors that influence our ability to be active, including childcare, sleep and energy levels to name just a few. What our bodies don't need is more stress and pressure, so how we approach it is key, as well as having realistic expectations. This is something that Lulu discusses extensively with her coaching clients and so I have asked her for her top tips for all of you:

1. Something is always better than nothing. Very often we're looking for the time and the space to get the 'perfect' workout in. But in motherhood, this isn't always as easy to find as it might have once been! Ten minutes of something is better than no minutes of a 40-minute full-body workout.
2. Learn to value rest. Rest is so undervalued in our society – and yet if we're looking for our body to adapt, to change, to get stronger, we need to recognise that it only makes those adaptations when we actually give it proper rest.
3. Don't undervalue activities like getting outside for a walk. It can be easy to get frustrated that we're not getting our 'workouts' in if life throws us curve balls in motherhood. But rather than wallowing in that frustration, start recognising the benefits of other activity: simply getting outside for a dose of fresh air can do us the world of good.

It can be easy to see the limitations on our lives, and what we *can't* do in this stage. However, what can help - and is often really powerful - is to actually think about what we *can* do and to see how that can bring about gradual change. This might look a bit like Figure 19.

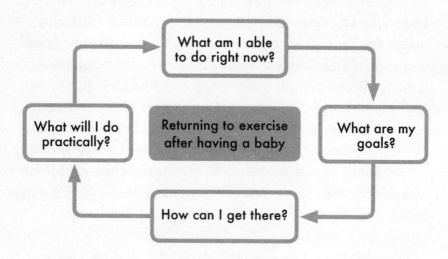

Fig. 19: Returning to exercise postpartum reflection using the Appreciative Inquiry Model

Figure 19 is based on the Appreciative Inquiry Model,[6] which is a positive approach to help leaders develop and organisations to change. Rather than focusing on the problem, they focus on the positives and what is working. I think we can use this as new mums to encourage ourselves, recognise our strengths and bring our physical recovery alongside how we think, feel and our goals. So how might this look in practice? Head to Figure 20 for an example.

Why not take a moment to turn to the Foundation Reflections section on page 199) and jot down how this might look for you right now. You can review it as many times as you need, and as things change you will see how far you have come.

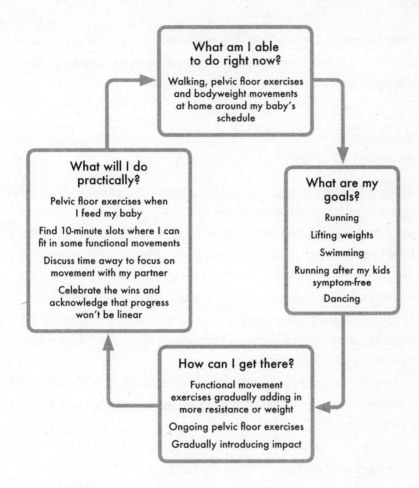

Fig. 20: An example of putting the Appreciative Inquiry Model into practice

Can I be active and exercise when breastfeeding?

This is a common question, and I am delighted to say that the answer is a resounding *yes*. You can exercise when breastfeeding and it doesn't impact your supply or quality of your milk.[7,8] On a practical level, having a good supportive sports bra is important and I would advise feeding before exercise, especially in those early months. Keep hydrated, especially with more vigorous exercise where you are sweating more, as we need to ensure you don't become dehydrated.

What symptoms should you look out for when returning to activity?

My hope is that women can return gradually to activity and exercise without symptoms, however, for some of us that isn't how our story goes. I still hear of women wearing black leggings to help hide urinary leakage that occurs during exercise, or wearing a pad just so they can be active. I want to challenge the narrative that is still very present, that urinary leakage is just part of motherhood. It is not. It isn't something we have to accept as normal and I want all of you to stand up and challenge the myth for yourselves, for your friends and for future generations.

Urinary leakage is what we often hear about, but is it the only symptom? Let's run through them all so you know what to look out for.

- **Urinary incontinence:** Leakage of urine during any form of activity – walking, running, lifting weights, lifting your kids, dancing and so on. This is called stress urinary incontinence. It can sometimes be hard to tell if we are leaking urine or just have more discharge, which can be common postpartum. This is when using a pad and seeing if there is a yellow stain or smell of urine can help to differentiate between the two.
- **Faecal or flatal incontinence:** Leakage of poo or wind during any form of activity. It's not as commonly talked about but is experienced by many and can be a real barrier to activity from fear of this happening in a public place.

- **Prolapse:** A heaviness or dragging sensation in the vagina aggravated by or felt more after activity. This does not mean you have to stop all forms of activity, but we need to just assess and support you in how to be active in the best way to help your body.
- **Diastasis rectus abdominis:** After birth this may present as a bulging up or dropping down of the tissues down the middle of the tummy. Again, it is not a complete barrier or stop to all activity but helping you to know what is best for your body at each stage is important.
- **Pain:** Pain felt anywhere in the body should not be ignored on returning to activity.

In the next chapter I am going to delve into incontinence, prolapse and diastasis rectus abdominis in a lot more detail, so if you want more information on any of these, I promise it is coming. Before we get there, however, let's consider what else we can be doing to support our body during this time.

SCAR TLC

The majority of women will have a scar after giving birth, whether this be an abdominal scar after a Caesarean birth, or a scar after a perineal tear which might be internal (in the vagina) or external (on the vulva). Once they are fully healed (at around six to eight weeks postpartum), scars can really benefit from being massaged. Scars are often quite tight and can have altered sensation, being either numb or actually hypersensitive. This might sound a bit crazy but trust me on this, it can help symptoms as well as build confidence.

Vaginal scar massage

A sensitive and tight scar in the vagina or on the vulva can cause discomfort day to day and feel like it is pulling, and naturally can make us cautious and worried about returning to intercourse. Gently massaging the scar once it has fully healed can help to reduce discomfort, tightness and make us more confident that intercourse will be OK. I advise women to do this before returning to intercourse if they have any concerns, because if we are apprehensive that intercourse is going to be painful our pelvic floor often tightens; this is vaginismus that we have discussed previously (see page 88). Preparing by doing some massage before we return to intercourse can help to prevent this occurring.

Massage technique

This is very similar to perineal massage recommended before birth. Try these steps:

- Ensure the scar has fully healed, which will take at least 6 weeks. If you have any concerns about your scar or are unsure if it has fully healed then please speak to your doctor.
- Wash your hands and use a natural oil or lubricant and apply to the vulva and your thumb.
- Use a mirror to have a look and locate any scar tissue. There may be some outside as well as inside.
- You can start massaging the external scar first. Start using little circles the whole way along the scar and then rubbing across it. This should be gentle and not cause redness. (See Figure 21.)
- Then place your thumb inside your vagina a couple of centimetres. Sweep side to side 10 times. This might help you to locate the area of scar tissue internally which might feel more tender or tight.

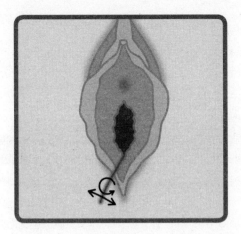

Fig. 21: External scar massage

- If you know where the scar is, you can gently hold a stretch into this area for 30 seconds. Then you can gently stretch either side of it for 30 seconds as well.
- Repeat this a few times a week and you should notice any pulling and discomfort decreases.
- If you have ongoing discomfort or pain, or the scar is too sore to touch and massage, then please flag this to your doctor for review.

Caesarean scar massage

Massaging a Caesarean section scar has so many benefits, and I asked Hannah Poulton, a UK leading C-section and scar expert, to share her wisdom and top tips on how to get started.

The benefits of scar massage:
- Helping us to reconnect with our bodies after surgery.
- Reducing any feeling of pulling around the scar.
- Increasing blood flow to the area.

- Softening of the scar.
- Reducing sensitivity.
- Changing the appearance of the scar.
- Reducing numbness around the scar.

How to start interacting and massaging your Caesarean scar:

- Look at your scar in a mirror or physically look at it to start with.
- Get used to patting it dry after a shower using a soft cloth, towel or muslin.
- Once the scab has fully gone, usually around 6 weeks, you can start to think about massaging around and onto the scar. Scar massage can only happen when your scar is fully healed, there is no infection, no stitches left, and you are happy to touch the scar.
- Lie on your back somewhere you feel relaxed, try some deep breathing and start with gentle light touch over your scar.
- You can then apply a natural oil onto the scar.
- Sweeping motions back and forth and circles over your scar are a great place to start.

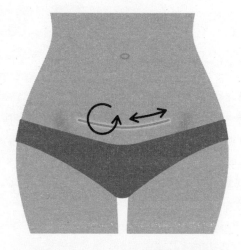

Fig. 22: Caesarean scar massage

- Start with light pressure. You are not aiming to cause discomfort or redness around the scar.
- Build up the time you are doing this for. Start with a few minutes and then gradually build up to 10–15 minutes a day.
- If you are struggling to physically touch your scar, use a clean make-up brush or cotton wool to sweep over the scar instead. Take your time and don't put pressure on yourself.
- It can be really helpful to use different textures over the scar as well.
- If your scar is red and raised, then using silicone may help.[9]
- Don't compare yourself or your scar to anyone else. This is your birth, your journey and your recovery. Your scar will heal in its own time with the correct gentle care and attention.
- If you find that looking at or touching your scar feels traumatic or brings back flashbacks of your baby's birth, please don't carry on; instead seek support.

IS IT ALL ABOUT OUR PHYSICAL RECOVERY?

Though my focus is often on physical recovery as a physiotherapist, this is absolutely only one part of the picture in the postpartum period. We must remember to support and look after the whole mother and empower you to care for and prioritise yourself. Caring for you is caring for your baby. Maternal mental health is such an important topic to discuss and conversation to open up. I am passionate about highlighting and acknowledging the very present link between pelvic floor symptoms and mental health struggles, as it has been shown that pelvic floor symptoms impact the mental and emotional health of 43 per cent of women.[10]

When we struggle with our pelvic health after birth it can bring with it so many emotions of anger, resentment, self-blame, shame, embarrassment, loneliness, I could go on and I am sure many of you would add to this list. Navigating motherhood, caring for children and managing pelvic floor symptoms is really challenging, and often you are then struggling to do the activity or exercise you love that could help your mental health. It really is a vicious cycle. It can also lead to us comparing ourselves to others' recovery journeys and being jealous of their progress when we are struggling. I know I've felt this for sure. When I was diagnosed with a prolapse and decided not to run for a while, I was so angry to see others doing something that I felt I would never be able to do again. It was no one else's fault but the feelings were very real. So, I want you to know that however you feel, those feelings are valid and part of the journey. They need to be discussed and you need to be supported. Don't bottle them up, share them with a medical professional or with family and friends.

I also want to be clear that you can be grateful for the birth of your baby *and* struggle with the symptoms it has left you with. One does not cancel out the other, despite women still being told to 'just be grateful you have a healthy baby'. Gratitude and sadness can co-exist together, and one amazing woman who has repeatedly helped me to remember this, along with thousands of other women, is my friend, psychotherapist and author Anna Mathur. Anna shares below her thoughts and tips for caring for your mental and emotional wellbeing as you navigate motherhood:

1. **Never overlook the chance to rest.** Rest for us is like plugging in your phone to charge. We recharge as we slow down, and this can be so hard to do during motherhood. Even small moments of rest are important. If your phone was low in battery you wouldn't think that charging it for 10 minutes before you left home wasn't worth it,

would you? You would take any charge you can get. We are the same. Finding small moments where you can slow down to recharge can help you through the days. In order to give out we need refuelling and recharging. We need energy to have fun, enjoy our kids, and navigate anxiety and emotions.

2. **Practise gratitude.** Motherhood can be full of moments of 'I've got to... do the laundry, get up at night with the baby or do the school run' but can we reframe this and try saying 'I get to... do the laundry, get up at night with the baby or do the school run.' It is important to acknowledge the challenges that we face but practising gratitude helps to bring balance.

3. **Recognising we don't have a village in the way we need.** As humans we were created to need and want community, and motherhood is the ultimate time when a village is needed. The phrase 'it takes a village to raise a child' doesn't come from nowhere. It could not be more true. However, the village that used to be the same few streets with kids playing in them and friends and family always around, are now communities spread across the country and the globe. We have to be intentional in building a village that we need. This can often require us to allow moments of vulnerability to forge new relationships and invest in existing ones. Ensure there are two or three people in your life that know beyond the 'I'm OK' phrase that we all use on a daily basis.

4. **Make sure you are in contact with someone every day.** Find small moments for interaction. Plan a phone call in the diary. A short walk with a friend or a girls' night out. Don't trust that life will always allow you to do those things; we have to make them happen. Connection is so important.

5. **Work out what your baseline is.** Note what are the basic things you need to feel OK day to day, whether that be a walk, a hobby, an exercise class or a daily shower. Every few months take a moment to think, 'am I functioning at my baseline or have I let things slip?'

6. **Think about your daily habits and basics of self-respect.** Are you drinking enough water? Taking a moment to go to the toilet? Ensuring you eat some food? When our body is dehydrated it is in a state of stress. If you struggle to follow through despite the best intentions, strip it back to something so small you can't not do it. For example, a glass of water when you wake up. In time, as you value the need to drink more and make it a habit, it will naturally increase. If you want to move more and miss it, why not aim for 5 minutes a day. Keep it manageable and then work up from there.

7. **Ask yourself 'what are my needs?'** We spend our days meeting our children's needs and it can be very easy to forget our own in the mix. In order to meet our children's needs though, we do need to have our needs met as well. We can start to lose the language of our own needs, meaning we can struggle to even identify what we need at any given moment. Practise this in the small moments when you are meeting your baby's or child's needs, like a nappy change; ask yourself at that time, 'what do I need right now?' too.

8. **Become aware of signs your body is under high stress and on high alert.**
   You may notice:
   - You are more sensitive to noise.
   - Your shoulders are up, you're getting tension headaches or tummy symptoms.
   - You're struggling with feeling 'touched out' by too much physical contact.
   - You are quick to get angry.
   - You feel you can't cope.
   - You feel overwhelmed most of the time.

   If you are feeling these things a lot of the time, think about how you can carve out more moments of rest and talk about it. This doesn't mean you need a full day of childcare to go to a spa, it means taking mindful moments throughout the day.

BIRTH TRAUMA

Many women experience traumatic births, and this can stay with them for ever. Recognising and supporting women who have experienced birth trauma is important. Birth trauma and pelvic floor trauma and symptoms frequently occur together; however, birth can be traumatic without any ongoing physical symptoms. Illy Morrison, my lovely friend, a midwife and author, specialises in supporting women after birth trauma, and she has shared some thoughts with us on this very important topic.

WHAT IS BIRTH TRAUMA?

Birth trauma is the shorthand term used for post-traumatic stress disorder (PTSD) after birth or the term used to describe the experience of women who have symptoms of PTSD, such as flashbacks or intrusive memories, hypervigilance or nightmares, but not full-blown PTSD.

WHAT CAN YOU DO IF YOU ARE STRUGGLING?

The first thing I would recommend is to speak to your care providers, either your midwife, doctor or health visitor. There are numerous treatment and support options for those suffering from birth trauma. Birth reflection is an option; this is something that is offered by most hospitals and is generally an opportunity to discuss the clinical elements of the birth experience by using the clinical notes as a reference. There are a few challenges with this approach, the most important one being that the rehashing of the clinical experience in a space that is not trauma-informed runs the risk of re-traumatisation and not the healing that was sought. There is also a risk of defensive practice. This is where the person facilitating the reflection session feels that they, their colleagues, or their hospital trust is under attack and, in defence, invalidates, gaslights or denies the lived experience of the woman and her family. That being said, for many, this service has been helpful. You can access birth reflections privately with a birth professional. This allows the aspect of impartiality, which can feel safer. The challenge with this approach is that the practitioner does not have access to the clinical notes, but the patient can request these via their hospital website (see page 223). Further treatment options include cognitive behavioural therapy (CBT), Eye Movement Desensitisation and Reprocessing (EMDR), or talking therapy with a specialist practitioner.

HOW CAN A BIRTH DEBRIEF HELP?

A birth debrief can be great as a starting point. It allows the opportunity for clarity on what happened, validation and understanding. For many this is sufficient, but for others, what a debrief allows is the space to narrow down areas of difficulty to then be able to seek further support.

TOP TIPS FOR ANYONE STRUGGLING AT THE MOMENT

1. **Share.** A problem shared is a problem halved. Find a safe space/ person. This could be a partner, professional or friend, but find someone you trust.
2. **Seek support** from healthcare professionals.
3. **Write it down.** Getting things out of your head and onto paper is an excellent start.
4. **Know that it is not for ever** and that it is not your fault.

RECOVERY FAQS

Q: How long until I feel more like myself?

A question I am frequently asked and found myself asking a lot as well. The honest answer is that it really depends. However, I would say, on average, women notice a shift between 6–12 weeks, then around 6 months and then again at 1 year postpartum. I honestly felt most like me again between 1–2 years postpartum. I know that sounds like a long time, but I think being honest and realistic is important as well. We all have our own stories, but you should know that it is totally normal not to feel yourself at 6 weeks postpartum – despite what you might see on social media.

Q: I am struggling with vaginal wind, what is going on?
Passing wind out of the vagina, or 'queefing' as it is known, can be super embarrassing. Queefing is where air passes into the vagina and then is forced out, through a certain change in position. This can be more common after birth or in certain positions, such as headstands. Optimising pelvic floor function and flexibility is key, so, if you are struggling, try all the tips in this book to support your pelvic floor rehabilitation.

Q: Water comes out of my vagina after I go for a swim or come out of the bath, why is this?
One of those questions a lot of us wonder about but don't want to ask! I remember this happening the first few times I went to baby swim lessons with my daughter and wondering what was happening. This can occur after pregnancy and birth as the vagina is more open, allowing more water to pass in. When you stand up and walk back to the changing room gravity and pressure changes cause the water to come out. Again, working on pelvic floor muscle rehabilitation and giving your body time is key. It definitely got better for me.

* * *

As we have established in this chapter the time going beyond the immediate postpartum recovery can be a bit of a rollercoaster of physical symptoms and emotions. There is so much to navigate during this time. Being kind to ourselves and meeting ourselves where we are at is so important and I encourage you to do this at whatever stage you are at. There is no set timescale, your journey will be individual and, at times, this is hard. I have finally got back to running nearly 6 years after having my first, and that isn't because I physically could not have done so before. It is just that there were so many factors that contributed to this being the right time for me. So, hold on to what is right for you and seek support along the way where you need it.

Foundation Reflections

Take a moment to jot down any thoughts or tips that you want to remember from this chapter and refer back to them as and when you need it. You could pop a couple of tips or reminders on Post-its and pop them on a mirror or near a light switch as little prompts throughout your day.

....

....

....

....

....

....

....

....

....

CHAPTER 10

What Is This I Am Feeling?

Incontinence, Prolapse and Diastasis Rectus Abdominis

Let's learn about:

- The different types of urinary incontinence
- What you can do to help if you struggle with incontinence
- Anal incontinence: the different types and treatment options
- Pelvic organ prolapse: what it is and what the symptoms are
- What you can do to help if you have prolapse
- Vaginal pessaries
- Exercise and prolapse
- Diastasis rectus abdominis in more detail
- How to assess for diastasis rectus abdominis
- FAQs about incontinence, prolapse and diastasis rectus abdominis
- How to prepare for an appointment when seeking support

There are many possible symptoms that we can experience after birth, during day-to-day life and when becoming more active. Most of which are still rather taboo, hard to talk about and difficult to access help for. In this chapter we are going to take a deep dive into each of these symptoms and conditions and help you understand what you might be feeling, as well as what you can do to help yourself and how to seek further support as needed. The message I want to come through loud and clear from the beginning is that there *is* help. These symptoms don't have to define your life, your motherhood journey, or be accepted as 'just one of those things'. They deserve time and support to help you feel like you again. I can't promise a quick fix but hope to make things feel more manageable, with incremental improvements along the way.

INCONTINENCE

When we hear the word incontinence most of us probably think of leaking urine. However, as mentioned before, we can experience incontinence of urine, faeces or wind. Let's look at each of these individually and understand them a bit more.

Urinary incontinence

Leaking urine is often laughed off as part of motherhood, but I think, if we are really honest, for most of us it is far from a laughing matter. The problem is when we don't know what to do about it, what else can we do but laugh! The reality is that the women I meet don't want to leak urine; they want to exercise without a pad, run after their kids in the park and not worry they will need to change their trousers. Around one in three women are living with urinary incontinence, so that is a lot of us struggling with this on a daily basis. There are different types of urinary incontinence, and we are going to take a look at the most common in a bit more detail.

Stress incontinence (SUI)
This is when leaks occur due to stress on the bladder and pelvic floor, for example, when coughing, sneezing, laughing, jumping or lifting a heavy object. This is often the one mums resonate with

most, avoiding trampolines like the plague for fear of leaks. It often occurs due to weakness or damage to the pelvic floor muscles, urethral sphincters or surrounding connective tissue.

Urge incontinence

This is where leaks occur when you get the urge to go for a wee but can't make it to the toilet in time. It can be really stressful and reduce your confidence in going out. It can start to feel like your bladder is controlling your life. It can occur at any stage of life and is particularly common postpartum in the early days after a vaginal birth. However, if it carries on past 6–12 weeks then this needs treatment and further support. When talking about urge incontinence we need to discuss overactive bladder.

Overactive bladder (OAB)

An overactive bladder is when you experience bothersome urgency to wee, with or without urge incontinence. This means to be diagnosed with OAB the urgency you experience needs to be affecting your day-to-day life. Women will also often report the frequency of needing a wee, as well as getting up at night to do a wee, which is called nocturia. Urgency can be very distressing and cause panic, as well as having a huge impact on a woman's life. Treatment of OAB is important whether there is leakage or not, so if you struggle with urgency of needing a wee that is distressing then please know there is help. You don't need to leak urine to get help with your bladder.

Women can experience stress and urge incontinence separately or together, known as *mixed incontinence*.

Coital incontinence

Leakage that occurs during sex, which can, understandably, be very distressing and upsetting. We will discuss this more in the next chapter if you are struggling.

What can I do to help incontinence?

Treatment will vary depending on the type of incontinence you are experiencing and your day-to-day symptoms, so, as always, seeking personalised care is best. However, there is lots you can start to help in the meantime.

Stress urinary incontinence

Pelvic floor exercises:
A good place to start, which probably won't surprise you, as pelvic floor muscle training is an effective treatment for stress incontinence.[1] It is important to remember all parts of the pelvic floor puzzle (see page 38), and ensure we are preparing our pelvic floor for the task we need it to complete. Guidelines state that women who experience stress incontinence should be offered 'supervised pelvic floor muscle training for at least 3 months'. Supervised means with a pelvic health physiotherapist, who can provide ongoing support. This will support you in completing your pelvic floor exercises at home, which are recommended to be done 3 times a day with at least 8 repetitions.[2]

Treat and prevent constipation:
As we have discussed, the bowels have such a close relationship with the bladder so ensuring we are emptying our bowels well can help improve stress incontinence symptoms.

Try using The Knack:
You are probably thinking, 'what on earth is this?' If you are, you are not alone. This is a technique that can be used to reduce urine leakage at moments when there is increased stress and pressure on the pelvic floor, for example, during coughing or sneezing. Try contracting your pelvic floor and hold the contraction when you cough or sneeze. I know this can be hard to predict, but actively

contracting the muscles has been shown to reduce leakage.[3] This isn't recommended for more active tasks such as running – we don't want to run actively squeezing our pelvic floor – it is just for isolated use for specific moments like coughing.

Trial an intra-vaginal device:

These come in different forms and are placed inside the vagina to provide support to the urethra, which can reduce stress incontinence. They are not recommended as routine management, but can be particularly helpful for women who struggle with leakage during exercise.[4]

Use pads if needed:

Sometimes we need to use pads to help manage symptoms. I never want women to feel this has to be their long-term management strategy, but while we work on rehabilitation and supporting your body to get better they can really help reduce embarrassment and give you the confidence to go out and about.

Don't avoid activity or impact exercise for ever:

Being active is so important for many reasons, as we have mentioned, but research also suggests that walking may decrease the risk of urinary incontinence.[5] We need to gradually introduce the pelvic floor back to impact as we are able. This road is different for all of us, but life comes with impact. I like to use graded impact as part of pelvic floor rehabilitation. Try introducing some stamping of your foot, coming up on your tiptoes and landing down heavily on your heels, or some small jumps when you feel ready.[6] Don't try and contract your pelvic floor while doing these, but let it respond naturally (see page 181). You have to work with where your body is at, but if we never challenge the pelvic floor and encourage it to handle impact, we are not supporting it to meet the demands we expect of it.

Urge urinary incontinence

Pelvic floor muscle rehabilitation:

Working on pelvic floor muscle rehabilitation is a good place to start.[7] Remember this doesn't just mean focusing on strength. Ensure you are working on the pelvic floor relaxing, as well as contracting. Some women will actually have a pelvic floor that needs support to relax fully first (see page 45) before introducing more strength and endurance work.

Treat and prevent constipation:

As we have discussed, the bowels have such a close relationship with the bladder, so ensuring we are emptying our bowels well can help improve urge incontinence symptoms.[8]

Trial reducing bladder irritants:

There are certain drinks that have been shown to irritate the bladder, and what I mean by irritate is you may feel you need to pass urine more urgently or frequently, or leak urine more after certain drinks. For years we have pointed the finger at caffeine as being one of the biggest bladder irritants, with women being advised to reduce or cut it out. Let's be honest: that's every mother's worst nightmare – there is no way I would get through a day without a cuppa or two. Research isn't fully conclusive on this, so you can all give a big sigh of relief. However, if you are experiencing urge incontinence it can be worth trying to reduce caffeine intake to see if it helps. Alongside this, try and reduce your intake of drinks with artificial sweeteners, and fizzy drinks. You may also benefit from reducing salt in your diet, if you have a high salt intake, as this has been shown to reduce bladder symptoms in those with OAB.[9] It is advised that adults should not consume more than 6g of salt daily, so it's worth checking in on your diet.

Pace your drinking:

Try to drink regularly throughout the day, rather than large volumes in a short amount of time.

Work on your fluid intake:

Make sure it isn't too high or too low. Aiming for around 1.5–2 litres a day is a good starting point.

Try urgency suppression techniques:

These can help to reduce the sensation of urge, improve confidence and take back control of your bladder. It is really normal that when we feel urgency to go for a wee, or experience leakage, that we rush off to the toilet when this occurs. However, this can actually make our leakage worse. You can try these techniques to regain control and calm the urge you feel:

- Try distracting yourself with a task or activity.
- Apply pressure to the perineum.
- Curl your toes and/or rise up and down on to your tiptoes in standing.
- Contract your pelvic floor and hold for 10 seconds. This helps to calm the bladder muscle and reduce urgency. This is why working on pelvic floor muscle rehabilitation is key so you have the strength and endurance in order to use this technique.

Use pads if needed:

Sometimes we need to use pads to help manage symptoms. I never want women to feel this has to be their long-term management strategy, but while we work on rehabilitation and supporting your body to get better they can really help reduce embarrassment and give you the confidence to go out and about.

As part of your treatment with a medical professional they might ask you to fill out a **bladder diary** so they can understand your bladder habits slightly better. This information can then be used to start bladder training, which should be done for at least 6 weeks.[10] If you experience these symptoms during perimenopause or postmenopause your doctor my prescribe **vaginal oestrogen** to help symptoms.[11]

INCONTINENCE FAQS

Q: Why am I being told to lose weight?

Guidelines state[12] that women with a BMI over 30 should be encouraged to lose weight to help their incontinence symptoms. Increased weight around the abdomen increases pressure and strain on the muscles and connective tissues around the bladder and can therefore increase symptoms.[13] However, for many women losing weight is just not that simple, and many women feel limited in their ability to be more active due to symptoms of incontinence. So it can become a bit of a catch-22 situation. What we need to do is keep this in mind as part of the bigger picture, but ensure women have the right physiotherapy and nutritional support on their journey.

Q: Should I get a pelvic floor device to help improve my symptoms?

First of all, we need to understand the two main types of pelvic floor device:

1. **Electrical stimulation:** a probe is placed inside the vagina which attaches to a hand-held device. The probe passes gentle electrical impulses through the pelvic floor muscles, which stimulates them. Over time the aim is to build up the

strength and bulk of the muscles through using this type of device.

2. **Biofeedback device:** a probe is placed inside the vagina and is connected to an external device either by wires or by Bluetooth. They don't stimulate the muscles but provide visual feedback about what your pelvic floor is doing as you squeeze and let go. They often have programmes for you to follow. They can help to increase your confidence and connection with your pelvic floor muscles, as well as keep you motivated.

Devices definitely have a place in pelvic floor rehabilitation, however, they are not recommended to be used routinely for everyone. My advice is to try and seek individual assessment to determine what the best course of action is for you. However, as help can be very difficult to access at times, I totally understand why women choose to get such a device.[14]

ANAL INCONTINENCE

Anal incontinence is struggling to control poo or wind, leading to incontinence. It is often broken down into faecal (poo) and flatal (wind) incontinence, which is what I will do as we discuss this topic a little further. It is common in the postpartum period, affecting around 30 per cent of new mothers.[15]

Faecal incontinence

Struggling to control your bowels is very distressing. Leaking poo can cause you to lose confidence and feel very embarrassed. This impacts around one in ten people, which is a large number I think you will agree. However, it is also hugely under-reported so the figure is likely to be even higher than this.

Symptoms may include:

- Being unable to hold in a poo, with an urge to go and leaking on the way to the toilet.
- Decreased awareness of needing a poo and leaking without urge.
- Passing a poo OK, but noticing soiling in underwear after a bowel motion or later in the day.

There are two main types of faecal incontinence:

1. **Urge faecal incontinence**: Leakage of poo when you feel the urge to go, but can't make it to the bathroom. This is typically leakage of a large volume.
2. **Passive faecal incontinence**: Leakage of poo without any urge or awareness, which is usually a smaller volume than with urge faecal incontinence. It includes smearing in underwear, which might only be a small amount but still bothersome.

PLEASE NOTE: if you have lost all awareness of needing a poo, and/or notice a change in the sensation of your vulva, this needs to be flagged urgently to your doctor.

Treating faecal incontinence
Supporting women who suffer with faecal incontinence is paramount. One-to-one support is important to understand the reason

and provide tailored help. I understand how hard and embarrassing it can feel to reach out for help if you are struggling with bowel symptoms, but please know that medical professionals talk about bowels and poo all the time. I always say to women, nothing is TMI with me.

Treatment often includes a variety of things to improve symptoms as well as quality of life. These might include:

- Pelvic floor muscle retraining.
- Improving bowel emptying techniques.
- Discussing food and fluid intake, with support from a dietitian as needed.
- Use of anal plugs to prevent or reduce leakage while you are out and about.
- Rectal irrigation, which is the use of water to help open your bowels.[16]

A NOTE ON RECTAL IRRIGATION

Rectal irrigation is where water is put into the bowel via the anus to help you to have a bowel movement. You can use irrigation at home independently to help you manage bowel symptoms. It can be used to help symptoms of faecal incontinence or constipation, as well as improve quality of life.[17]

For **incontinence** it can help you to empty your bowels before you are going out somewhere, so you know there is less chance of having any leaks if you have already opened your bowels. This can give you freedom and your confidence back.

For **constipation** it can help you to open your bowels if you are struggling to initiate a bowel movement. It is used for those who have long-term problems with constipation, rather than short term.

Assessment by a trained professional is required before starting to use rectal irrigation, so please do speak to a doctor or pelvic health physiotherapist if you would like to know more.

Flatal incontinence

Flatal incontinence is the inability to hold in wind, which is more common than we think. So many women report this, and many are too embarrassed to talk about it. Treatment mainly consists of pelvic floor rehabilitation, improving the strength as well as the flexibility of the muscles, and considering how diet might be contributing. Just know this is another symptom that doesn't merely have to be accepted as part of life and motherhood.

Why might women experience bowel symptoms?

After third- or fourth-degree tears, which involve the anal sphincters (see page 135), women can experience anal incontinence. This most commonly occurs after a 3c or fourth-degree tear.[18] These symptoms are not exclusive to those with third- or fourth-degree tears though. They can occur in the short term postpartum due to impact on the nerves that send messages to the anal sphincters and pelvic floor. Unfortunately, there are some women where a third- or fourth- degree tear has occurred but was not picked up at delivery and therefore was not repaired. This is called a missed obstetric anal sphincter injury (OASI). If you have ongoing bowel symptoms and unable to control faeces or wind, whether you have had a third- or fourth-degree tear or not, please don't suffer in silence. Speak to your doctor, seek support and assessment.

PELVIC ORGAN PROLAPSE (POP)

This is a topic that I find women either don't know much about, *or* their lives have been dramatically impacted by it. Having been on the receiving end of the words 'you have a prolapse' myself, I know how life-changing they can be and feel. I guess if there is a section of this book I have wanted to write the most, it is this one. It is probably the section I needed to read 6 years ago, and one that I know so many women I meet are desperate to find. To any of you reading this, either worried you have a prolapse or sat there post diagnosis, wondering if you will ever feel like you again, I know how that feels. It does get better. It can be quite the ride at times, but let's journey together and please know you are not alone. And if I can give you one piece of advice before we start, the first rule of prolapse is, do *NOT* google prolapse!

What is POP?

POP is the movement of one or more of the vaginal walls downwards in the vagina, due to changes and damage to the structures that support them, which is symptomatic. These structures include the muscles, fascia and ligaments, which are impacted through various activities and events through life. We most commonly talk about prolapse that involves the bladder, uterus and bowel; however, the urethra and small bowel can also be involved. It is important to know that POP does not mean that there is damage to the organ.

- **Anterior-wall prolapse:** occurs when the front wall of the vagina, which supports the bladder and urethra, bulges down into the vagina. This may also be referred to as a cystocele or cystourethrocele.

- **Posterior-wall prolapse:** occurs when the back wall of the vagina that supports the rectum bulges into the vagina. This may also be called a rectocele. If the small bowel bulges down, then this is called an enterocele.
- **Uterine prolapse:** occurs when the uterus moves down into the vagina.
- **Vault prolapse:** can occur after a hysterectomy (removal of the uterus) where the top of the vagina moves down into the vagina.

There are four grades of prolapse, numbered 1–4, depending on the severity.

Grade 1: prolapse that is within the vagina.
Grade 2: prolapse to the entrance of the vagina.
Grade 3: prolapse that comes outside the vagina.
Grade 4: prolapse that is fully out of the vagina.

This all sounds pretty scary, right? The thought of our organs moving from where they were and the fear of them falling out is a huge source of understandable anxiety for women. It is a tricky one, because the more we tell women this can occur, the more fearful they can become. However, if we don't tell them and it does occur then they feel totally unprepared. I believe we need to inform women, but we should give them the whole picture, not one small part of it without any idea of how to live and thrive with a prolapse.

What might you feel?

Most commonly women report:

- A heaviness or dragging sensation within the vagina.
- The presence of something in the vagina that should not be there.

- The feeling of a tampon being too low and rubbing.
- Difficulty opening their bowels or feeling they cannot completely empty them.
- Feeling they do not completely empty their bladder and/or noticing they dribble more urine when they stand up.
- Discomfort or reduced sensation during sex.
- Pain in the lower back or tummy.

Why does POP occur?

There are a variety of risk factors that include:

- Pregnancy
- Childbirth
- Being overweight
- Chronic constipation and straining
- Persistent cough
- Our genetics

The important thing to note here is that though often childbirth can be the trigger for us to develop symptoms, there is often more to the story. When we consider the other factors we can often start to see how they might have also contributed to our symptoms. When we think about the important 'why did this happen to me?' question, it is key to try and keep a balanced view. In the same way, saying to a woman that her main focus should be on losing weight misses all other aspects of her story and is not balanced or helpful.

Let's understand prolapse further

The interesting, or maybe rather confusing, part of POP is that women can have changes to the vaginal walls observed on examination but have no symptoms. Only around 6 per cent of women will report symptoms despite significantly more women actually having a prolapse if examined.[19] In fact, stage 1 prolapse of the front or back wall of the vagina has been shown to be present in 50 per cent of women who have not had children.[20,21] Therefore, it is now considered that stage 1 changes to the front or back wall of the vagina are likely to be within normal range.[22] To diagnose a prolapse there should be movement of at least one of the vaginal walls to the vaginal opening or beyond, as well as bothersome symptoms or other medical conditions that are a consequence of the prolapse.[23]

Alongside any discussion of stage or grade, the most important parts of the picture are *your* symptoms and *your* story. Let's see beyond the grade and structures and see you as a woman, your life and what this means for you. Yes, these labels help us as medical professionals work out what might help you best, but it can be too easy to forget the woman behind the medical jargon at times, and the significance that these words have on a woman's mental and emotional wellbeing. However, what I think this does helpfully show is that birth is not the only factor at play. Yes, it will be part of the picture but potentially not all of it. I think this is often a helpful shift for women mentally, who can end up blaming themselves for elements of their birth. Widening the lens and gaining more of a bird's-eye view can really help. We need to keep focused on your life, your goals and what you can do to improve your symptoms.

What can you do to help?

Treat and prevent constipation:

If you are struggling to do a poo, first the rectum has to store it, and as we have discussed before, a rectum that is filled with poo will put pressure on the other pelvic organs, vaginal walls and surrounding tissues. It often leads to women straining as well, which can further weaken tissues and worsen symptoms. Therefore, I am here again to say take care of your bowels. Head back to page 75 to consider top tips on how to help and see a doctor if you need further support.

Pelvic floor rehabilitation:

Guidelines state that women should be offered guided pelvic floor muscle training, i.e., with a physiotherapist, for at least 16 weeks as first-line treatment, if they have a grade 1 or 2 symptomatic prolapse. Rehabilitation should focus on the whole pelvic floor puzzle as we have discussed before, ensuring that a woman feels able to relax the pelvic floor muscles as well as contract them. Naturally if you feel your pelvic organs are falling out of your vagina, you are going to squeeze your pelvic floor to hold them in. Lots of women often struggle to let go out of fear – there's no judgement here; I've been there. However, working on overall function is key, alongside strengthening exercises.[24]

Lose weight if necessary:

This is such a difficult topic to talk about at times and, in my opinion, there is too much pressure put on women to lose weight, while also often being told not to exercise in certain ways. Losing weight might help to reduce symptoms, though it is unlikely to change the prolapse that is already present.[25] However, it may help to prevent further progression of the prolapse.[26]

Support to open your bowels:

Women who have a prolapse of the back wall of the vagina can struggle to open their bowels and can experience a feeling of incomplete emptying. To help you can either apply pressure to the perineum using your fingers, to help support externally, or place your thumb inside the vagina onto the back wall and apply some pressure, while opening your bowels. This can help to support the prolapse and make it easier to pass a poo.

Tips to help completely open your bladder:

If you are struggling to fully empty your bladder, try rocking forwards and backwards a few times after you have initially emptied and see if this helps you to pass any more urine. Don't bear down. You can also try a double void, where you do a wee, stand up, walk around a bit and then sit back down and try again.

Try different rest positions:

Lying with your legs elevated on a chair, sofa, or up against a wall for short periods can help reduce symptoms. You might also find positions where you elevate your hips also help. For example, lying on your back with a pillow under your pelvis.

Speak to your doctor about vaginal oestrogen:

This comes as a small tablet or cream put into the vagina and aims to replace oestrogen at times when levels are naturally lower in the body, which can lead to dry or thin vaginal tissues that can worsen prolapse symptoms. It is most commonly used during or after menopause, or when breastfeeding, as oestrogen levels are lower than normal.

Consider a vaginal pessary:

These can play a significant role in helping to manage prolapse symptoms and improve quality of life. Sadly they are still viewed as just for 'older women', which just isn't true. They can help women of all ages, and we need to continue to challenge this narrative. In order to do this we need to understand what they are better, so I have asked my friend Tracey Matthews, a pelvic health physiotherapist who fits pessaries, to share some more information with us, overleaf.

A NOTE ON PESSARIES

What is a pessary?

A vaginal pessary is a device worn in the vagina to provide support to the vaginal walls and pelvic organs to reduce symptoms of prolapse. They can help to improve quality of life by allowing you to go about day-to-day tasks without symptoms, as well as be active and do exercise that you enjoy.

There are different types of pessaries that are used for different types of prolapse. Most commonly used are ring, cube or gelhorn pessaries. They all work in slightly different ways to provide support to the vaginal walls. The most appropriate one for you can only be determined by thorough assessment. Sometimes it takes a little while to find the right pessary and size for you. Unfortunately, they don't work for everyone, and sometimes it can be a bit of trial and error.

A ring or gelhorn pessary can be left in for 3 months before review is required, whereas a cube pessary is taken in and out on a daily basis. What is consistent with all pessaries is that once they are in you should not feel them or have any discomfort.

Do I need to use a pessary for ever?

No, they can be used either short term or long term. Their use should always be tailored to your symptoms and needs. When you have a pessary, you will need ongoing review and monitoring to ensure the vaginal tissues are not impacted by the pessary.

Who can fit a pessary?

Gynaecology doctors, along with some specialist physiotherapists and GPs.

Exercising with a prolapse

Too often women are told to stop exercising, to not run or lift any weights when diagnosed with a prolapse. I honestly think this is one of the most disempowering things we can say to a woman, to a mother. How does she care for her children, put an infant into a buggy or car seat, pick up a tantruming toddler in the supermarket, or exercise for her mental health if she has been told not to 'lift anything heavy' or 'exercise'? The reason this sort of advice has been given is down to reducing strain and increases in intra-abdominal pressure to protect and prevent further progression of a prolapse. Let's take a moment to consider intra-abdominal pressure (IAP) a little further. (To remind yourself what IAP is, turn back to page 31.)

Changes to our pelvic floor muscles and surrounding tissues, through pregnancy, birth and life in general, can change their ability to respond to changes in IAP as they did before. This can be why we may start to experience leaks with sneezing, laughing or running, and is why advice around prolapse can be to stop exercises where IAP will significantly increase to protect weakened tissues. It is easy to make assumptions about what movements and activities cause the biggest increases in IAP, leading us to label activities as good and bad, or dos and don'ts. However, the list of activities below, going from the highest to lowest IAP shown to be put on the pelvic floor, may surprise you:

1. Jumping
2. Seated cough
3. Standing valsalva (the valsalva manoeuvre is a technique where effort is made to exhale without letting air escape through the nose or mouth. This is often done by pinching your nose and closing your mouth, whilst forcefully trying to breathe out. This is how we are often taught to clear our ears when on a plane.)

4. Abdominal crunch

5. Standing still[27]

So, it is easy for us to say don't do any crunches, but would we ever tell a woman to not cough sitting down? I don't think so. So how we need to reframe this is that IAP fluctuates all day, throughout the day and with different activities. What we need to do is help our bodies to be ready for these changes, help the pelvic floor to be ready to respond. This takes time, training and support, and the right level of challenge at the right time.

I want you to hear me loud and clear: a prolapse doesn't mean it is the end of the road for your relationship with exercise. It also doesn't mean we head straight out for a run and ignore that it is there. Gradual and graded return to exercise is the best approach, and individual support on how best to do this for *your* body is needed, as we do need to understand the facts to shape the way ahead. The journey may be slower than that of our peers, it might be harder to get there, but trust me, it is worth the journey. It is totally understandable to feel frustrated, jealous of others whose journeys seem easier, and angry that you can't get back to what you love straight away. Until we have explored all options to get someone back to what they love, with rehabilitation and the use of a pessary as needed, then nothing should be taken off the table.

I wanted to share a little bit of my own journey, which I briefly mentioned in the last chapter, with regards to exercise and prolapse before we continue. I honestly found this one of the hardest parts of having a prolapse. The fear and frustration of not being able to do what I loved and did before pregnancy. I was jealous of others, I felt let down by my body and didn't have a lot of hope that it would change. A year after diagnosis I started to work with a specialist personal trainer who had brilliant knowledge of the pelvic floor and prolapse, and could encourage and guide me carefully and gently to do a bit more over weeks and months. My confidence grew and grew, and it honestly changed my life. After my second pregnancy I did all the rehab and gradually started to do more. I always had the goal that I wanted to learn to lift weights and return to running, and in the last year, which is 6 years from diagnosis, I have started lifting weights on a weekly basis and have returned to running. Things I never imagined I would do on initial diagnosis, but here I am. I know this isn't everyone's story but I hope it gives some of you confidence and courage that there can be a way ahead.

There can often be a lot of attention on what is 'bad' and 'good' for our pelvic floor, a desire for clear labels, however, we don't have them. Therefore, I think our energy and attention is best placed working on getting our pelvic floor ready for the tasks and activities we want to do. Doing the rehabilitation and thinking of all the ways we can support the pelvic floor and body are key. This might include the use of a vaginal pessary as already discussed. Think about if you had a hamstring injury or tear, it would need graded and gradual rehabilitation to get it ready to deal with the load of running again. The pelvic floor is the same. The body has an amazing ability to adapt and change, we just need to help it on its way and throw in a good amount of patience as well. When trying to return to impact exercise like running or jumping with a prolapse it can feel scary. Using graded return to impact exercises, as we discussed on page 204 when talking about incontinence, can be really helpful for women with prolapse as well. I would always advise this is done with support and under the watchful eye of a physiotherapist if possible.

Sometimes it is not always possible to get women back to everything they want without symptoms just through physiotherapy – I don't pretend we are miracle workers. However, it is about finding what the woman *can* do, rather than presenting her with a huge list of what she can't. Another aspect we need to consider is how restricting women's activities and removing impact and resistance training can have a knock-on effect on other areas of health – bone health especially being a hugely important factor for women as we head into menopause. We will discuss this more in Chapter 13; however, I think it highlights again the link our pelvic health has to many aspects of our health as women.

Emotions and feelings

Being diagnosed with a prolapse can be life-shattering, anxiety-provoking, confusing and embarrassing. It can leave you feeling angry, resentful and full of grief. Often, once we fully understand what it means, how we can go about our daily life with it, and identify and confront our fears, we find a way through. However, I will be honest: for most women it can feel like a challenging journey at times. In the words of Ronan Keating, 'Life [with a prolapse] is a rollercoaster, just gotta ride it.' My main message to you is that your feelings are valid, it is understandable to feel all the emotions you do, and seeking support from a medical profes-sional who can help to guide you and make sense of what you are feeling can be very powerful. I know I have said it before, but you are not alone, and there is help.

PROLAPSE FAQS

Q: Do I have to have surgery if I have a prolapse?

If you google prolapse you will definitely come away feeling that surgery is the main treatment option, which can feel rather daunting.

However, the short answer is no. It does depend on the grade of prolapse and symptoms though, and this is why it always needs individual assessment. First-line treatment for the majority of women should be supervised pelvic floor muscle rehabilitation, however, surgery might be something that you choose at a later stage.

Q: Can I have another vaginal birth if I have a prolapse already?

The short answer is yes, lots of women do go on to have a vaginal delivery with a prolapse and have positive birth experiences that do not worsen their prolapse. However, for many women it is not a simple decision. Weighing up whether you have a vaginal or Caesarean delivery takes time and needs to be informed with support from a medical team. I don't believe there is a clear-cut right or wrong decision. I believe you need to be supported to look at all parts of the picture, including your pelvic health, mental health, general health, the baby's health, home support and your desires and wishes for the birth. Looking at the risks and benefits for both types of delivery and making an informed decision from there. My top tips if you are navigating this:

1. Speak to your medical team early on in pregnancy to start the conversation.
2. Ask for your previous birth notes and seek answers to any questions you have. You can apply to receive any medical records via your hospital's website. There is paperwork to complete and ID checks and then notes are posted out to you. These will be a direct copy of any notes written by medical professionals at the time of birth and a discharge summary. I would advise going through the notes with a midwife or medical professional who is caring for you

during a subsequent pregnancy to help explain what things mean. I personally did this with my midwives in my second pregnancy and found it really helpful.

3. Seek assessment from a pelvic health physiotherapist to understand how your pelvic floor muscles are functioning to help you keep strong through pregnancy.

4. Pregnancy alone has an impact on the muscles and connective tissue, and Caesarean deliveries do not remove all risk of prolapse progressing or symptoms worsening. This is why it is not a simple decision, but with the right discussions, space to explore your feelings and emotions, you will come to the right decision for you and your baby.

Q: Why are my symptoms worse around ovulation and my period?

Women often report they only feel their prolapse around ovulation or just before their period, or that symptoms are worse around this time. Reasons that this might be experienced are that during ovulation oestrogen levels are higher, which causes the connective tissues to be softer and this can mean slightly less support and more symptoms. The vaginal and vulval tissues have a very high proportion of oestrogen receptors compared to other parts of the body, and therefore are very sensitive to oestrogen changes. This can be relevant when the levels rise and fall as they do during the menstrual cycle, or if they drop consistently low, for example, while breastfeeding. Also, during the menstrual cycle the uterus changes size as the lining plumps up ready for a fertilised egg (if there is one). The pelvic organs are not rigidly held in the same position all the time, and they can respond to this small change in the uterus. Women also often report changes to their bowel habits around their period and so for some this may contribute to symptoms.

Q: Should I stop breastfeeding to help my prolapse?

The short answer is no. Women are often told, just wait until you finish breastfeeding and your symptoms will resolve. This often gives false hope that stopping breastfeeding will improve or cure their prolapse and symptoms. For some, symptoms do improve, however, for many this is sadly not the case and I think it is unfair for women to feel the pressure to choose between breastfeeding their baby and experiencing prolapse symptoms. The key is to understand why it might help and what else we could do to support you in the meantime.

When you breastfeed, levels of prolactin rise and as this happens oestrogen is suppressed. Therefore, oestrogen levels are consistently low and this can lead to the vulvar and vaginal tissues being less plump, drier and more sensitive. This can therefore make women more symptomatic and aware of their prolapse, and when oestrogen levels return to normal they feel it less. If you wish to keep breastfeeding then you can try using a vaginal moisturiser or speak to your doctor about using a vaginal oestrogen, which is a cream or tablet that provides oestrogen just to the vulvar and vaginal tissues. We should be supporting women to find ways to carry on breastfeeding, if they wish to, and be informed that breastfeeding is unlikely to delay their pelvic floor recovery.[28]

Q: Can I lift my children if I have a prolapse?

Being told not to lift anything heavy when you have a prolapse leaves every mother thinking 'how on earth do I look after my kids?' Kids are heavy, car seats are heavy, carrying a toddler and a scooter while pushing a buggy is heavy! Therefore, we can't tell a mother not to lift anything, because she cannot physically meet the demands of motherhood. This is why we need to support women to take care of their pelvic health, return to exercise and be strong so they can lift their kids without fear, as well as supporting them to consider additional help, like pessaries, to allow them to continue day-to-day life without discomfort or fear. If you are worried, then you can try and contract your pelvic floor as you lift, the technique called The Knack discussed on page 203. There might be a time when it is appropriate to modify and minimise unnecessary lifting, like in the early weeks postpartum or after vaginal surgery. However, for the average woman we need to support her to feel confident to lift her kids. I always encourage women to listen to their body and how it feels, of course, and they may need to gradually build up to carrying for longer times, for example.

Q: Can I have sex with a prolapse?

Yes, absolutely you can. Some women may report that they feel some discomfort, but for many they are pleasantly surprised. I would say the biggest barrier for women is feeling unconfident in their body, feeling self-conscious that their partner will feel something is different or feeling afraid intercourse will make their prolapse worse. Sharing these feelings and fears with your partner is key, as well as exploring different positions that you might feel are more comfortable. It is safe to have intercourse, but it is understandable if you need time to feel ready. Just know that there is support and help if you are struggling.

Q: Should I try hypopressives?

This is a FAQ that comes up time and again as women seek support for their symptoms, and I always signpost them to Alice Housman, a hypopressives teacher and trainer and founder of Hypopressives by Alice. Below Alice shares what hypopressives is and how it might benefit you if you want to try.

Hypopressives is a movement and breathwork technique which combines different poses with a 'vacuum breath'.

Although it's tempting to focus on achieving the vacuum alone, the full pelvic health benefits come when it's combined with a variety of poses. The vacuum breath generates an involuntary contraction and lift through the pelvic floor through its relationship with the diaphragm. Hypopressives gets the pelvic floor to work better in the background without us thinking about it, which can in turn help to improve symptoms like prolapse and incontinence, as well as overall pelvic floor function. International research is positive and evolving about the benefits of hypopressives for pelvic floor dysfunction, as well as posture, diastasis, body image and sense of wellbeing.

It was originally developed as a postnatal core recovery technique by physiotherapist Dr Marcel Caufriez and has been widely used in countries such as Spain, France and Belgium for over 40 years to improve prolapse and incontinence symptoms, and for fitness. Hypopressives has only been taught in the UK for the last decade, as prior to this, much of the teaching and research was in Spanish.

Q: Why is pelvic floor muscle training not working for me?
Unfortunately, pelvic floor muscle training doesn't work for everyone to improve symptoms of prolapse (or incontinence), and there are different reasons for this. It can be very demoralising if you are putting in the hours to do pelvic floor exercises and nothing is happening. So I want to highlight a few reasons that you might be struggling to make progress, after you have worked on your technique and all aspects of the pelvic floor puzzle.

1. **Realistic timescales.** Muscles often take longer to strengthen than we imagine or wish. It can take weeks and months for us to notice changes in strength and symptoms.

So keep your focus on the long term, even though it's really hard.

2. **Nerve supply.** Birth can lead to nerve damage that can impact the pelvic floor muscles. This can recover and repair over time, but it does often take months.

3. **Scar tissue** that comes from a perineal tear during delivery can restrict the muscles and connective tissue. Gentle massage of the scar tissue and muscles can help to improve flexibility of the muscle, aiding their strengthening and recovery (see page 188 for tips on how to get started).

4. **Levator avulsions** can occur where part of the pelvic floor muscles pulls away from the bone where it is normally attached. This means that it is unable to function as normal and can be a reason for incontinence and prolapse symptoms not improving despite you doing all the right things.

5. **Viewing the pelvic floor in isolation.** As you have probably realised by now, it is always important to consider all contributing factors to the symptoms you experience. As we discussed back in Chapter 4 (see page 83) we need to consider other muscles around the pelvis and hips as well when considering pelvic floor symptoms. Equally, we need to consider our breathing – the diaphragm's movement and, linked to this, how our thoracic spine moves. Our thoracic spine is the upper part of our back, below our neck, where our ribs attach and its movement and position can influence our breathing dynamics, which can in turn impact our pelvic floor function. Working on thoracic rotation through exercises like Thread the Needle on page 178 can be helpful. Taking a step away from the pelvic floor, having a bird's-eye view and considering all angles can be the key to improving your symptoms.

Individual support should help to identify if any of the above might be relevant to you, but I want to ensure that you know that there are many factors influencing our recovery, and that you are not alone if pelvic floor muscle training doesn't seem to be working for you.

DIASTASIS RECTUS ABDOMINIS (DRA)

Diastasis rectus abdominis (DRA) is something that women are becoming more aware of, which is great, because understanding our body and the changes it goes through is important. However, there can also be a lot of scaremongering about it, and women can be left unsure whether they have it, or what they should be doing about it. Let's take a look at it together, to help you understand it in more depth. As we discussed in Chapter 6, DRA is the separation of the rectus abdominis muscles, with thinning of the linea alba, the connective tissue between the muscles. It is important to remember that this is a totally natural process that occurs during pregnancy and is not to be feared. There is natural recovery in the initial weeks after birth, but around a third of women will have ongoing DRA.[29] We don't know exactly why, but potential contributing factors could be twin or multiple pregnancies, as there is often a larger stretch on the abdominal wall, a history of chronic constipation and straining on the toilet, or genetics. I want to walk you through what to look out for, how to assess yourself and what to do to help. You are not broken if you have ongoing DRA, it doesn't mean you have to avoid all exercise, despite what you might hear, and there is help available.

I do want to say at this point that struggling with how your body looks after having a baby is totally understandable. There

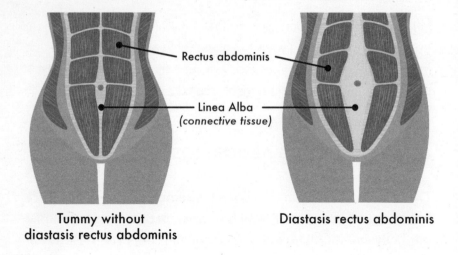

Rectus abdominis

Linea Alba
(connective tissue)

Tummy without
diastasis rectus abdominis

Diastasis rectus abdominis

Fig. 23: Diastasis rectus abdominis

still seems to be a societal expectation for women to 'bounce back' after having a baby, and this can lead to us feeling insecure and self-conscious about how our bodies look and feel. It is totally normal to want to feel and look like yourself again. There can be too much pressure at times for women to feel that they have to accept all changes to their body with love and gratitude because they have the gift of a baby. However, I truly believe we can be grateful and beyond delighted for the gift of a baby *and* struggle with our postnatal body. There needs to be space for all emotions and feelings, they are all valid. We need to accept our bodies for where they are at the present moment, but it is also OK to want to understand and explore how to help your body strengthen and change over time. Research has shown that DRA does lead to struggles with body image and lower quality of life, therefore this is why we need to educate and support women about DRA and where to find help.[30]

What might you notice if you have DRA?

You may see a bulging up or a dropping down of the tissues down the centre of your tummy, or feel that your tummy just doesn't look right or feel that you still look pregnant. You might also notice some discomfort or tenderness.

How can you assess yourself?

Assessing yourself can help to give you an idea of whether you need to seek further help or not. If you are early postnatal try this after 6 weeks; your body will be doing lots of natural recovery before this point.

1. Lie comfortably on your back on the floor with your knees bent.
2. Take two fingers and feel down the centre of your tummy from the bottom of your breastbone all the way down to your pubic bone. See if you can feel the edges of the rectus abdominis muscles or not when at rest. If you can, note how many fingers you can fit in between.
3. As you press down, note how the connective tissue feels between the muscles. Does it feel soft or firm?
4. Then, gently lift your head up, bringing your chin to your chest. Stay in this position as you feel down the centre of your tummy again, from breastbone to pubic bone. It is important to check down the whole length of the linea alba as it is possible to have separation at any part along it.
5. You are looking to see how many fingers you can fit in between the rectus abdominis muscles, as well as how far you can drop your fingers down between the muscles. Take

note again of how the connective tissue feels: is it soft and you can drop quite far down, or is it firm?

If you can feel a gap between the muscles, as well as softness in the connective tissue with your fingers easily dropping down between the muscles, you may well have DRA. However, if you don't feel any gap between the muscles, and the connective tissue is firm, stopping you from dropping your fingers down, then it is unlikely that you do. It can be really hard to assess this on yourself, so if you have tried and struggled or don't know what you felt, you are not alone. If you feel you have identified a DRA – and this can be at any stage of life – or you are unsure, please do seek an assessment from a doctor or pelvic health physiotherapist to help understand more. The key message is that it is not all about the size of the gap, the tension of the connective tissue is very important too.

Diastasis and movement

Any time we learn of changes to our body, it can make us fear movement, feel broken and be unsure what we can and can't do. If you search the internet or social media you will come across various exercise programmes that are labelled 'diastasis safe', which can lead us to think that some movements are not safe for us, making us afraid. You can absolutely exercise if you have DRA. Individual support to establish what is best for you at each phase is recommended, but we should not be telling women they cannot exercise. This includes core exercises too. Now I am not saying that means you should head off and do a hundred sit-ups, but I am saying we should not avoid doing any exercises that involve the abdominal muscles. In fact, we really need to use them to help them get stronger. As we discussed with prolapse, a lot of it comes down to how you can manage intra-abdominal pressure and perform a certain exercise, rather than the exercise being right or wrong, safe or unsafe per se. It is about doing the right exercise for you at the right time, and unfortunately there isn't a one-size-fits-all programme for that.

Top tips to help you on your journey:

Though I can't give you individualised help through these pages, there are some things you can put in place today to help if you think you have DRA, while you seek further support:

Connect to your breathing:

Work on the diaphragmatic breathing that we went through on page 42. Remember how movement of the diaphragm is key for the whole of the core. It is also natural, if we are self-conscious about how our tummy looks or feels, to hold it in throughout the day. Practicing diaphragmatic breathing can help the abdominal muscles to relax and move, which is important in their recovery.

Don't strain on the toilet:

I know, I am back to talking about bowels again. However, in the same way that straining on the toilet to do a poo is not great for our pelvic floor muscles and connective tissue, neither is it for our abdominal muscles and connective tissue.

Don't fear movement:

Going about your daily life is not going to harm you; your body is stronger than it probably feels. A physiotherapist will guide you through how to return to the exercise you love, gradually and in the right way for your body.

Talk about how you are feeling:
As I've said, your feelings are valid. Share them with family, friends and medical professionals who can support you.

Prepare to be patient:
Rehabilitation and recovery can take time. You need to give yourself a few months of consistent and specific rehabilitation before you can expect to see much change. It is so hard to keep motivated, but trust me, it is worth the hard work.

Remember the basics:
Ensuring you are eating well, keeping up a good fluid intake and getting enough sleep, or as much as you can with kids, is important for any recovery.

DIASTASIS FAQS

Q: Can I do a sit-up if I have a diastasis?
The short answer is yes, it is possible and OK to do a sit-up with DRA. However, it isn't quite that simple. Whether sit-ups are the best exercise for you right now is another question. The rectus abdominis muscles do need to be used, worked and loaded as part of rehabilitation for DRA, it is just about gradually doing this in the right way for you. So sit-ups are likely to form part of your rehabilitation and exercise programme at some point.

Q: Should I use an abdominal binder or support?
There is definitely a place for abdominal binders or supports for certain women, however, they are not advised as routine care for all women. They come in various forms, from supportive leggings to Tubigrip or more structured binders. Some women choose to use

them for comfort, and I totally understand this personal choice. The most important thing is that they don't replace exercise and individualised support but play a role alongside this.

Q: Do I need surgery?

As we have discussed for incontinence and prolapse, rehabilitation and physiotherapy do not always resolve symptoms or help you reach your goals. This is also the case for DRA, and therefore for some women having surgery is the right decision. It is often a big decision for women as there are some limitations on what they can do immediately after surgery, so they need help with caring for their children. Support from a physiotherapist and medical team is essential to help you make the best decision for you with regards to surgery.

* * *

As we come to the end of this chapter, exploring some of the symptoms that you might experience after having a baby – or anytime in life – I want you to continue to hear the main message: there *is* help. It can be so hard to reach out for help and make the first appointment, but I promise you it will be worth it. To anyone who has tried to reach out and didn't receive the response, empathy or care they expected, please don't let that put you off. Try and seek support from someone else.

Here are a few top tips to help you as you navigate seeking help:

- Write down some information about your symptoms. What are you feeling, where are you feeling it and when do you feel it most? Is it after certain activities or at a certain time of day?
- Write down how you are feeling about your symptoms and any fears you have.

- Write down what you have tried doing to date, or information that you have learnt so far.
- Jot down any questions you have, however big or small.

Writing all this down prior to an appointment and having the information in front of you during it can really help if you are feeling anxious or nervous. I love it when women turn up with a list of questions and thoughts as it means I can shape the session to her individual needs. Knowing how to help and care for your body is so valuable and empowering and I see in women, and know personally, how life-changing it is. So, however you end this chapter, take a moment to reflect. Jot down any thoughts, observations, or answers to the above bullet points in the Foundation Reflections section opposite, to help you prepare for or prompt you to make an appointment if you haven't already.

Foundation Reflections

There is a lot to digest in this chapter, but if any of these symptoms or feelings feel familiar then make a note. Take the notes with you as you seek support from a doctor or physiotherapist.

....

....

....

....

....

....

....

....

....

....

....

CHAPTER 11

Sex – Nothing is TMI

Let's learn about:

- What the pelvic floor muscles have got to do with sex
- The mind–body connection
- Why intercourse might be painful
- Sex after having a baby
- Sex during menopause
- How a pelvic health physiotherapist can help with sexual pain
- Psychosexual therapy

Sex is a topic that for many is not easy to talk about. I am sure we can all remember those sex education classes where everyone was giggling away – if you were even privileged enough to receive this education of course. Sex is a personal and private thing and may not be something that you desire to share openly on a daily basis. However, if we don't feel confident to talk about it, then what do we do if we go on to have problems or struggles with it? We don't need to be oversharing constantly, but we need to have a few safe places where we can share if and when needed. This is often what my clinic room becomes, and why I always say 'nothing is too much information' – and I really do mean it! This is what this chapter is about; it is about opening up about this important topic, why our pelvic floor is even relevant, problems we might face, and help that is available. I am delighted and privileged that Candice Langford, a pelvic and sexual health physiotherapist, has contributed throughout this chapter. Together, we share the information we feel all women need to know to thrive in this area of their life.

Let's remind ourselves of some key facts before we start. Sex is 'any physical or psychological act that uses your body or mind for sexual pleasure or expression'.[1] 'Sex' does not equal intercourse. Intercourse involves vaginal penetration. 'Sex' is a unique experience inclusive of all forms of sexual activities that lead to pleasure and maybe even orgasm. Sex and intercourse should be pleasurable and not painful. You have a right to pleasure! When we define sex as intercourse, requiring penetration, and don't include external stimulatory activities, we exclude how the majority of women achieve pleasure and orgasm. A survey found that only 4 per cent of women rely on penetration alone to reach orgasm, which acknowledges that sex is far more than just intercourse.[2]

On the topic of defining sex and having a right to pleasure, I feel that it is valuable to bring to light the orgasm gap, because an educational system and a narrative that excludes 'outercourse' – sexually relevant stimuli of erogenous zones (which may or may not include the vulva) – is primed to further perpetuate the issue of female sexual satisfaction being overlooked.[3] Studies have found that heterosexual women were significantly less likely to have experienced orgasm than males (65–69 per cent, compared with 95 per cent).[4,5] I think we can all agree that that is quite a significant gap, and the only way we can change this and the narrative is by opening up this conversation and understanding our bodies and pleasure better, as well as how to help pain and problems we might face.

There are many reasons why we may struggle with sex and intercourse at any stage and any age in life. If you find intercourse (i.e., penetration) painful, whether it has always been this way, or there has been a recent change, this isn't something you need to accept. There is help.

WHAT HAVE THE PELVIC FLOOR MUSCLES GOT TO DO WITH SEX?

The pelvic floor muscles wrap around the vaginal opening, and as we have previously discussed, these need to be relaxed enough to allow for penetration. If there is increased tone of the muscles, which can feel like too much tension, and the pelvic floor is 'switched on' or in protect mode a lot, this can make penetration difficult or painful. The pelvic floor muscles are a bit like the gate-keepers to the vagina, so we need nice flexible pelvic floor muscles to allow penetration, but do they need to be strong to help improve our pleasure? During orgasm there is rhythmic contraction of the pelvic floor muscles, which you may never have noticed or connected with before. Therefore, stronger pelvic floor muscles may improve arousal, orgasm and pleasure.[6,7] So, if there was ever inspiration to do your pelvic floor exercises, let it be this! Remembering always that it is strength *and* flexibility that we want. It is always essential to remember that sex and intercourse are not purely physical acts, though I think many view them that way. Sex is also hugely influenced by our mind, our emotions and our relationships. So though, as a physiotherapist, I am focused on the physical parts of anatomy, I will always chat to women about the whole of them, and work with other specialists to ensure they have all the support they need. Physical symptoms can be a sign and result of thoughts and feelings that we cannot see.

THE MIND–BODY CONNECTION

Understanding the mind–body connection is foundational to so many parts of physiotherapy and I am therefore delighted that Dr Sula Windgassen, a health psychologist, has provided a detailed explanation to help us learn more about this:

We are implicitly socialised to think of the mind and body as separate. In fact, we are implicitly taught to view the internal systems within the body as separate. This is because our healthcare systems are divided up into specialities and sub-specialties organised around specific areas of the body. For example, women are often referred to gynaecology for anything 'pelvic' or reproductive and to gastroenterology for anything to do with the bowels. A common frustration is that quite often, due to the proximity of these organ systems and, indeed, the similar effect of hormones and biochemical reactions in these regions, women find themselves ping-ponged across departments, when in fact what they need is an integrated approach that looks at how these organs are interacting. This is the same issue when it comes to the mind and body. For every thought and emotion, there is an underlying biochemical process that has a distinct (even if not consciously noticed) effect on the body. Furthermore, it is not a linear or causal relationship between the two but an ongoing interaction.

Have you ever had an argument with someone where the culmination of the argument ends up so far from the starting point? This is often due to things escalating as one responds to another. Maybe one person uses a scathing tone, to which the other goes to leave and then the other person shames them for this tendency and so it erupts. By the end of it, it doesn't really matter 'who started it', but how the interaction played out to get to the end point. It is in this same way that our minds and bodies are communicating. A physiological event such as tissue damage, strain or infection may initiate pain. This pain can quite automatically come with an increase in bodily stress, which may soon lead to the experience of psychological stress. It is then that the interaction starts building. Stress, low mood, anxiety all depletes our capacity to deal with demands. As these are depleted, it breeds more stress. The experience of negative affective states (stress, low mood, anxiety, etc.) is well-established to influence physiological processes in the body. This includes suppressing immune system functioning, increasing muscle tension, heart rate and blood pressure, and exacerbating the experience of pain.

THE MIND AND PAIN

Understanding how pain works is fundamental for managing it. Advances in pain research over the last 20 years have helped us come to a much more rigorous understanding of pain and how we come to experience it. So much so that the definition of pain has been revised by the International Association for the Study of Pain, to 'An unpleasant sensory and emotional experience associated with, or resembling that associated with, actual or potential tissue damage.' Integral to this definition is that pain has sensory and emotional components and can occur without actual tissue damage. It is also reflective of the recent developments in pain science that conceptualise pain as a biopsychosocial phenomenon. This means that the determining of whether someone experiences pain is influenced by a combination of interacting biological (physiological), psychological and social factors.

This challenges a common assumption held by many that pain is purely a physiological process, determined only by the firing of nerve signals from point A (the site of damage/physical issue) to point B (the brain, which then tells us to feel pain). Pain science has now clarified that whether or not an individual experiences pain is determined by an equation. The specifics of this equation will vary across individuals, but the broad parameters are:

Nociception + Psychological and Social context
= Pain experience

Nociception refers to the sensory nerves that receive and transmit information about sensory experiences and may be activated due to stimulation such as tissue damage, pressure or physical irritation. We can think of this as the point A to B relay referred to previously. Nociception signals to the brain that something has occurred, but this in itself will not necessarily result in the experience of pain. That is to some degree determined by the other part of the equation, which we can think of as acting like an amplification dial. Psychological and social factors that influence the amplification (or de-amplification) of the pain experience include:

- **Appraisal and perception:** How bad is the damage? Will it continue for a long time? Can you control it?
- **Emotions:** Anxiety and low mood are associated with an exacerbation of the pain experience.
- **Past experiences:** These will inform appraisal and perception.
- **Social context:** Can you get support? Do you have resources to cope or the possibility for rescue/alleviation from the pain?
- **Attention:** Are you distracted or is a lot of the attentional focus on the sensory experience?
- **Reactivity of the nervous system:** Is the nervous system generally hypervigilant and hyperalert to threat and danger or is it generally regulated and able to re-regulate in the face of stress?
- **Feedback from immediate and past social contacts:** Are others worried? Are they supportive? Do they fill you with confidence in this being handled or alert you to potential dangers of pain?

The above are just some of the psychosocial factors that can influence the pain amplification. Some will be more relevant than others, depending on the context and sensory experience.

Regardless of the pain experience, it is clear that addressing the role of thoughts, emotions and relationships/social support when experiencing pain can take a burdensome layer off the pain experience.

DIFFERENT TYPES OF THINKING

While people often find the mind–body connection theoretically intuitive, when faced with the realities of this in real life it can feel much more unfathomable and, perhaps more importantly, scary. The assumption that can make the role of the mind in determining bodily experiences scary is that you have little control over the mind. A common piece of evidence for this is that people often report having symptoms but not feeling particularly stressed, or being in a really good place, and then being hit by symptoms. It simply doesn't feel like it marries up. Or it may feel like you don't really know how you feel. That is a scary prospect!

This is where it can be useful to divide up our 'mental experiences' broadly into conscious and subconscious categories. Conscious processing is the type of intentional thinking we are more aware of day to day. It involves deliberate consideration of information, its evaluation and analysis. In contrast, subconscious processing is automated and intuitive. Every human will have a healthy mix of both types of processing, but a vast majority of our cognitive processing will be automated. That saves the brain energy and saves us time.

If you were to make a cup of tea, you'd likely not have to think about a single step, coasting on subconscious processing. However, if you went to get the tea bags and saw they were gone, your more conscious processing would kick in: 'Did I forget to buy tea? Do we have some elsewhere? What do I want instead?' Understanding that unconscious processing is a normal part of everyday life can help to take the threat out of it. Reassuringly, once we are alerted to the role of the mind in unwanted experience, the antidote isn't as complicated as we may fear. It can be as simple as bringing to our awareness what has been below our consciousness and working with that. This does not necessarily mean rooting around for past traumas (although sometimes these play a significant role). It can be identifying a previously unspotted thought that just blended into the fabric of experience and acknowledging that it is there. If we aren't aware to begin with, this can build resistance and, with that, tension. All of which can impact muscles and communication of nerve cells.

An example: Shelly has been experiencing urinary incontinence and this has caused her a lot of embarrassment. Her partner doesn't know this as she's been trying to hide it, but she's been googling to try and work out what is wrong. This evening, after the kids have gone to bed, her partner turns towards her with an excited smile that they have the evening to themselves. It's been a while and Shelly knows that he's expecting to have sex. From that moment to the moment they are in bed, is a blur. Shelly has been somewhere between panic and resignation. When the penetration hurts, she braces herself for it to continue hurting and questions whether this is another symptom of whatever is 'wrong down there'.

In this short excerpt we can see that Shelly has many unarticulated thoughts:

'This is shameful.'
'I need to hide it.'
'He might look at me differently if he knows.'
'What if I wet myself if we have sex.'
'Something is wrong.'
'I should have sex because it's been a while, even if I am
    uncomfortable.'

The list could go on. All these thoughts add pressure, add difficult emotions and, consequently, manifest in the body through increased tension and perhaps heightened sensitivity. Bringing that awareness to the unarticulated mental experience can help to transform it because it brings more choices. The choice to share the burden or to say no in that moment. The choice to focus on relaxing the body rather than following the thought stream. There are many potential choices that we are precluded from if we are unaware of the role of the mind.

Of course, that's not to say that simply becoming aware is easy or that the choices themselves are. With every challenge there is a starting point, without which there would be no progress at all. Practising becoming aware to the role of the mind is the fundamental starting point for any journey with health and wellbeing.

WHY IS INTERCOURSE PAINFUL?

You are not alone if you find yourself asking this question, if you have just accepted pain and discomfort as the norm, or if you now avoid intercourse to prevent feeling pain. As we explored in Chapter 5, there are various conditions that can cause painful intercourse (known as dyspareunia) involving the skin of the vulva and pelvic floor muscles. There are also different life stages that can lead to challenges as well, including postnatal and during the menopause. Let's take a look at these first.

LET'S TALK ABOUT SEX (AFTER) BABY!

For many, sex and intercourse is so far from their mind when they have just given birth, or when their doctor asks about contraception during a postnatal check. Having a small baby can feel like the best contraception you can ever have. Exhaustion, being up all night, breastfeeding and having a baby in your room can be enough to put anyone off! All jokes aside, contraception is very important to consider as you return to intercourse as you can still fall pregnant before your periods return and while breastfeeding. A common question is 'when can I have sex [intercourse] after birth?' and the general advice is once any wounds have healed and vaginal bleeding, known as lochia, has stopped, which is usually around 6 weeks. However, equally as important is when you feel ready, which will be different for everyone. For some it is 6 weeks, and for others it is months down the line. It can be so frustrating when you've spent the time to sort contraception and you finally feel up to it, to find when you do it's far from enjoyable, quite painful or just impossible. There are a number of reasons why this can occur, so let's talk through them:

1. **Hormones:** when breastfeeding, the levels of prolactin increase in our bodies, which suppresses the release of oestrogen. Our oestrogen levels are therefore lower during this time and oestrogen is the hormone that keeps the vaginal tissues plump and healthy. With less oestrogen the tissues become drier, less flexible and more sensitive. This means the tissues may be less resistant to friction, often resulting in what is often referred to as a 'paper cut' sensation at the vaginal entrance. The increase in sensitivity may also mean that you are now unable to use the lube that you previously did. Prolactin itself has a negative impact on your desire to engage in intimacy, so if you are breastfeeding or expressing, it's not surprising if you are not 'in the mood'.[8]

2. **Scar tissue:** after an episiotomy or perineal tear there will be new scar tissue that forms in the perineum and vagina. This can be very sensitive and tender, or it can feel quite

numb. It can also be and feel quite tight. The scar itself may be your source of discomfort during intercourse, or the anticipation of pain may be resulting in active guarding by your pelvic floor muscles, which in turn may increase a painful or difficult intercourse experience.

3. **Granulation tissue:** is a normal part of the healing process of wounds, however, sometimes there is excessive growth and some remains on top of the wound once it has healed. This is often red in appearance and tender to touch. It requires review with a doctor and sometimes needs to be removed through a small procedure.

4. **Birth trauma:** if your birthing experience has been traumatic and you are struggling to process and come to terms with what has happened, this can lead to your body and pelvic floor protecting you, resulting in painful, difficult, or uncomfortable attempts at intercourse. It can also lead to you feeling disconnected from your body, which makes it that much more difficult to identify behavioural responses to trauma such as breath-holding, pelvic floor tension, withdrawal or avoidance. This is true for any woman, whether they have had a vaginal or Caesarean birth.

What if pain isn't the issue, what else might be a barrier?

Pain isn't the only barrier to sex and intercourse after birth, other common barriers are:

1. **Reduced libido:** you are *not* alone if you are feeling this. It is so understandable, and many women are distressed by altered desire in the postpartum period. This can be in part hormonal, but also can be down to the fact of being needed by a baby or children all day that when it comes to

any time with our partner, we are so 'touched out' the last thing we feel like doing is being intimate. In this instance, what was previously considered sensual and suggestive touch may now feel annoying and unwelcome. If we have experienced pain at any point this can also influence our libido as anticipation of pain can definitely reduce our desire or interest. Sleep deprivation can also hugely impact our libido, and having small children is certainly a time when this is very common![9]

2. **Altered sensation and pleasure:** as the pelvic floor muscles and vaginal tissues have had a big stretch during vaginal delivery, this can lead to the vaginal canal feeling more open and reducing sensation during intercourse. Nerves may also be recovering after vaginal delivery or Caesarean birth, leading to altered sensations, including numbness or a crawling sensation at rest or during intercourse. Since intimacy is largely a sensory experience, it makes sense that this may lead to an avoidance of engaging in intimacy with a partner.

3. **Reduced body confidence:** you have experienced a rapid rate of change, from a growing belly in pregnancy to postpartum where the role of your body has changed to, for some, feeding and nourishing a baby, all in a matter of months. This can be overwhelming! You may struggle with these changes and be lacking in confidence. We know that a negative body image has the potential to impact arousal, desire and even pain.[10] This can influence how you feel during sex. You may be familiar with feeling distracted, while wondering what your partner might be thinking or feeling; you may also feel worried about how your vulva looks and if your partner will notice any difference during intercourse. We over-analyse the context. This is called

'spectatoring', an out-of-body experience that is the opposite of what we need for intimacy. Our brains are our most powerful sex organ and if we are distracted, critical or dissociating, we can't expect relaxation, enjoyment, spontaneity and pleasure. You are not alone in this; coming to terms with our body after birth can be really hard but it is possible!

4. **Struggling with incontinence:** if you are experiencing incontinence day to day, you can be anxious about leaking during sex. Understandably this is going to impact your libido and confidence. Leaking urine during sex is called coital incontinence.

A NOTE ON COITAL INCONTINENCE

Coital incontinence is leakage of urine that occurs during intercourse. It can be very embarrassing and greatly affect how a woman feels about sex and impact her libido. It is treatable but needs thorough assessment. It can sometimes be related to an overactive bladder and isn't just down to the pelvic floor muscles. Therefore, establishing the cause is key to finding the best treatment. Don't suffer in silence, seek help so you can get back to having intercourse without symptoms or fear.

Top tips if you are struggling with sex after birth:

Take a look at your vulva:

I know this can feel scary, and you may fear what you might see, but most women are often pleasantly surprised. Many women are also not sure if there is anything different as they haven't looked before! We can often fear the worst but knowing what your body looks like is so important to help you reconnect with it. Sex education, including anatomical awareness, has the potential to improve symptoms of sexual dysfunction.[11] It is never too late to get to know your body, and sometimes this time in our lives is a wonderful opportunity to do just that.

Body TLC:

It can be so hard to love and accept your postnatal body – trust me, I know. Focusing on the amazing things it has done and acknowledging the stage you are at are important. Showing your body love through practical ways – a warm bath, using a lovely body moisturiser, gentle movement and good nutrition – are all ways to work on loving your body, even if you struggle with what you see in the mirror. Coming to a place of acceptance and love for what your body has done and where it is right now can really help how you feel when it comes to being intimate. It is a process, and I am not saying it is easy but just take it one step at a time.

Talk to your partner:

It might seem obvious but being open and honest with where you are at is key. You might feel that it is obvious how you are feeling considering you have just had a baby, but don't underestimate the power of clear communication and honesty. You may not always agree but hearing each other out will help understanding and reduce arguments.

Scar massage:

Gentle massage of any perineal tear, episiotomy or Caesarean scars can help to reduce discomfort or tightness. See pages 188 and 190 for more information on how to do this.

Work on pelvic floor reconnection:

Starting with breathing and relaxation and building up to contractions is a good place to begin. Exact pelvic floor treatment will depend on your symptoms, so personalised assessment and treatment is best where possible. This isn't all about pelvic floor function, but also about reconnecting with your body and understanding it better.

Lube, lube, lube!

Use a water-based, glycerine-free lubricant during the early postpartum period, or for as long as you need help while vaginal tissues are drier from reduced oestrogen levels. Avoid scented, flavoured or coloured products. If you are uncertain of a new product or how your body may respond to it now compared to before pregnancy or birth, start with a 2-minute patch test on your inner thigh.

Acknowledge a change in preference:

The way we express and experience ourselves sexually (our sexuality) changes over time. And this may very well be one of those times. Things that you desired and enjoyed before having a baby may, at present, be the very last things that you would consider pleasurable. This highlights point 3 on page 249: you'd need to communicate that this is no longer working for you. See this as an opportunity to explore other avenues of pleasure.

Use boundaries where necessary:

If painful penetration is something that you are experiencing, consider taking penetration off the table while you work on those symptoms. You can still experience the value of support, connection, intimacy and pleasure with a partner in the absence of penetration.

I think a hugely important thing for anyone struggling with sex and intercourse, whether before or after having children, is to know that you are not alone. I wanted to share a story from someone who has been there and done the journey, so I am so thankful to Clio Wood, author, journalist and mum of two for sharing her story with us. Clio's passion to ensure that no woman feels alone and without help is infectious, and here she shares her story in her own words.

During pregnancy with my first daughter, I was so convinced that the only problem I'd face with sex after birth was a loose vagina, that I became obsessed with pelvic floor exercises. I did them everywhere. Standing on the platform at the tube station, sitting at my desk, lying in bed, watching TV. All good in theory, except that I was doing my pelvic floor exercises wrongly and developed a tighter pelvic floor. I had never been taught them in person, and had no idea that I needed to release them after the squeeze!

So postnatally, I found myself with an inflexible pelvic floor, which, coupled with a traumatic birth and vaginal scarring from an episiotomy meant that penetrative sex was incredibly painful. Summed up, the cause sounds simple now, but in the moment, I didn't know any of those reasons and when the pain of intercourse felt like shards of glass in my vagina, I was (understandably) worried! I asked my GP what could be wrong, and I could see she was unsure. She suggested swabbing for infection, despite my episiotomy having fully healed and looking healthy – the swabs didn't find anything, so I was sent on my way with the message that it would get better. It didn't, so I came back and asked again. I was swabbed, again; but again to no avail.

I pushed for a referral to somebody else, so I was sent to a gynaecologist. She didn't examine me physically but peered briefly between my open legs before sending me for an internal ultrasound. The internal ultrasound (with a wand inside my vagina) was highly painful, but ultimately fruitless as it found nothing wrong in my uterus or ovaries. So back to the gynaecologist I went. With weeks between appointments this whole process took nearly a year to conclude, and I still didn't have the answers I needed.

It was a friend who suggested I meet up with Amanda Savage, an incredible woman and the first time I'd met a pelvic health physiotherapist. Her knowledge and explanations left my jaw hanging. She articulated the movement and rehabilitation needs of the pelvic floor, scarring and body more generally after birth so well; I was just confused as to why I hadn't heard any of this information before. When I saw Amanda for an assessment and treatment, she put her finger on the problem (literally and metaphorically) right away. I was tense from birth trauma and my body was closing in on itself trying to protect itself. She identified scarring and my tighter pelvic floor and some incredibly tight glutes. It was no wonder that I could barely tolerate penetration at all. She helped me to perfect my pelvic floor technique, taught me to relax, encouraged me to process my birth trauma (which I continued to do with a therapist too) and showed me how to do scar massage.

All this work changed my experience of intercourse (and my body more generally) entirely. It didn't recover overnight, but over the course of the next year I worked on myself mentally and physically and with my husband found my way back to pleasure again.

If you resonate with Clio's story, please know there is help. Take this as a prompt to take the first step, and though it might feel scary and difficult to do I promise you it will be worth it.

NAVIGATING SEX AND THE MENOPAUSE

Menopause is another time in life when women can report difficulty and pain with sex and intercourse, whether this be during perimenopause or after menopause. This is often predominantly down to hormonal changes. During the perimenopause, oestrogen levels start to fluctuate and drop, and postmenopause they remain lower. As mentioned previously, oestrogen is what keeps our vaginal tissues plump and lubricated and reduced levels can lead to something called genitourinary syndrome of menopause (GSM). GSM describes a whole multitude of symptoms that might present as a woman journeys through menopause, including changes to the vulvar and vaginal tissues. Understandably, if the vaginal tissues are drier then intercourse can be uncomfortable or painful. For some it can cause splitting of the tissues, a bit like paper cuts, which can be very sore after intercourse as well. Using a vaginal moisturiser regularly can aid in tissue hydration to prevent trauma to the tissue, and a water-based glycerine-free lubricant during intercourse can provide relief from symptoms associated with friction. Some women may benefit from the use of vaginal oestrogen, which may be in the form of a tablet or cream placed inside the vagina and/or applied directly to the external vulvar tissue. The choice of product depends on your symptoms but essentially it helps to replace the oestrogen that the tissues need to reduce dryness and discomfort.

Hormone changes don't only impact the vulvar and vaginal tissues though, they affect the whole body, as we will explore more in the next chapter. These hormonal shifts can cause our libido to change. For some they might experience increased desire and arousability, which may be a welcomed change or tough to navigate if you have a partner who is experiencing age-related changes in sexual health, for example age-related erectile dysfunction. On the other hand, you may experience reduced desire and arousability; this may be associated with a history of painful intercourse or other menopause-related symptoms such as insomnia, mood changes or fatigue.

HOW MIGHT A PELVIC HEALTH PHYSIOTHERAPIST HELP IF INTERCOURSE IS PAINFUL?

Supporting women to return to pain-free and pleasurable inter-course, enabling them to grow in confidence and understand their body better, is an absolute privilege. I want to discuss in more depth two of the key conditions that we support women with, that we first discussed in Chapter 5: vaginismus and vulvodynia.

A quick recap before we discuss what the help and treatment might look like:

Vaginismus occurs when we try to insert something into the vagina but the pelvic floor tightens up involuntarily.

Vulvodynia is generalised pain in the vulvar area lasting over 3 months without a clear identifiable cause, which can be either unprovoked or provoked. Pain can be quite widespread across the vulva or in a more specific area.

Treatment, as always, will vary depending on your own individ-ual symptoms and story, but may include:

- **Information about the condition:** Understanding what you are feeling and experiencing is step one in things improving. It helps to reduce fear knowing what is going on and that you are not broken. A plan and a way forward can really help how you feel mentally. It can be really helpful to share this with your partner, or invite them to the appointment so they are part of the conversation from early on.
- **Education about pain and the brain's involvement:** Understanding pain is complex, but understanding our brain's involvement and why we need to take a holistic and full-body approach to your symptoms helps to get the best results. You

are *one* body, and we can't detach your vulva and vagina from it. As I mentioned previously, when it comes to sex it is not just a physical act and, therefore, we need to consider all contributing factors when discussing symptoms. This does not mean we are saying that your symptoms are 'all in your head', far from it. However, we need to explore and understand how our brain and mind is involved in our experience. I hope that Dr Windgassen's wisdom on this topic shared earlier in the chapter has helped you to understand more about this.

- **Encouragement to get to know your body:** You've already done a lot of this through this book, so you are one step ahead, but this is a very important part of any physiotherapy input, especially when it comes to sex.
- **Support and encouragement to touch your vulva:** When you can't see your anatomy it can be very hard to know what is what. Equally, if you are used to touch being painful it is natural to avoid this, whether this be your own touch or a partner's. A big part of treatment is graded and gradual touch, helping your body and mind to learn that touch is safe. This often needs to start with you feeling more confident to touch any painful areas, including any scars.
- **Scar massage:** As explored previously we will advise you on how to reconnect with and massage scars, whether they are vaginal or abdominal scars.
- **Breathwork:** This is probably unsurprising by this stage in the book, but teaching you to connect with your breath, diaphragmatic breathing and its connection with the pelvic floor are foundational to our treatment and support.
- **Pelvic floor rehabilitation:** Education and feedback on restoring movement and flexibility of the pelvic floor, as well as incorporating strengthening exercises when the time is right. This may involve the use of biofeedback machines to help

provide you visual feedback about what your pelvic floor is doing, as well as gentle stretching done by the physiotherapist or yourself in your home programme. It is all about helping you to understand your body and pelvic floor better.[12]

- **Use of vaginal dilators:** Vaginal dilators are silicone or plastic and can be used to gently stretch the vaginal tissues, as well as help you to gradually learn that penetration is not painful. They start small, around the size of a finger, and go up to the size of an erect penis. Over weeks or months, we support you to work up the sizes, using breathing techniques. The goal isn't just to get up to the biggest size, but how your body feels and responds as well. Initially it can feel a bit daunting to use them, but I see on a weekly basis how helpful they are and love seeing women build in confidence as they use them.

- **Considering movement and muscles away from the pelvic floor:** Though pelvic health physiotherapists have a huge passion and focus on the pelvic floor, we also assess other muscles as well. It is about understanding the pelvic floor better, why the muscles are functioning in the way they are, as well as their relationship with other muscles in the body. Therefore, treatment may also include exercises for other muscles, not just the pelvic floor.

- **Discussing other contributing factors:** It is often helpful and important to look at the whole of life and think about how we can influence and change other factors that could also be contributing to symptoms. Two big ones are stress and sleep. Working on ways to reduce stress and improve sleep can help our symptoms and ability to engage in treatment.

- **Sex education:** Depending on your pelvic health physiotherapist's special interest and their qualifications, they may help by answering questions you may have regarding 'sex'. There is no shame in feeling a little lost and uncertain

about 'the basics' since most people can agree that their sex
education has been little to none. Having an understanding
about human sexual responses might be just what you need
to reduce the anxiety and tension relating to intimate
encounters.

- **Home programme and control:** You will be sent home with a
bespoke home programme that comprises important and
relevant elements of what has been done in the sessions.
Your personalised programme will not only help you with
symptom management but also help you to establish an
element of control and autonomy. A physiotherapist is there to
be your guide and cheerleader; a 'facilitator not a fixer'.

Psychosexual counselling

As we have touched on the importance of the mind–body connection and how sex is far from just a physical act, I am sure it won't surprise you to know that we often recommend women to also see a psychosexual therapist. It can really help to support you further and complement what you are doing in your physiotherapy sessions. It also provides a safe place for you and your partner to explore how you are feeling. I am delighted that my friend and psychosexual therapist whom I refer to regularly, Kate Moyle, has answered some questions about what to expect from psychosexual therapy.

WHAT IS PSYCHOSEXUAL THERAPY?

It is talking therapy to help you work through any difficulties or problems that you might be having with your sex life. It aims to examine how we think and feel about sex, our emotional and physical reactions to it, as well as how we view ourselves as a sexual being. It aims to support a range of symptoms including challenges with desire, difficulties with orgasm, pain, anxiety and trauma.

WHAT CAN SOMEONE EXPECT FROM A SESSION?

During a session, in person or virtually, conversation will aim to tackle our thinking around sex. It provides a safe space to explore what we feel about sex, understanding ourselves in context of our world and what we have been taught about it. It is likely to go into personal and sexual history so that the therapist can help you explore what has contributed to your current thoughts and feelings. The sessions will aim to teach you about your anatomy, body and how it works. Building a positive relationship with your body and exploring what feels good is important. It is also foundational to work through shame that may have developed over time. The therapist may also set you up with a programme and some exercises or practices to work on at home.

HOW CAN IT HELP SOMEONE WHO IS HAVING PAIN WITH SEX?

We often need to start by redefining sex. We have a very ingrained belief that penetration is sex, so when it is painful we feel we can no longer enjoy sex or intimacy. A therapist will explore further what sex really is for you and how we can find pleasure and be intimate in other ways that are pain free. This will often involve exploring what feels good for us and understanding our body better. Mindfulness-based and body-awareness exercises can help to increase desire and reduce pain.[13] The goal is to empower and educate you on how to feel safe and experience pleasure through sex, however this might look for you.

ARE PARTNERS ALWAYS PRESENT?

Partners are not always present and lots of people come alone. You don't need to be in a relationship to benefit from psychosexual therapy. Some women do come with their partners as it can be helpful to work on the dynamics in a relationship as well.

GENTLE MOVEMENT AND EXERCISES THAT MIGHT HELP YOU ON YOUR JOURNEY

As mentioned previously, treatment is not just focused on the vulva, vagina and pelvic floor muscles, and I wanted to share some of the stretches and movements I encourage women to do at home as part of their treatment programme.

Child's pose

- Kneeling on a mat, walk your hands forward.
- Sit back onto your heels with your arms stretched out in front of you.
- As you rest in this position practise taking some deep diaphragmatic breaths.
- As you breathe in visualise your sitting bones widening and moving apart.

Happy Baby

- Lying down on a mat lift both legs up one at a time into the position shown in the picture.
- The soles of your feet should be facing up to the ceiling.
- Spread your knees apart and hold on to the side of your feet or your ankles.
- You may feel stretching in your inner thigh muscles.
- Practise some deep diaphragmatic breathing and visualise your sitting bones widening as you breathe in.

These positions should not cause pain, so please don't push into or through pain. You can use them regularly throughout your day.

MYTH BUSTING

'The best advice if you are struggling with painful sex is "to just have a glass of wine and relax"'

I am always surprised and shocked that any woman has ever been told this, and yet sadly I still hear it being said. This type of comment not only invalidates a woman's experience and symptoms but also

*plays into the narrative that it is all down to her and her fault. It tries
to simplify something that is often far more complex and with
multiple contributing factors. So if you have been told this, or are
told this, please politely ignore it and know that there is much better
advice and help elsewhere!*

'The pain is all in your head!'
*I hope that through this chapter you have learnt more about the
mind-body connection and why we need to consider the mind when
discussing pain. It can be so hard if you've seen a doctor, who has
done swabs and scans that all come back as normal, for it therefore
to feel suggested that this is not a physical problem. However, as we
have discussed, it is often more complicated than using one label.
Just because it is related to our thoughts and feelings does not mean
it is 'all in your head'. Equally, just because the pain is in the vulva
and vagina doesn't mean it isn't in part related to our thoughts,
feelings, beliefs and brain. You are one, your body and mind are
connected, and caring for the whole of you is the answer.*

Foundation Reflections

Take a moment as you finish this chapter to jot down any thoughts or feelings you have. Are you struggling with sex or intercourse at the moment? Can you try and identify any of the issues discussed in this chapter that might be relevant to you? Can you use your notes to chat to your partner? Would it help to book an appointment with your doctor?

....

....

....

....

....

....

....

....

....

PART IV

Moving Through Life – Perimenopause and Beyond

CHAPTER 12

Menopause Matters

Let's learn about:

- The perimenopause and its extensive symptoms
- What menopause means for our pelvic health
- The treatment options available to us, including HRT
- Top tips to help your personal journey
- Key pillars of health to focus on

There are not many things certain in life, but something that is for all women is menopause. It doesn't get much good press, is often viewed pretty negatively and for years it has been rather taboo to talk about. So, much of women's struggles were done alone and in silence, with the view that 'there is nothing that can be done'. However, thankfully tides are changing, awareness is increasing, and the menopause army is marching on to bring about changes. When it comes to pelvic health, menopause has frequently been viewed as just a time when 'symptoms will inevitably get worse', or a time when women experience symptoms for the first time and therefore menopause gets all the blame. Understanding what to expect and how to be proactive during this time in our lives is key. Let's take a more in-depth look at this all together so we can be prepared, or, if you are already in or moving beyond this season of life, can be empowered to take care of yourself now and in the years ahead.

Let's start with some definitions as this is key to our whole understanding. Though we hear the term menopause most frequently, there are actually a few important terms we need to consider:

Menopause is a single point in time, which is a year from your last period. The average age for this is 51 years old.

Premature menopause is when menopause occurs before the age of 40.

Early menopause is when menopause occurs before the age of 45.

Premature ovarian insufficiency (POI) is a condition where your periods stop suddenly and spontaneously, either early or prematurely. POI isn't the same as premature or early menopause, because with POI there's a chance your period will come back. People with POI may still ovulate, menstruate or become pregnant.

Perimenopause is the time running up to menopause where women might experience a whole host of symptoms, including irregular periods. On average it can last between 4 and 8 years running up to our final period. Women in their forties can often be told that they are 'too young' to have menopause symptoms, but this simply isn't true.

Postmenopause is any time after that 1-year mark from your last period.

This helps us to understand that it is often the **perimenopause** we refer to when talking about the menopause. The common symptoms we hear about are the night sweats, the hot flushes, the brain fog and emotional outbursts, but do we all experience the same symptoms during this time?

Some women may pass through the perimenopause without much notice, but for many it can be a time of real struggle dealing with a whole host of symptoms. Below is an extensive list that shows the large variety of symptoms that women can experience.

PERIMENOPAUSE SYMPTOMS

- Acne
- Itchy skin
- Anxiety
- Depression
- Irritability
- Mood swings
- Panic disorders
- Incontinence
- Vaginal dryness
- Reduced libido
- Bloating and digestive problems
- Recurrent UTIs
- Brain fog
- Burning mouth syndrome
- Gum tenderness
- Breast tenderness
- Body odour
- Dizziness
- Fatigue
- Low motivation
- Reduced concentration
- Poor memory
- Loss of self-confidence
- Headaches
- Heart palpitations

- Hot flushes
- Night sweats
- Irregular periods
- Joint pain
- Reduced bone density and osteoporosis
- Muscle tension
- Weight gain
- Brittle nails
- Sleep disruption and insomnia
- Tingling hands and feet
- Hair loss

Wow! That is a lot of symptoms, right? No wonder menopause gets a bad reputation, but why do these symptoms and changes occur?

During the perimenopause, some of the key female hormones, which we first looked at in Chapter 1 (see page 35), start to fluctuate and change. I used to think that our hormone levels carried on as normal and then one day there was a ski slope-style drop down to a flat line and that was menopause. How wrong I was! It is much more of a rollercoaster, which seems to be a bit of a theme in this book, of up and down fluctuations with a gradual decline. There are some circumstances where women might experience a more abrupt menopause, for example, after surgery where the ovaries are removed or during cancer treatment.

The two main hormones that are often discussed during this time are oestrogen and progesterone. Oestrogen, as we have said a few times already, is a hormone that is important for regulating our menstrual cycle, as well as for keeping our tissues pumped and plumped, ready for action. It is also important for our mind, mood, bone strength and heart health. Progesterone is also a key player in our menstrual cycle and plays a significant role in preparing our body for and supporting it during pregnancy. Though we often discuss fluctuations and declines in oestrogen and progesterone as being the main drivers of symptoms during the perimenopause, testosterone is also a key player. You might be surprised to hear this, as we often associate testosterone as a male hormone, but women have it too. Testosterone is important for bone density, muscle mass and energy levels, as well as our mood, libido and brain function. Therefore, as it declines, alongside oestrogen and progesterone, this can also contribute to symptoms. Testosterone declines more gradually, with less fluctuations than the other hormones, and individual assessment is required to understand if this is a potential contributing factor for a woman's symptoms.

WHAT DOES THIS MEAN FOR THE VAGINA AND PELVIC FLOOR?

The sheer number of symptoms that can occur during the perimenopause can feel overwhelming, so I am just going to focus on the ones that relate to the vagina, vulva, bladder, bowels and pelvic floor (your pelvic health squad), which I am sure won't come as a surprise! The hormonal changes, particularly the reduction in oestrogen, that I have mentioned impact the pelvic health squad significantly, especially the vulva and vagina, as they have large numbers of oestrogen receptors. They therefore love oestrogen and so this time in life can cause a bit of chaos among them.

It isn't necessarily a case of lower oestrogen levels making the pelvic floor muscles weaker that causes bladder, bowel or prolapse symptoms to start or worsen,[1] but more the changes to the vaginal, vulvar, bladder and urethral tissues. Ultimately, like most things we have learnt through this book, there can be a variety of factors that can contribute and cause symptoms to develop. It could be that the pelvic floor muscles were already weak going into the perimenopause and then the gradual changes to the tissues as well has led to symptoms. This, alongside changes to bowel habits that can also occur during this time, particularly constipation, can all come together and leave the pelvic health squad needing a bit of help. Also, as we age our muscle mass naturally decreases – approximately between 3 and 8 per cent each decade from the age of 30.[2] This gradual loss of muscle mass as we age is called sarcopenia and it impacts all skeletal muscle. Our pelvic floor muscles are skeletal muscle and so are not immune from this process either.

It is important at this stage to revisit genitourinary symptoms of the menopause (GSM), which we briefly mentioned in the last chapter. GSM is an umbrella term for a whole variety of symptoms that can occur during the perimenopause and postmenopause that relate to the bladder, vagina, vulva and sex, including:

- Vaginal and vulvar dryness
- Pain or discomfort with intercourse
- Decreased vaginal lubrication
- Decreased arousal, orgasm and desire
- Itching, irritation or burning of the vulva or vagina
- Increased urinary frequency and/or urgency
- Recurrent urinary tract infections[3]

You may also hear these symptoms be referred to as urogenital atrophy, as it is important to note that these symptoms can start after the menopause.

We also need to consider lifestyle changes in this stage of life for women. During perimenopause you may still have young children who need lifting, alongside elderly parents who need physical support. This can leave you feeling pulled in all directions, finding very little time to exercise or focus on your own needs. Then as you move through to being postmenopausal you may become a grandmother for the first time, suddenly lifting and carrying a heavy baby again in awkward positions. During this time you may also retire and your pace of life changes drastically, allowing a lot of down time leading to deconditioning, or allowing more time to increase your activity levels and challenge your body more. These changes in our lifestyle, alongside hormone levels, can lead to us developing a variety of symptoms.

Common symptoms women report during this time are:

1. **New or worsening prolapse symptoms.** There can be a lot of scaremongering that goes on around menopause and prolapse, suggesting that it is a foregone conclusion that a prolapse will just get worse during this time. Thankfully this isn't necessarily the case. There is always a risk that a prolapse could progress and worsen, for many different reasons. However, just because we might become symptomatic for the first time, or more symptomatic, doesn't mean that anatomically a prolapse has progressed. I know this sounds confusing, and I encourage you to head back to Chapter 10 (see page 214) to have a reread of the section around prolapse. Lower levels of oestrogen lead to the vaginal tissues becoming drier, thinner and more sensitive, which can increase our symptoms and awareness of prolapse.[4,5]

2. **New or worsening incontinence symptoms.** Similarly to prolapse, we may experience new or worsening bladder symptoms, but that doesn't mean they aren't treatable. The hormonal shifts can be the final straw that leads to us developing symptoms. Whereas before you might have only

had symptoms occasionally if you had a really bad cough, you might start to notice them happening more often. You may start to notice more stress incontinence, as well as urge incontinence (see pages 201 and 202). It isn't always a dramatic change, but a more subtle and gradual one. This may be down to existing pelvic floor muscle weakness, as well as changes to the urethral and bladder tissues as a result of reduced oestrogen.

3. **New or worsening symptoms of urinary urgency or frequency.** As oestrogen levels decline women can also start to experience symptoms of an overactive bladder (head back to page 202 for a recap), which is one of the symptoms of GSM. Changes to the cells of the urethra and bladder can make them less compliant and more sensitive, which can lead to increased overactivity of the bladder muscle. Feeling a more urgent need to do a wee, and/or needing to go more frequently, can hugely impact quality of life and our ability to carry out everyday tasks like going to the supermarket.

4. **Pain with intercourse.** As we have established by now, this is never normal, and shouldn't be accepted at any time in life. Hormonal changes can lead to increased sensitivity or pain. These symptoms are widely under-treated and unsupported in the UK.[6] Turn back to page 255 for a recap of some top tips to help, and head to your doctor for review and support.

5. **Recurrent UTIs.** Another symptom of GSM is recurrent UTIs, which aside from being uncomfortable can require repeated trips to the doctor and courses of antibiotics. Reduced oestrogen levels can make the bladder and

urethral tissues more susceptible to bacteria that lead to UTIs. Oestrogen also influences blood flow to the vaginal tissues, which is necessary to support the important and good bacteria lactobacillus, which helps to maintain a lower pH level in the vagina. This helps to prevent overgrowth of yeast, i.e., thrush, and is protective against UTIs.

6. **Changes to bowel habits.** There can be a variety of bowel symptoms that develop during this time in our lives. For some they might find themselves more constipated, for others they may find they are experiencing more diarrhoea, or bloating, or aggravation of their IBS symptoms. This can be due to reduced oestrogen and its link with the stress hormone cortisol – however, this can also just be a time in life when we are more stressed anyway, so hormones are not solely to blame.

WHAT TREATMENT IS AVAILABLE?

Treatment for symptoms of perimenopause needs to be as varied as its symptoms, and it is never too early or too late to flag symptoms to your doctor. For pelvic floor, vulvar, vaginal, bladder and bowel symptoms there is also a wide variety of treatments available to support you. Let's explore these together.

Medical management

I wanted to start by acknowledging the importance of assessment for and use of medication and hormone replacement therapy (HRT) during this time. I am delighted that Dr Anna Cantlay, a

GP with a specialist interest in the menopause, has answered some important questions so we can be more informed and prepared:

When should you see your GP if you think you are perimenopausal or menopausal?

We welcome all women to come and talk to their GP if they feel they are perimenopausal or menopausal. A recent report from the All-Party Parliamentary Group for Menopause recommended that all women be invited for a health check at 45 where menopause should be discussed.[7] Even if you don't have many symptoms, it's a really important time to discuss your general health as the risk of certain conditions, such as osteoporosis and cardiovascular disease, can increase after menopause.

What can you expect from a menopause consultation?

A good menopause consultation should offer a holistic approach to assessing your symptoms, their impact on you and the treatment options available. It's often helpful to come armed with a symptom diary as this can help use the time effectively, particularly given most NHS GP appointments are only 10–15 minutes. See the Helpful Resources (page 325) for some options you might like to use. Your GP will ask questions about your current health and past medical history so they can better advise you on lifestyle and possible treatment options available to you to treat perimenopausal and menopausal symptoms.

What treatment options are there?

The most commonly prescribed and effective treatment to manage the perimenopause and menopause is Hormone Replacement Therapy (HRT). There are, however, other options available for treatment if you choose not to have HRT, or when HRT may not be recommended.

Hormone Replacement Therapy (HRT)

Systemic HRT is an effective treatment to manage the symptoms of perimenopause and menopause. We have oestrogen receptors all throughout our body and replacing oestrogen through hormone therapy helps to improve menopausal symptoms and health consequences. HRT normally consists of two main female hormones – oestrogen and progestogen. (Progestogen refers to a sex steroid hormone that has progesterone-like activity and may be body identical or synthetic.) Whether you need one or both depends on your personal health history. Women without a uterus will normally be offered oestrogen-only HRT (there are some exceptions to this such as a history of severe endometriosis), whereas a combined oestrogen and progestogen preparation will be offered to those with a uterus.[8] A third hormone, testosterone, may also be prescribed by some specialist clinics for symptoms of low libido.[9]

HRT comes in many forms, including patches, gels, sprays and tablets, and your GP or healthcare professional will help you choose the most appropriate preparation for you. Most doctors will recommend body-identical HRT, which consists of a transdermal oestrogen (gel, spray or patch applied to the skin) and an oral micronised progesterone called Utrogestan. This is the safest and most regulated way to prescribe HRT and are precise duplicates to the natural hormones produced by your ovaries. This is different from compounded bio-identical HRT, which are unlicensed and unregulated hormonal preparations made up by specialist pharmacies. They are not recommended by the British Menopause Society due to concerns regarding their safety and efficacy.[10]

Vaginal oestrogens

Vaginal oestrogens, also sometimes referred to as topical oestrogens, can be used to help support vaginal and bladder symptoms relating to the perimenopause and menopause known as GSM, mentioned previously. Vaginal oestrogens work locally on the vagina, vulva and nearby pelvic tissues with minimal systemic absorption. They therefore do not carry the same risks as systemic HRT and can be used safely by the majority of women. Vaginal oestrogens come in the form of pessaries (tablets inserted into the vagina), creams and rings. They can be effective at reducing vaginal dryness and irritation, and urinary symptoms such as urgency, frequency, urinary incontinence and recurrent UTIs, and can be used long term.[11, 12] Systemic HRT, applied to the skin or taken orally as mentioned above, can be safely used with additional vaginal oestrogens so please do speak to your GP for assessment.

Benefits of HRT

In addition to helping with the symptoms related to menopause, there are also health benefits of taking HRT. Osteoporosis risk is reduced, and for women starting HRT within the first 10 years of the menopause it is likely to be associated with a reduction in cardiovascular disease. There may also be a reduction in the risk of colorectal cancer, type 2 diabetes and dementia but further research is needed.

Is HRT safe?

For the majority of low-risk women, starting HRT within the first 10 years of the menopause or under the age of 60, HRT is a safe and effective treatment. The risks are small and will depend on the type of HRT used and the duration of use. Risks such as blood clots (deep vein thrombosis), breast cancer and endometrial cancer will vary depending on the type and duration of HRT used. Body-identical HRT is the safest of all HRT – transdermal oestrogens do not have a clot or stroke risk, and studies have shown Utrogestan-containing HRT does not increase breast-cancer risk for the first 5 years of use.[13] As with all medications, your doctor will take a detailed history of your symptoms and past medical history and fully discuss any risks, potential side effects and benefits so you can make an informed choice.

Non-hormonal options

Most prescribed alternatives have been evaluated for their effectiveness to support hot flushes, but some will also help with mental wellbeing. Some can have some side effects that need to be considered in choosing an appropriate alternative. Examples include some antidepressants, clonidine, gabapentin, pregabalin and oxybutynin.

Alternative therapies

There are several alternative and complementary therapies available for menopause care. Acupuncture, yoga, herbal treatments (black cohosh or red clover), aromatherapy and reflexology may be helpful to some women looking for a holistic approach to their health and wellbeing, but research is limited into their effectiveness. While some treatments may provide partial relief from some menopausal symptoms, their effects are often transient. For this reason, they are not normally recommended for the sole treatment of the menopause.

Pelvic floor muscle training

I am sure it comes as no surprise that pelvic floor muscle training is important at this time in life, especially to help with symptoms of incontinence, prolapse and GSM. Though we might think of pelvic floor muscle training as purely improving the strength of the muscles, there is actually more to it. Pelvic floor muscle training has been shown to improve blood flow to the tissues of the vulva and vagina, pelvic floor function and flexibility, as well as tissue elasticity in postmenopausal women.[14] The good news is that pelvic floor muscle training is effective for women of all ages.[15,16] Another reason that we should be talking about this loud and clear is that it is never too late to benefit from taking care of our pelvic floor. Head to Chapter 2 to recap on how to give your pelvic floor muscles maximal TLC.

Think about what you are drinking

As we explored in Chapter 10, what we drink can have an influence on bladder symptoms, especially when struggling with urgency, frequency and recurrent UTIs. Ensure you are drinking enough fluid, aiming for around 1.5 litres a day, as well as cutting down on caffeine, artificial sweeteners, alcohol and fizzy drinks.

Take care of your bowels

Constipation and straining to open our bowels need to be addressed to support all pelvic floor symptoms. At a time in life when we can start to notice new or worsening bowel symptoms, there is never a more important moment to take control. Always remember the foundations of fluid, fibre and movement, while also working on reducing your stress levels. Much easier said than done, of course, but we will explore this a little more in a moment. It can sometimes feel like a shock experiencing new bowel symptoms, especially faecal or flatal incontinence. Sometimes these occur as the result of an old injury to the anal sphincter and pelvic floor during birth, and hormonal shifts and tissue changes are now resulting in symptoms. It is never too late to improve things, but making sense of changes can be hard. Our gut also influences hormone production and so taking care of our gut microbiota is essential at this time. Go back to Chapter 1 (see page 17) to reread the wisdom from Kristy Coleman.

The power of a pessary

Vaginal pessaries can be so beneficial for improving symptoms of prolapse, and menopause might be a time when you need to consider one for the first time. Turn back to page 218 to reread the section on pessaries, and speak to your doctor if you would like to be assessed to try one. Postmenopausal women will often be advised to use a vaginal oestrogen alongside a pessary to take care of the vaginal tissues, if there are signs of urogenital atrophy.

Lubricants and moisturisers

In the same way we reach for various moisturisers to support our facial skin through life, and with an ever-growing market of 'anti-ageing creams', let's not forget that our vulval skin and vaginal tissues love moisture too. Using a vaginal moisturiser, such as those from YES organics, Sylk or Replens, regularly can aid in tissue hydration and day-to-day comfort. These can be bought online or from a local pharmacy. Using a water-based glycerine-free lubricant during intercourse can provide relief from symptoms associated with friction.

WHAT ELSE SHOULD WE CONSIDER AT THIS TIME OF LIFE?

Though my focus is always predominantly on a woman's pelvic health, we always need to support a woman with taking care of all parts of her health. As Dr Cantlay highlighted, there are a number of health problems that can arise during this time of life, and these, alongside the wide variety of symptoms, need a fully holistic and nurturing approach. Therefore, I wanted to discuss some foundational pillars that I think are vital for the whole of life, but are even more paramount during this phase when we can feel really up against it.

The power of sleep

Since having kids sleep is honestly something I think and talk about more than most things! Any sleep-deprived parent can tell you what the lack of sleep can do to you, so it is unsurprising that it plays such an important role in our health. There can be many factors influencing our sleep at this time of life. As many of us are having children later in life than previous generations, the gap between our postpartum period, small children and perimenopause starting can sometimes not be that long – or in fact overlap. Six years into this motherhood journey and there are still plenty of reasons that I am woken in the night. I remember my mum saying she never slept the same after having kids as she was always listening out, even when I was in my early twenties and had moved back home! Even if our children are sleeping well, hormones may start to cause problems as oestrogen levels decline. Oestrogen helps to decrease the length of time it takes us to fall asleep, how many times we wake up, and increases total sleep time.[17] It also plays a key role in regulating our body temperature, and its decline can cause the famous hot flushes we hear about. It is therefore unsurprising that oestrogen decline can play havoc with our sleep. Though we can't control the hormonal changes, there are things we can do to try and help.

HRT can be helpful at improving sleep, as can focusing on our overall sleep hygiene. Aiming for 7–8 hours of sleep a night is a good place to start – not always easy I know, but something I am constantly working towards. However, it is not all about the length of time we are in bed but what we do in preparation. Reducing screen time before bed, not consuming caffeine after lunchtime, having a consistent bedtime routine (just like our kids), reducing alcohol consumption and doing regular physical activity can all help improve our sleep.

Unfortunately, even if we focus on all of these factors, our pelvic health squad can be responsible for causing sleep issues as well. Women can find themselves getting up more overnight to do a wee, and though once might not be too disturbing, if you find yourself getting up multiple times a night this can be a sign of an overactive bladder (head to page 202 to recap). There is help for these symptoms, so don't let your bladder cause sleep issues.

Nutrition: food, fuel and fibre

Perimenopause and postmenopause is a time when thinking about what we are eating could not be more important. As for many other stages of a woman's life, the focus and pressure can be on weight management, and though this is important for many reasons, flipping our focus onto the power of nutrition and what it can do to help fuel us can be really helpful: focusing on what will benefit us and what we should be eating *more* of, rather than what we should restrict. Nutrition is not all about our weight, it also has a large impact on our bone and heart health as well. One main area of focus during this time should be managing blood sugar (glucose) levels. Put simply, when our blood glucose levels keep going up and down in large peaks and troughs, the body is put on high alert and has to focus on managing them, taking attention away from focusing on regulating hormones like oestrogen and progesterone. These peaks and troughs can also impact our mood and eating habits, as we are more likely to experience cravings and reach for that cake. Personalised nutritional advice can be hugely beneficial during this time, but here are some key principles to follow:

1. **Pack in the plants:** Focus on increasing your intake of fruit, vegetables and legumes (such as lentils, beans and chickpeas) while aiming for a wide variety of colours as well. Try for a minimum of 30 different plant-based foods a week. It can be quite an exciting challenge and makes our food a lot more pretty to look at! This is also so important for our gut microbiota.

2. **Aim for wholegrains:** Increasing our wholegrain intake can help our heart health. Making some simple swaps from white bread and pasta to wholegrain, eating oats, wholegrain cereals or brown rice are good places to start.

3. **Think about fats:** Fats in our food have often been seen as the enemy. I am sure lots of us will have seen 'low fat diets' advertised. However, fats are essential for our body; they help to make our hormones, as well as supporting the absorption of essential fat-soluble vitamins A, D, E and K. So, it isn't about avoiding them, but focusing on understanding the different types and what to incorporate into your diet. Try to get the majority of fat in your diet from unsaturated fats, such as oily fish (aim for two portions of fish a week, one of which is oily, for example, salmon or mackerel), nuts and seeds, avocados and olive oil or rapeseed (vegetable) oil, and reduce saturated fats like butter, coconut oil and fatty cuts of meat.

4. **Prioritise protein:** Protein is a powerhouse and needed for so many of our body's functions. Think about how you can incorporate it into each meal and snack that you eat. It isn't all about building muscle, which is often what we associate

with protein. There are so many sources that we can add in: fish, lean meat, grains such as quinoa or oats, dairy, chia seeds, lentils and nuts. Protein can also help to regulate our blood (sugar) glucose level by lowering the glycaemic index (GI) of a meal. The glycaemic index refers to how quickly foods affect your blood sugar levels. High GI foods include white bread, white rice, potatoes and some sugary foods. Low GI foods include wholegrains, pasta and pulses. Being mindful of the glycaemic index of a meal can help in the management of blood glucose levels.

5. **Find calcium-rich food:** Calcium is vital for our bone health, which we will explore a bit more in the next chapter. We often think of dairy as providing the calcium we need, for example, milk, cheese and yoghurt, however, calcium can be found in other sources as well. These include tinned fish, for example, sardines, fortified cereals, fortified plant-based milks and some leafy green vegetables. For calcium absorption we also need Vitamin D, which we get from food such as eggs, oily fish and mushrooms, as well as from sunlight. Government guidelines in the UK recommend that everyone takes a Vitamin D supplement, 10mcg a day, in the autumn and winter months. Others may be advised to take Vitamin D all year round, especially if they are not able to get outside much.

6. **Focus on fibre:** You will know by now I talk about fibre a lot, and its importance for our bowel health, but it has also been shown to lower our risk of heart disease.[18] Another good reason to think about how to get that 30g of fibre into your diet every day. Turn to page 23 for a recap.

7. **Include soya:** Eating soya-based food such as tofu, edamame beans, soya-based milks or tempeh can reduce the severity and frequency of hot flushes.[19]

8. **Reduce alcohol and salt:** As we have explored, reducing these can help with our bladder health and sleep, but it is also beneficial for our heart health. Reducing alcohol (and caffeine) can also help with the severity of hot flushes. Aim for no more than 14 units of alcohol a week, and 4–5 cups of caffeinated drinks a day (400mg). With regards to salt, adults are advised not to consume more than 6g a day, so it is worth checking your diet as most of us don't know how much we are consuming.

Mental and emotional wellbeing

If the symptoms were not enough to make us feel anxious and stressed, perimenopause is often a time in life when we are juggling a lot day to day. School runs, multiple activities to get children to, keeping careers going and navigating an ever-changing world. While also feeling the demand to eat well, exercise and maintain relationships, of course. I feel exhausted thinking and writing about it. It is therefore not surprising that with hormonal changes on top of everything else that we do at this time we can struggle mentally and emotionally. First and foremost, there is no shame in finding yourself needing more support or struggling with your mental health at any stage of life and motherhood. Acknowledging when we need help is the key, and that can be harder than it might seem.

You might start to notice that anxiety and depression start to creep in over time, or they can hit you all of a sudden. Speaking to your doctor and exploring the options for support is the best place to start. Cognitive Behavioural Therapy (CBT), a type of talking therapy, is recommended in guidelines as a treatment option for anxiety during the perimenopause and menopause.[20] Alongside medication and CBT, looking at your life and working out how to prioritise self-care, hobbies and stress-relieving activities is also really important. Managing stress could not be more important during this time in life. It can be hard but sometimes taking a step back and looking at work, life, the balance between the two and the support you have around can be helpful to show you how you can reduce stress day to day. Managing stress isn't only important for our mental and emotional wellbeing though, it can play into our hormone production. When our body is stressed, it goes into 'fight or flight' mode, producing cortisol and adrenaline that can interfere with the production and balance of oestrogen and progesterone. Reducing alcohol and caffeine can help reduce anxiety, stress and improve sleep. I am not here to ruin all your fun, but just take a moment to think about how to find the best balance for you.

Activity and exercise

This is such an important part of the conversation for the health and wellbeing of women during perimenopause and after menopause. So much so that I have dedicated a whole chapter to it, which is coming up next. It is very easy to advise women to aim for 150 minutes of moderate-intensity activity a week, including resistance training and impact exercise, however, there can be so many barriers to this being possible and a huge one is often our pelvic health. Being active has so many benefits, reducing stress, improving sleep, managing weight, helping our heart and bone health as well as maintaining muscle mass, there is no doubt we need to support women to maintain or increase their activity levels.

* * *

I know menopause can seem like a very unknown, overwhelming and in some ways quite scary time. I hope that this has started to open up the conversation for you and that you feel more empowered to know what help is available and what you can do to help at home. It isn't all doom and gloom. If you can be proactive and have the necessary conversations at the right time it can make navigating this season just that little bit easier.

MYTH BUSTING

'Symptoms will just get worse during the menopause'
This is definitely not a foregone conclusion. You may become more symptomatic or develop new symptoms but, as we have discussed, there are lots of things that can be done to help. It is never too late to get started.

'You are too young for menopausal symptoms'
Women are still being told they are too young for menopausal symptoms. We must remember that the perimenopause might last up to 10 years before the menopause, and so though a woman might be in her early forties and a long way off from her last period, that doesn't mean she doesn't have symptoms that need support. If you are struggling with symptoms and are told this, ask questions or gently challenge this narrative, or try and see another medical professional.

Foundation Reflections

If you identify that you are struggling with any of the symptoms highlighted jot them down, book an appointment with your doctor and take the list with you to start the journey to seeking support. You may also like to write down a few take-home messages that you want to refer back to at a later date.

....

....

....

....

....

....

....

....

....

CHAPTER 13

Moving Through Menopause

Let's learn about:

- Important health implications of the menopause transition
- Why being active and exercising are so important
- Different types of exercise and their benefits
- Some of the barriers to being active
- The long game: moving beyond menopause and why we need to take care of our future selves

---

There is no question that being active and exercising is good for our minds and bodies, and you will have probably gathered throughout this book that I am passionate to support women to feel confident in their bodies so they can be active. Exercise plays such a vital role in so many aspects of our health, especially when we are going through the perimenopause or are postmenopausal. I wanted to take a whole chapter to look at this all in a bit more detail, because it is easy to hear 'being active is important' and to know the guidelines, but what is the reason behind them? Equally, there are so many limitations that can hold us back from meeting the advised activity levels, and pelvic floor symptoms can be a big one.

It is important to note that we all enter this stage of life differently, and, as we established in the last chapter, we experience different symptoms to differing severities. For some we may have been consistently active throughout adult life and found it easy to get back to exercise after having kids, but for others we may have never found a real groove with exercise, and with the demands of life found it hard to carve out the time and space. The health implications of the menopause transition are true for everyone regardless of their symptom experience, and understanding these can really help our motivation to be physically active. I'm going to walk you through some of the key health implications that are not so widely known about, and how exercise plays a significant role in their prevention and treatment. We will also explore in more detail what can hold us back and how to tackle these barriers.

Before we start, let's consider what the UK Chief Medical Officer's guidelines suggest regarding physical activity, which is that we should aim for 150 minutes of moderate-intensity activity a week. When broken down, that is around 30 minutes a day, 5 days a week.[1] This can feel like a lot, and initially feel difficult to factor in, but starting small and building up makes this incredibly manageable.

'DEM BONES' – BONE HEALTH

Bone health is not a topic that many of us give much thought to, until it is a problem. Trust me, you don't want to first start thinking about your bone health once you are sitting in hospital with a hip fracture. Having seen my grandmother experience two of these, I can tell you now that it is quite a challenging road, especially once you are 80. I really don't mean to be negative, but I did think when chatting with my grandmother during this time that I wished someone had spoken to her, and everyone else in her generation, about their bone health at a much younger age. We have the privilege of knowing so much more now, and bone health is a very important foundation for our bodies. We reach our peak bone mass in our thirties, after which it often plateaus and then declines. This is why we need to consider this part of our health much earlier than we often do and think about preventing issues, rather than trying to play catch up.

Osteoporosis is a condition where reduction in bone mass and density mean that bones are more likely to break. There are around 3.5 million people living with osteoporosis in the UK, and it affects more women than men. Around one in two women over the age of 50 will break a bone because of osteoporosis.[2] That is a lot of us and is why this conversation is so important! Osteopenia is the stage before osteoporosis, where scans show that your bone density is lower than average for your age but you do not have osteoporosis. Not everyone with osteopenia goes on to develop osteoporosis, and there are lifestyle changes we can make to help our bone density, which we will come to soon. The reason osteoporosis is more common in women is in part due to the hormonal shift of menopause and the decline in oestrogen. Oestrogen is key in maintaining bone structure, and so with its decline the bone mass and density decline as well. Though this all sounds a bit doom and gloom, there are ways we can be proactive to help. A significant one is exercise, in particular resistance and impact training, alongside looking at our nutrition, especially our calcium and Vitamin D intake, and stopping smoking.

THE TICKER – HEART HEALTH

Another important aspect of health that all women need to be more aware of is our heart health, more medically known as cardiovascular health. This refers to the health of the heart muscle and the blood vessels that supply it. Heart disease is the number one cause of death for women in the UK, and worldwide. It kills more than twice as many women as breast cancer each year, which might come as quite a shock.[3] The broader term of cardiovascular disease (CVD) refers to any condition that impacts the heart and blood vessels, including heart disease, heart attack, high blood pressure and stroke.

Oestrogen helps to keep blood vessels flexible, keeping blood flowing freely and helping to manage blood pressure. Declining levels of oestrogen during and after the menopause can impact the blood vessels, leading to increased risk of CVD. Oestrogen also helps to regulate cholesterol, and when it declines the levels of 'good' cholesterol decrease and those of 'bad' cholesterol increase. This can lead to more fatty deposits in the blood vessels, which can increase the risk of heart attack or stroke. Again, it is not all doom and gloom, there is plenty that we can do to help and prevent developing problems, including stopping smoking, exercise, maintaining a healthy body weight and focusing on a diet low in saturated fat. Taking oestrogen as HRT may have a protective role in preventing heart disease, especially when started before 60 or within 10 years of the onset of menopause.[4]

THE POWER STATIONS – MUSCLE HEALTH

Sarcopenia is the gradual loss of muscle mass and strength as we age, as we briefly discussed in the last chapter. As we age, our muscle mass naturally decreases, approximately by between 3 and 8 per cent each decade from the age of 30.[5] This gradual decline accelerates for everyone after the age of 60, and this acceleration has also been observed with menopause. So as women we really need to think about our muscles sooner rather than later.[6] To be honest, sitting here as a woman in her mid-thirties, I am reminded that this is a prime time for me to be thinking about these aspects of my health. It is one of the reasons I started lifting weights more consistently last year, but more on that in a moment.

It is hard to imagine what loss of muscle strength will be like as we grow older, but it can hugely impact our mobility, independence and quality of life, and increase risk of falls. With many of us living into our eighties and nineties, these are all aspects we need to consider. Thankfully there are things we can do to help and prevent – you may start to notice a bit of a theme here as well. Regular physical activity, including resistance and weight-training, as well as good nutrition and overall lifestyle, alongside improving sleep and reducing stress.[7] Though these issues can feel like they are many years away, actually our thirties, forties and the perimenopausal years can be the most opportune time to start making lifestyle shifts and ensuring we are investing now for the future.[8] None of us need more things or stresses to think about, however, I think bitesize changes and addressing barriers at this stage is fundamental. Saying that, it isn't too late; you can continue to build muscle and improve balance at any age. I have seen that first hand through many years of working with elderly patients. We need to be proactive without living in fear.

THE HEADQUARTERS – BRAIN HEALTH

Some of the symptoms related to the menopause are brain fog, forgetfulness and reduced memory, which seem to occur due to changes in oestrogen and testosterone levels. It can be really frustrating and hard, especially if you are someone who has always relied on having a brilliant memory. Many women struggle with this and you are not alone. Lifestyle changes and focusing on good nutrition, being active and our sleep can all help with these symptoms. Alongside the brain fog can come anxiety and depression that can really knock a woman sideways. Speaking to a medical professional should always be our first port of call, alongside considering how exercise can play an important role.

A condition that probably most of us will have heard about is dementia, and this impacts more women than men. We don't fully know why this is, but one factor could be hormonal changes and the variety of ways that oestrogen helps the brain. Therefore, with its decline come changes to the brain. There is exciting and evolving research showing the role HRT could have in decreasing the risk of Alzheimer's and dementia, however we need more research to come to a concrete conclusion on this.[9] It is so important to remember that HRT can play a role far beyond managing the immediate symptoms of menopause that we might experience day to day, and to keep a lifelong mindset and viewpoint.

LET'S TAKE A DEEPER DIVE INTO THE TYPES OF EXERCISE

Now that we have established the importance of why we need to be active and exercise, let's think a bit more about what this might look like. Ultimately, I always say to women that finding what we enjoy and can realistically commit to is a priority, otherwise it can be really hard to be active or exercise consistently. However, I want to walk you through different types of exercise and their benefits. I am delighted that Kate Rowe-Ham, a menopause fitness coach and founder of Owning Your Menopause, has joined us to share her thoughts on this important topic. She regularly reminds women that we need to 'reframe fitness, moving away from aesthetics to focus on the multiple other benefits that exercise has throughout life, but particularly during menopause and beyond'.

Resistance or weight-training

This type of exercise helps to improve and maintain muscle strength, as well as bone density through the tension that muscles and tendons apply to the bone. This tension and stress stimulate the bone to make more bone tissue.[10] This type of training is also great for our heart health, mental health and confidence in how strong our bodies can be. Weight-training can be for everyone, however, it can also feel really daunting if you are new to it. Don't worry, you don't need to head straight to the weights section of a gym to do this type of exercise. You can start with bodyweight movements, such as squats, lunges and press-ups, and try using resistance bands as well. You might like to try some of the exercises over on pages 172–8 if you are new to this type of training. Building in functional movements, like squats and lunges, are a brilliant place to start. It is advised by the UK Chief Medical Officer to aim to do this type of training twice a week.[11]

Over time as you build in confidence you might like to try using some smaller hand-held weights, or try more heavy lifting under the guidance of a personal trainer. Recently I have started lifting heavier weights and I really love it. My main focus has been on nurturing my bones and muscles for the future, as well as creating space in the busyness of life and all the mental health benefits of exercise. I was nervous to start and didn't put myself down as someone who could do it, but I have been amazed what my body can do. So, if you have ever discounted or avoided using weights, then take this as an opportunity to maybe give it a try, your bones and muscles will thank you!

Weight-bearing and impact exercise

Weight-bearing exercises are where we are upright, standing on one or both feet. They include walking, jumping, running and skipping, ranging from low impact to high impact. Impact exercise helps to improve bone density through repetitive stress on the bones, which stimulates the bone to make more bone. Aiming for brisk walking, walking interspersed with jogging – for example Couch to 5K – and building up to running can be a good way to introduce this type of exercise.[12]

Aerobic exercise

Aerobic exercise, sometimes known as cardio exercise, is really good for our heart health – the hint is in the name! It is any exercise that increases our heart rate and includes a whole variety of activities. Running, swimming, cycling or using a cross-trainer are the most common, however you might prefer dancing, playing tennis, hiking or team sports.

* * *

Getting started with exercise or exercising consistently at this stage of life can feel overwhelming. If you are already exercising regularly, just think about if you are managing to incorporate some form of resistance and/or impact exercise into your routine. If you are struggling to get started, maybe try and find a local class with a friend that you commit to once a week, or find a programme you feel comfortable doing at home. It is also important to remember that activity and exercise don't need to fully focus on bone density and heart health alone, they are also so important for our overall wellbeing, mental health, weight management and to reduce stress. This is why a variety of activities really is the spice of life.

Though many of us know being active and exercising is important, there are still many barriers to women meeting the advised levels. If you are reading this and feeling worried, like a failure, or just overwhelmed at the prospect of this topic, you are not alone. Sport England have found that 38 per cent of women aged 45–54 do not meet the recommended levels of physical activity and 23 per cent are considered inactive, which means doing less than 30 minutes a week.[13] This is a lot of women, and we therefore need to consider some of the barriers that are holding women back.

WHAT CAN HOLD US BACK FROM ACTIVITY AND EXERCISE?

Life

Need I say any more?! In all seriousness though, life and mother-hood can feel like one of the biggest barriers to activity. The mental load, the exhaustion and the feeling of there always being something on the to-do list can leave us feeling burnt out, always prioritising everyone else's needs and seeing time disappear in front of our eyes. This is certainly how I feel at times. Kate Rowe-Ham has seen this with a number of the women she works with:

> Midlife is a time when we may find ourselves juggling family life, home life, work life, elderly, or sick parents and many of our needs fall by the wayside. This often coincides with some of the perimenopause symptoms that can make life seem that extra bit harder and, feeling lost, we may put our own health and wellbeing on the back burner.

Pelvic floor symptoms

I am sure that it will come as no surprise to you that pelvic floor symptoms can be a huge barrier to us being physically active, especially when thinking about lifting weights and impact exercise. Whether it be urinary or anal incontinence, prolapse symptoms, or fear of making a prolapse worse, there are many reasons that women avoid or pull away from being active. This is where pelvic health is so much more influential on other parts of our health than we probably ever think. If women are avoiding impact and resistance training due to their pelvic floor symptoms then this can have an impact on their bone, heart and mental health. For me, this is why we need to be having conversations about pelvic health more freely and openly, ending any taboo around the topic.

I remember speaking at an event a few years ago and asking a room of around 60 women how many avoided impact or resistance training due to their pelvic floor, and around half of the room put their hands up. This was a huge wake-up call for me. One survey of over 4,000 women found that one in three women would say their pelvic floor symptoms were a substantial barrier to exercise.[14] I am hoping you know by now that pelvic floor symptoms are treatable and there is help. It might take time and there might not be a simple answer, but we must keep supporting women so that pelvic floor symptoms are not the barrier to them being active.

Loss of confidence and not knowing where to start

As we've mentioned, it can be so hard to get started. I hope that this chapter has highlighted a few ways that you can do so. I've also shared a few platforms in the Helpful Resources section (see page 325) that you might find helpful on your journey. It is natural to feel less confident or self-conscious, especially if you are still struggling with how your body has changed, including pelvic floor symptoms. I promise there is a way forward that will work for you; it might not be exactly what you expect but there will be a way.

Society

Society's view of women, women and exercise and women in sport, and a largely aesthetic-driven fitness industry, have all hugely impacted our relationships with being active and with exercise. Jacqueline Hooton, a women's health coach, challenges the narratives that can hold women back from being active and does so to raise awareness of the power of exercise and lifting weights through midlife and beyond. She shared with me her thoughts on this topic:

> Women have been convinced that exercise is about dropping a dress size and shrinking, with society continuing to place a huge onus on aesthetics and not health. This can end up with women having a negative relationship with exercise and having a focus just on how they look, rather than the health benefits.

Though there is nothing wrong with caring about how you look or wanting to manage and maintain your body weight and appearance, when our sole focus is on this it can lead to certain challenges. The tide is changing, and more and more women are speaking out about the multiple health benefits of being active, moving away from the aesthetic narrative that so many of us grew up with. We are seeing women's sport grow and more awareness of women's health topics such as endometriosis, periods and returning to competitive sport after having a baby, thanks to high-profile athletes talking about these topics openly. Menopause awareness is growing too, with amazing women like Davina McCall showing us all the importance of exercise through this time, walking the walk as well as talking the talk.

Aches and pains

Aches and pains can hold us back, which can feel so frustrating, especially if you have carved out time in a busy schedule, prioritised yourself and then find yourself unable to exercise. Musculoskeletal pain (MSP) is prevalent in perimenopausal and postmenopausal women, affecting around 71 per cent of perimenopausal women in some way.[15] MSP refers to new or ongoing pain that impacts the muscles, tendons, bones or ligaments.

Tendons are the strong connective tissue that attach muscles to bones, and there is an increased incidence of tendinopathy in perimenopausal and postmenopausal women. Tendinopathy is where there is some degeneration of the tendon, which commonly causes some pain, swelling and difficulty with certain movements or exercises. Gluteal tendinopathy (impacting the tendons of the bottom muscles) is common in women of menopausal age, affecting one in four women over 50.[16] The increased incidence of tendinopathy in women at this stage of life is thought to be related to decreased oestrogen levels, as this decline seems to affect collagen formation and tendon strength. Joint pain is also commonly reported, and there are many reasons and conditions that result in women developing joint pain. Osteoarthritis is a common condition and more common in women than men after the age of 50, which of course coincides with the menopause transition. Hormones are likely to play their part, which is a bit of a running theme here, but that doesn't mean that all hope is lost. Assessment should always be completed and pain shouldn't just be blamed on hormones. A collaborative approach is always best, and treatment is likely to include education and exercise to improve function.

Previous experience

Our previous experience of exercise can play a huge role in how it sits within our lives as we age. As Jacqueline Hooton shares, 'poor relationship with exercise can go back to school days, of not feeling included or good at sport'. It is easy to label ourselves as 'not into fitness' and feel unable to see how we could build more activity or exercise into our lives. I can absolutely guarantee that you don't need to be into fitness, have a gym membership, or have exercised regularly up until this day for this to be a possibility. What is key here is to come back to the word *activity*. Being active is often much more achievable and approachable than a formal exercise programme. So, if ditching the word 'exercise' helps you, then focus purely on how to fit moments where you can be slightly more active than you are today into your life, and see where the weeks and months take you. You might surprise yourself how much you enjoy it.

TOP TIPS FOR BEING ACTIVE DURING THIS TIME OF YOUR LIFE

Jacqueline and I have put together our top tips to help break down barriers and support you to become more active today:

1. Start simple. Aim to get out for a short walk daily and start forging a new routine.
2. Something is better than nothing. Don't discount what you are able to do because it doesn't seem enough.
3. Work activity into your normal everyday life. A walk in your lunch break, walking part of your commute, going to a class with a friend after work before you hit the sofa exhausted, running errands by foot instead of in the car, or meeting a friend for a walk before having lunch together.
4. Find a friend who is on this journey so you can support and motivate each other, as well as keep each other accountable.

5. Find a podcast series you love and listen to it as a treat while being active.
6. Know that *all* activity counts.
7. Celebrate all the wins.
8. Don't compare yourself to others.
9. If one form of activity doesn't work for you, try something different. We all connect with and enjoy different things.

HEADING BEYOND THE MENOPAUSE

If the average age of menopause is 51 and life expectancy for women in the UK is 83, there are a large number of years in which we are postmenopausal. This is why we need to ensure that our pelvic health not only doesn't impact our day-to-day life, mental health and quality of life, but also doesn't act as a huge barrier to physical activity and all the additional health benefits we need to lap up as we age. Urogenital atrophy can be an ongoing problem many years after menopause, so know that if you are struggling with any of the symptoms we discussed on page 272 at any point, there is help and please speak to your doctor.

Another important factor to consider as we grow older is our risk of falls. Falls are common, in fact around 33 per cent of those over 65, and 50 per cent over 80, will have at least one fall a year.[17] Using exercise, alongside nutrition, to improve and support bone density to reduce the risk of fractures if we do fall is key. However, it is also important to consider how to help reduce the risk of a fall in the first place. There are various medical conditions that might contribute to falls, however, exercise, including resistance and balance-specific exercises, has been shown to be effective in reducing falls.[18,19] Another incentive for us all to consider is how we can build more activity and exercise into our lives!

One significant risk factor for falls is, in fact, urinary incontinence.[20] It is understandable that if you are experiencing urinary incontinence, particularly alongside urgency, you may find yourself rushing to the toilet, increasing your risk of falling over on the way.[21] The reason falls are such a significant problem as we age is there is significant correlation with hip fractures. It has been found that over 95 per cent of hip fractures are due to a fall.[22] The sad reality is that the mortality rate after hip fracture is high, and so we really want to do everything we can to reduce the risk of falls and fractures. As I have said, falls are multifactorial, but if we could aim to reduce one key contributor by reducing incontinence then we should.

I feel this really brings home why pelvic health is so important, why it is so much more than just pelvic floor symptoms, and why we need to continue to work together to raise awareness and improve pelvic health for all. Take a moment as we end this chapter, and nearly end our journey together, to reflect and jot down any thoughts in the Foundation Reflections section on page 306. Whatever age or stage of life you are at I hope this inspires you to be more active and tackle any barriers that are currently in your way.

MYTH BUSTING

'It is too late to make changes to my pelvic health'
Thankfully it is never too late to make changes to your pelvic health – whether this be constipation, pelvic floor strength or bladder symptoms. Whatever your age, improvement can be made. We need to shout this from the rooftops and share this with our friends and family and spread the word!

'I don't need to think about my bone health until after menopause'
*Our bone health is something we should be thinking about if possible
before we reach menopause. Remember there is a gradual reduction
in bone density after it reaches its peak in our thirties. I honestly
think this is one of the most important conversations we can have
with women, including the role nutrition and exercise play and the
barrier our pelvic health can be. The good news is that it isn't too
late, we can still make changes as we age and move past menopause.
I just love to encourage women to be as proactive as possible.*

Foundation Reflections

Whether you love routine, or being spontaneous trying lots of different things, take a moment to consider where you are at right now. Think about all that your mind and body needs as you plan your activity and exercise for the weeks ahead. Jot down some ideas or even a little plan for what you could try this week. Start small and see where it takes you.

....

....

....

....

....

....

....

....

....

Before You Go...

Thank you for joining me on this journey. I hope you finish these pages feeling informed, educated and empowered. Before we leave each other I want to conclude with a few thoughts. Pelvic health doesn't stand alone. It is part of a wonderful web that comes together to form our overall health, and I hope you more fully grasp its role in your life after our journey together. I hope you now understand your own pelvic health better, what you can do to get started in taking care of this vital part of your health, and that you are absolutely not alone if you are navigating any of the symptoms we have discussed. Thank you for joining me, for taking the time to be part of the mission to change the landscape around pelvic health, as we all aim to build our own strong foundations.

Notes

INTRODUCTION

1. National Institute for Health and Care Excellence (2021), 'Pelvic floor dysfunction: prevention and non-surgical management'. 9 Dec. 2021, www.nice.org.uk/guidance/ng210.

CHAPTER 1 – DEAR BODY

1. Public Health England (2016) 'Government Dietary Recommendations: Government recommendations for energy and nutrients for males and females aged 1 - 18 years and 19+ years.' Accessed online: May 2023.
2. Quartly, E. et al., 'Strength and endurance of the pelvic floor muscles in continent women: an observational study'. *Physiotherapy*, 2010;96:311-16.
3. Eickmeyer, S.M., 'Anatomy and physiology of the pelvic floor', *Phys. Med. Rehabil. Clin. N. Am.*, 2017; 28:455–60.
4. El-Hamamsy, D. et al., 'Public understanding of female genital anatomy and pelvic organ prolapse (POP); a questionnaire-based pilot study'. *Int. Urogynecol. J.*, 2022;33:309–18.
5. O'Connell, H.E. et al., 'Anatomical relationship between urethra and clitoris'. *J. Urology*, 1998;159(6):1892–7, doi: 10.1097/00005392-1998 06000-00031.
6. National Health Service (2023). 'Periods and fertility in the menstrual cycle' www.nhs.uk/conditions/periods/fertility-in-the-menstrual-cycle'. Accessed: May 2023.

CHAPTER 2 – PELVIC FLOOR FOUNDATIONS

1. Frawley, H. et al., 'An International Continence Society (ICS) report on the terminology for pelvic floor muscle assessment'. *Neurourol. Urodyn.*, 2021 Jun;40(5):1217–60, doi: 10.1002/nau.24658.
2. Ben Ami, N. and Dar, G., 'What is the most effective verbal instruction for correctly contracting the pelvic floor muscles?' *Neurourol Urodyn.*, 2018 Nov;37(8):2904–10, doi: 10.1002/nau.23810.
3. Naess, I. and Bø, K., 'Can maximal voluntary pelvic floor muscle contraction reduce vaginal resting pressure and resting EMG activity?' *Int Urogynecol. J.*, 2018 Nov;29(11):1623–7, doi: 10.1007/s00192-018 -3599-1.
4. Laycock, J., 'Concepts of neuromuscular rehabilitation and pelvic floor muscle training', in K. Baussler, B. Shussler, K.L. Burgio, K.H. Moore, P.A. Norton and S. Stanton (eds.), *Pelvic Floor Re-education*, 2nd edn (London: Springer, 2008).

CHAPTER 3 – WHERE DID IT ALL BEGIN?

1. ERIC, 'Children's Bowel Health – What's normal and what can go wrong?' www.eric.org.uk/childrens-bowels/. Accessed May 2023.
2. Bongers, M.E. et al., 'Long-term prognosis for childhood constipation: clinical outcomes in adulthood'. *Pediatrics*, 2010 Jul;126(1):e156–62, doi: 10.1542/peds.2009-1009.
3. Van Ginkel, R. et al., 'Childhood constipation: longitudinal follow-up beyond puberty'. *Gastroenterol.*, 2003;125:357–63.
4. Jansson, U.-B. et al., 'Voiding pattern and acquisition of bladder control from birth to age 6 years-a longitudinal study'. *J. Urol.*, 2005 Jul;174(1):289–93. doi: 10.1097/01.ju.0000161216.45653.e3.
5. National Institute for Health and Care Excellence (2010), 'Bedwetting in under 19s'. Clinical guideline [CG111] Published: 27 October 2010.
6. Loening-Baucke, V., 'Prevalence rates for constipation and faecal and urinary incontinence'. *Arch. Dis. Child.*, 2007;92:486–9, 10.1136/adc .2006.098335.
7. ERIC, 'Giggle Incontinence'. www.eric.org.uk/childrens-bladders/giggle -incontinence. Accessed May 2023.

CHAPTER 4 – A DEFINING SEASON

1. Verkuijl, S. et al., 'The influence of demographic characteristics on constipation symptoms: a detailed overview'. *BMC Gastroenterol.*, 2020;20:168.
2. Chang, Y.M. et al., 'Does stress induce bowel dysfunction?' *Expert Rev. Gastroenterol. Hepatol.*, 2014, Aug;8(6):583–5, doi: 10.1586/17474124.2014.911659.
3. The Rome Foundation, 'Rome IV Criteria'. Accessed May 2023, www.theromefoundation.org/rome-iv/rome-iv-criteria.
4. Kim, Y.S. and Kim, N., 'Sex-gender differences in irritable bowel syndrome', *J. Neurogastroenterol. Motil.*, 2018 Oct;24(4):544–58, doi: 10.5056/jnm18082.
5. Van der Velde, J. and Everaerd, W., 'The relationship between involuntary pelvic floor muscle activity, muscle awareness and experienced threat in women with and without vaginismus'. *Behav. Res. Ther.*, 2001 Apr;39(4):395–408, doi: 10.1016/s0005-7967(00)00007-3.
6. Beisel, B. et al., 'Clinical inquiries. Does postcoital voiding prevent urinary tract infections in young women?' *Fam. Pract.*, 2002 Nov;51(11):977.
7. National Institute For Health and Care Excellence (2018), 'Urinary tract infection (recurrent): antimicrobial prescribing'. NICE guideline [NG112], Published 31 October 2018, www.nice.org.uk/guidance/ng112
8. Haylen, Bernard T. et al., 'An International Urogynecological Association (IUGA)/International Continence Society (ICS) joint report on the terminology for female pelvic floor dysfunction'. *Int. Urogynecol. J.*, 2010 Jan;21(1):5–26, doi: 10.1007/s00192-009-0976-9.
9. Foster, Stefanie N. et al., 'Hip and pelvic floor muscle strength in women with and without urgency and frequency predominant lower urinary tract symptoms', *J. Women's Health Phys. Therap.*, 2021 Jul–Sep;45(3):126–34, doi: 10.1097/jwh.0000000000000209.

CHAPTER 5 – SOME KEY PELVIC HEALTH PLAYERS

1. Corsini-Munt, S. et al., 'Vulvodynia: a consideration of clinical and methodological research challenges and recommended solutions'. *J. Pain Res.*, 2017;10:2425–36, doi: 10.2147/JPR.S126259.

2. Benoit-Piau, J. et al., 'Fear-avoidance and pelvic floor muscle function are associated with pain intensity in women with vulvodynia'. *Clin. J. Pain.*, 2018, Sep;34(9):804–10, doi: 10.1097/AJP.0000000000000604.

3. Krapf, J.M. et al., 'Vulvar lichen sclerosis: current perspectives'. *Int. J. Women's Health*, 2020;12:11–20, doi: 10.2147/IJWH.S191200.

4. Johnston, J.L. et al., 'Diagnosing endometriosis in primary care: clinical update'. *Br. J. Gen. Pract.*, 2015 Feb;65(631):101–2, doi: 10.3399 /bjgp15X683665.

5. Lazaridis, A. et al., 'Nonsurgical management of adenomyosis: an overview of current evidence'. *Curr. Opin. Obstet. Gynecol.*, 2022 Oct;34(5):315–23, doi: 10.1097/GCO.0000000000000810.

6. Royal College of Obstetricians and Gynaecologists (2015), 'Long-term pelvic pain patient information leaflet', www.rcog.org.uk/for-the-public /browse-all-patient-information-leaflets/long-term-pelvic-pain-patient -information-leaflet/.

7. Leung-Wright, A. 'Physiotherapy for chronic pelvic pain: a review of the latest evidence', *J. Pelv. Obstet. Gynaecol. Physio.*, 2020 Autumn;127:26–38.

CHAPTER 6 – BUMP – AN INTRODUCTION

1. Sanghavi, M. and Rutherford, J.D., 'Cardiovascular physiology of pregnancy'. *Circulation*, 2014 Sep 16;130(12):1003–8, doi: 10.1161 /CIRCULATIONAHA.114.009029.

2. Da Mota, P.G. et al., 'Prevalence and risk factors of diastasis recti abdominis from late pregnancy to 6 months postpartum, and relationship with lumbo-pelvic pain'. *Man. Ther.*, 2015 Feb;20(1):200–205, doi: 10.1016/j.math.2014.09.002.

3. Dufour, S. et al., 'Establishing expert-based recommendations for the conservative management of pregnancy-related diastasis rectus abdominis: a Delphi Consensus Study'. *J. Women's Health Physical Ther.*, 2019 March;43(2):1.

4. Slater, Diane et al., 'Sit up straight': time to re-evaluate'. *J. Orth. Sports Physical Ther.*, 2021;49(8):562–4.

5. Aldabe, D. et al., 'Pregnancy-related pelvic girdle pain and its relationship with relaxin levels during pregnancy: a systematic review'. *Eur. Spine J.*, 2012 Sep;21(9):1769–76, doi: 10.1007/s00586-012-2162-x.

6. Clinton, S.C. et al., 'Pelvic girdle pain in the antepartum population: physical therapy clinical practice guidelines linked to the international classification of functioning, disability, and health from the section on women's health and the orthopedic section of the American Physical

Therapy Association'. *J. Women's Health Physical Ther.*, 2017 May;41(2):102–25, doi: 10.1097/JWH.0000000000000081.

7. Wuytack, F. et al., 'Risk factors for pregnancy-related pelvic girdle pain: a scoping review'. *BMC Pregnancy Childbirth*, 2020 Nov 27;20(1):739, doi: 10.1186/s12884-020-03442-5.

8. Mackenzie, J. et al., 'Women's experiences of pregnancy-related pelvic girdle pain: a systematic review'. *Midwifery*, 2018 Jan;56:102–11, doi: 10.1016/j.midw.2017.10.011.

9. Dufour, S. et al., 'Association between lumbopelvic pain and pelvic floor dysfunction in women: a cross sectional study', *Musculoskelet. Sci. Pract.*, 2018 Apr;34:47–53, doi: 10.1016/j.msksp.2017.12.001. Keizer, Alexzandra et al., 'Predictors of pelvic floor muscle dysfunction among women with lumbopelvic pain'. *Phys. Ther.*, 2019 Dec 16;99(12):1703–11, doi: 10.1093/ptj/pzz124.

10. Sonmezer, E. et al., 'The effects of clinical Pilates exercises on functional disability, pain, quality of life and lumbopelvic stabilization in pregnant women with low back pain: a randomized controlled study'. *J. Back Musculoskelet. Rehabil.*, 2021;34(1):69–76, doi: 10.3233/BMR-191810.

11. Olsson, Christina B. et al., 'Catastrophizing during and after pregnancy: associations with lumbopelvic pain and postpartum physical ability'. *Phys. Ther.*, 2012 Jan;92(1):49–57, doi: 10.2522/ptj.20100293.

CHAPTER 7 – BUMP – TO CARE AND PREPARE

1. Woodley S.J. et al., 'Pelvic floor muscle training for preventing and treating urinary and faecal incontinence in antenatal and postnatal women.' *Cochrane Database Syst. Rev.* 2020 May 6;5(5):CD007471. doi: 10.1002/14651858.CD007471.pub4. PMID: 32378735; PMCID: PMC7203602.

2. Yang X. et al., 'The effectiveness of group-based pelvic floor muscle training in preventing and treating urinary incontinence for antenatal and postnatal women: a systematic review'. *Int. Urogynecol. J.*, 2022 Jun;33(6):1407–20, doi: 10.1007/s00192-021-04960-2.

3. National Institute for Health and Care Excellence (2021), 'Pelvic floor dysfunction: prevention and non-surgical management'. 9 Dec. 2021, www.nice.org.uk/guidance/ng210.

4. Sobhgol, S.S. et al., 'The effect of antenatal pelvic floor muscle exercises on labour and birth outcomes: a systematic review and meta-analysis'. *Int. Urogynecol. J.*, 2020 Nov;31(11):2189–203, doi: 10.1007/s00192-020-04298-1.

5. Davenport, M.H. et al., 'Prenatal exercise is not associated with fetal mortality: a systematic review and meta-analysis'. *Br. J. Sports Med.*, 2019 Jan;53(2):108–15, doi: 10.1136/bjsports-2018-099773.

6. Mottola, M.F. et al., '2019 Canadian guideline for physical activity throughout pregnancy', *Br. J. Sports Med.*, 2018;52:1339–46, doi:10.1136/bjsports-2018-100056.

7. Ibid.

8. Prevett, C. et al., 'Impact of heavy resistance training on pregnancy and postpartum health outcomes'. *Int. Urogynecol. J.*, 2023 Feb;34(2):405–11, doi: 10.1007/s00192-022-05393-1.

9. Johnson, K.T. et al., 'The importance of information: prenatal education surrounding birth-related pelvic floor trauma mitigates symptom-related distress'. *J. Women's Health Physical Ther.*, 2022 Apr 6;46(2):62–72.

10. Skinner, E.M. et al., 'Psychological consequences of pelvic floor trauma following vaginal birth: a qualitative study from two Australian tertiary maternity units'. *Arch. Women's Ment. Health*, 2018 Jun;21(3):341–51, doi: 10.1007/s00737-017-0802-1.

11. Royal College of Obstetricians and Gynaecologists, 'Third and fourth degree tears'. Accessed May 2023, https://www.rcog.org.uk/for-the-public/perineal-tears-and-episiotomies-in-childbirth/third-and-fourth-degree-tears-oasi/.

12. Abdelhakim, A.M. et al., 'Antenatal perineal massage benefits in reducing perineal trauma and postpartum morbidities: a systematic review and meta-analysis of randomized controlled trials'. *Int. Urogynecol. J.*, 2020 Sep;31(9):1735–45, doi: 10.1007/s00192-020-04302-8.

13. Ibid.

14. Bø, K. et al., 'Too tight to give birth? Assessment of pelvic floor muscle function in 277 nulliparous pregnant women'. *Int. Urogynecol. J.*, 2013;24(12):2065–70.

15. Bø, K., Fleten, C. and Nystad, W., 'Effect of antenatal pelvic floor muscle training on labor and birth'. *Obstet. Gynecol.*, 2009;113(6):1279–84.

CHAPTER 8 – BIRTH RECOVERY

1. Svabík, K. et al., 'How much does the levator hiatus have to stretch during childbirth?' *BJOG*, 2009 Nov;116(12):1657–62, doi: 10.1111/j.1471-0528.2009.02321.x.

2. Lien K.C. et al., 'Levator ani muscle stretch induced by simulated vaginal birth'. *Obstet Gynecol.* 2004 Jan;103(1):31-40.

3. NICE, 'Pelvic floor dysfunction: prevention and non-surgical management'. NICE guideline [NG210] Published 9 Dec. 2021.

4. Elenskaia, K. et al., 'The effect of pregnancy and childbirth on pelvic floor muscle function'. *Int. Urogynecol. J.*, 2011. Nov;22(11):1421-7, doi: 10.1007/s00192-011-1501-5.

5. Sigurdardottir, T. et al., 'Can postpartum pelvic floor muscle training reduce urinary and anal incontinence? An assessor-blinded randomized controlled trial'. *Am. J. Obstet. Gynecol.*, 2020 Mar;222(3):247.e1-247.e8, doi: 10.1016/j.ajog.2019.09.011.

6. Royal College of Obstetricians and Gynaecologists, 'Assisted Vaginal Birth'. www.rcog.org.uk/for-the-public/browse-all-patient-information-leaflets/assisted-vaginal-birth-ventouse-or-forceps/.

7. Di Mascio, D. et al., 'The efficacy of abdominal binders in reducing postoperative pain and distress after cesarean delivery: a meta-analysis of randomized controlled trials'. *Eur. J. Obstet. Gynecol. Reprod. Biol.*, 2021 Jul;262:73-9, doi: 10.1016/j.ejogrb.2021.05.014.

8. Albert, H. et al., 'Evaluation of clinical tests used in classification procedures in pregnancy-related pelvic joint pain'. *Eur. Spine J.*, 2000;9:161-6.

CHAPTER 9 – BEYOND

1. Evenson, K. R. et al., 'Summary of international guidelines for physical activity following pregnancy'. *Obstet. Gynecol. Surv.*, 2014;69(7):407-14.

2. Goom, T. et al., 'Returning to running postnatal – guidelines for medical, health and fitness professionals managing this population'. Published March 2019.

3. The National Institute Health and Care Excellence (2021), 'Pelvic floor dysfunction: prevention and non-surgical management'. NICE guideline [NG210]. Published 9 December 2021.

4. Goom, T. et al., 'Returning to running postnatal – guidelines for medical, health and fitness professionals managing this population'. Published March 2019.

5. Donnelly, G.M. and Moore, I.S., 'Sports medicine and the pelvic floor'. *Curr. Sports Med. Rep.*, 2023 Mar;22(3):82-90, doi: 10.1249/JSR.0000000000001045.

6. Cooperrider, D.L. and Srivastva, S. 'Appreciative inquiry in organizational life'. In R.W. Woodman and W.A. Pasmore (eds.), *Research in Organizational Change and Development*, vol. 1 (Stamford, CT, JAI Press, 1987), 129-69.

7. American College of Obstetricians and Gynaecologists Committee Opinion No. 650, 'Physical Activity and Exercise During Pregnancy and the Postpartum Period'. *Obstet Gynecol.* 2015 Dec;126(6):e135-e142. doi: 10.1097/AOG.0000000000001214. PMID: 26595585.

8. Cary, G.B. and Quinn, T.J., 'Exercise and lactation: are they compatible?' *Can. J. Appl. Physiol.*, 2001 Feb;26(1):55-75, doi: 10.1139/h01-004.

9. Jiang Q. et al., 'Silicone gel sheeting for treating hypertrophic scars'. *Cochrane Database Syst. Rev.*, 2021;9:CD013357, doi: 10.1002/14651858.CD013357.

10. Johnson, K.T. et al., 'The importance of information: prenatal education surrounding birth-related pelvic floor trauma mitigates symptom-related distress'. *J. Women's Health Physical Ther.*, 2022 Apr 6;46(2):62-72.

CHAPTER 10 – WHAT IS THIS I AM FEELING?

1. Todhunter-Brown, A. et al., 'Conservative interventions for treating urinary incontinence in women: an Overview of Cochrane systematic reviews'. *Cochrane Database Syst. Rev.*, 2022 Sep 2;9(9):CD012337, doi: 10.1002/14651858.CD012337.

2. The National Institute for Health and Care Excellence (2019), 'Urinary incontinence and pelvic organ prolapse in women: management'. NICE guideline [NG123], Published: 2 April 2019.

3. Miller, Janis M. et al., 'Clarification and confirmation of the Knack Maneuver: effect of volitional pelvic floor muscle contraction to preempt urine loss in stress incontinent women'. *Int. Urogynecol. J. Pelvic Floor Dysfunct.*, 2008 Jun;19(6):773-82.

4. The National Institute for Health and Care Excellence (2019), 'Urinary incontinence and pelvic organ prolapse in women: management'. NICE guideline [NG123], Published: 2 April 2019.

5. Bø K. and Nygaard I.E., 'Is Physical Activity Good or Bad for the Female Pelvic Floor? A Narrative Review.' *Sports Med.* 2020 Mar;50(3):471-484.

6. Keeble, H., 'Functional Female Pelvic Floor: The High Impact and Weight-Lifting Webinar'. Helen Keeble Physiotherapy, September 2021.

7. Todhunter-Brown, A. et al., 'Conservative interventions for treating urinary incontinence in women: an Overview of Cochrane systematic reviews'. *Cochrane Database Syst. Rev.*, 2022 Sep 2;9(9):CD012337, doi: 10.1002/14651858.CD012337.

8. Akan, S. et al., 'Effects of the constipation treatment in women who have overactive bladder and functional constipation'. *Ann. Med. Res.*, 2020;27(4):984-7.

9. Matsuo, T. et al., 'Efficacy of salt reduction for managing overactive bladder symptoms: a prospective study in patients with excessive daily salt intake'. *Sci. Rep.*, 2021 Feb 18;11(1):4046, doi: 10.1038/s41598-021 -83725-9.

10. The National Institute for Health and Care Excellence (2019), 'Urinary incontinence and pelvic organ prolapse in women: management'. NICE guideline [NG123], Published: 2 April 2019. Last updated: 24 June 2019.

11. Xiao Yun Lin, 'An update on vaginal oestrogen for overactive bladder: reporting the literature'. *Australian and New Zealand Continence J.*, 2021;27(2):40–46.

12. NICE, 'Urinary incontinence and pelvic organ prolapse in women: management'. NICE guideline [NG123], Published: 2 April 2019. Last updated: 24 June 2019.

13. Doumouchtsis, S.K. et al., 'The role of obesity on urinary incontinence and anal incontinence in women: a review'. *BJOG* 2022 Jan;129(1): 162–70.

14. Hagen, S. et al., 'Effectiveness of pelvic floor muscle training with and without electromyographic biofeedback for urinary incontinence in women: multicentre randomised controlled trial', *BMJ*, 2020;371:m3719, doi: 10.1136/bmj.m3719.

15. Everist, R. et al., 'Postpartum anal incontinence in women with and without obstetric anal sphincter injuries'. *Int. Urogynecol. J.*, 2020 Nov;31(11):2269–75, doi: 10.1007/s00192-020-04267-8.

16. The National Institute for Health and Care Excellence (2019), 'Faecal incontinence in adults: management'. NICE Clinical guideline [CG49], Published: 27 June 2007.

17. Mekhael, Mira et al., 'Transanal irrigation for neurogenic bowel disease, low anterior resection syndrome, faecal incontinence and chronic constipation: a systematic review', *J. Clin. Med.*, 2021 Feb 13;10(4):753, doi: 10.3390/jcm10040753.

18. Gommesen, D. et al., 'Obstetric perineal ruptures – risk of anal incontinence among primiparous women 12 months postpartum: a prospective cohort study'. *Am. J. Obstet. Gynecol.*, 2020 Feb;222(2):165. e1–165.e11, doi: 10.1016/j.ajog.2019.08.026.

19. Barber, M.D. and Maher, C., 'Epidemiology and outcome assessment of pelvic organ prolapse'. *Int. Urogynecol. J.*, 2013 Nov;24(11):1783–90, doi: 10.1007/s00192-013-2169-9.

20. O'Boyle, Amy L. et al., 'Pelvic organ support in nulliparous pregnant and nonpregnant women: a case control study'. *Am. J. Obstet. Gynecol.*, 2002 Jul;187(1):99–102, doi: 10.1067/mob.2002.125734.

21. Larsen, W.I. and Yavorek, Trudy A., 'Pelvic organ prolapse and urinary incontinence in nulliparous women at the United States Military Academy'. *Int. Urogynecol. J. Pelvic Floor Dysfunct.*, 2006 May;17(3):208–10, doi: 10.1007/s00192-005-1366-6.

22. Dietz, H.P. et al., 'Association between ICS POP-Q coordinates and translabial ultrasound findings: implications for definition of "normal pelvic organ support"'. *Ultrasound in Obstetrics and Gynaecology*, 2016 Mar;47(3):363–8.

23. Collins, S.A. et al., 'International Urogynecological Consultation: clinical definition of pelvic organ prolapse'. *Int. Urogynecol. J.*, 2021 Aug;32(8):2011–19, doi: 10.1007/s00192-021-04875-y.

24. The National Institute for Health and Care Excellence (2019), 'Urinary incontinence and pelvic organ prolapse in women: management'. NICE guideline [NG123], Published: 2 April 2019, Last updated: 24 June 2019.

25. Gozukara, Y.M. et al., 'The improvement in pelvic floor symptoms with weight loss in obese women does not correlate with the changes in pelvic anatomy'. *Int. Urogynecol. J.*, 2014 Sep;25(9):1219–25, doi: 10.1007/s00192-014-2368-z.

26. Kudish, B.I. et al., 'Effect of weight change on natural history of pelvic organ prolapse'. *Obstet. Gynecol.*, 2009 Jan;113(1):81–8, doi: 10.1097/AOG.0b013e318190a0dd.

27. Cobb, W.S. et al., 'Normal intraabdominal pressure in healthy adults'. *J. Surg. Res.*, 2005 Dec;129(2):231–5, doi: 10.1016/j.jss.2005.06.015.

28. Iris, S. et al., 'The impact of breastfeeding on pelvic floor recovery from pregnancy and labor'. *Eur. J. Obstet. Gynecol. Reprod. Biol.*, 2020 Aug;251:98–105, doi: 10.1016/j.ejogrb.2020.04.017.

29. Sperstad, J.B. et al., 'Diastasis recti abdominis during pregnancy and 12 months after childbirth: prevalence, risk factors and report of lumbopelvic pain'. *Br. J. Sports Med.*, 2016 Sep;50(17):1092–6, doi: 10.1136/bjsports-2016-096065.

30. Fuentes A. et al., 'Self-reported symptoms in women with diastasis rectus abdominis: a systematic review'. *J. Gynecol. Obstet. Hum. Reprod.*, 2021 Sep;50(7):101995, doi: 10.1016/j.jogoh.2020.101995.

CHAPTER 11 – SEX – NOTHING IS TMI

1. Dr Karen Gurney (2020), *Mind The Gap: The truth about desire and how to futureproof your sex life.* Headline Publishing Group, London.

2. Mintz, L.B., *Becoming Cliterate: Why Orgasm Equality Matters - And How To Get It* (New York: HarperOne, 2017).

3. Mahar, E.A. et al., 'Orgasm equality: scientific findings and societal implications'. *Current Sexual Health Reports*, 2020;12:24–32.

4. Frederick, D.A. et al., 'Differences in orgasm frequency among gay, lesbian, bisexual, and heterosexual men and women in a U.S. national sample'. *Arch. Sex Behav.*, 2018 Jan;47(1):273–88, doi: 10.1007/s10508 -017-0939-z.

5. Richters, J. et al., 'Sexual practices at last heterosexual encounter and occurrence of orgasm in a national survey'. *J. Sex Res.*, 2006 Aug;43(3):217–26, doi: 10.1080/00224490609552320.

6. Lowenstein, L. et al., 'Can stronger pelvic muscle floor improve sexual function?' *Int. Urogynecol. J.*, 2010 May;21(5):553–6, doi: 10.1007 /s00192-009-1077-5.

7. Vilas Boas Sartori, D. et al., 'Pelvic floor muscle strength is correlated with sexual function'. *Investig. Clin. Urol.*, 2021 Jan; 62(1): 79–84.

8. Carosa, E. et al., 'Management of endocrine disease: female sexual dysfunction for the endocrinologist'. *Eur. J. Endocrin.*, 2020 Jun;182(6):R101.

9. Kalmbach, D.A. et al., 'The impact of sleep on female sexual response and behaviour: a pilot study'. *Sex. Med.*, 2015 May;12(5):1221–32, doi: 10.1111/jsm.12858.

10. Quinn-Nilas, C. et al. 'The relationship between body image and domains of sexual functioning among heterosexual, emerging adult women'. *Sex. Med.*, 2016 Sep;4(3):e182–e189. Gillen, Meghan M. and Markey, Charlotte H., 'A review of research linking body image and sexual wellbeing'. *Body Image*, 2019 Dec;31:294–301.

11. Kaviani, M. et al., 'The effect of education on sexual health of women with hypoactive sexual desire disorder: a randomized controlled trial'. *Int. J. Community Based Nurs. Midwifery*, 2014 Apr; 2(2):94–102.

12. Ghaderi, F. et al., 'Pelvic floor rehabilitation in the treatment of women with dyspareunia: a randomized controlled clinical trial'. *Int. Urogynecol. J.*, 2019 Nov;30(11):1849–55, doi: 10.1007/s00192-019 -04019-3.

13. Brotto, L.A. et al., 'Mindfulness and cognitive behavior therapy for provoked vestibulodynia: mediators of treatment outcome and long-term effects'. *J. Consult. Clin. Psychol.*, 2020;88(1):48–64.

CHAPTER 12 – MENOPAUSE MATTERS

1. Dietz, H.P. et al., 'Does estrogen deprivation affect pelvic floor muscle contractility?' *Int. Urogynecol. J.*, 2020 Jan;31(1):191–6, doi: 10.1007 /s00192-019-03909-w.
2. Volpi, E. et al., 'Muscle tissue changes with aging'. *Curr. Opin. Clin. Nutr. Metab. Care*, 2004 Jul;7(4):405–10.
3. Portman, D.J. and Gass, M.L.S., 'Vulvovaginal Atrophy Terminology Consensus Conference Panel. Genitourinary syndrome of menopause: new terminology for vulvovaginal atrophy from the International Society for the Study of Women's Sexual Health and the North American Menopause Society'. *Menopause*, 2014;21(10):1063–8.
4. Awwad, J. et al., 'Prevalence, risk factors, and predictors of pelvic organ prolapse: a community-based study'. *Menopause*, 2012 Nov;19(11):1235–41, doi: 10.1097/gme.0b013e31826d2d94.
5. Miedel, Ann et al., 'Short-term natural history in women with symptoms indicative of pelvic organ prolapse'. *Int, Urogynecol. J.*, 2011 Apr;22(4):461–8, doi: 10.1007/s00192-010-1305-z.
6. Domoney, C. et al., 'Symptoms, attitudes and treatment perceptions of vulvo-vaginal atrophy in UK postmenopausal women: results from the REVIVE-EU study'. *Post Reprod. Health*, 2020 Jun;26(2):101–9, doi: 10.1177/2053369120925193.
7. All-Party Parliamentary Group on Menopause. Inquiry to assess the impacts of menopause and the case for policy reform. Concluding report. Accessed www.menopause-appg.co.uk.
8. Hamoda, H. et al., 'The British Menopause Society and Women's Health Concern 2020 recommendations on hormone replacement therapy in menopausal women'. *Post Reprod. Health*, 2020;26(4):181–209, doi:10.1177/2053369120957514.
9. Scott, A. and Newson, L., 'Should we be prescribing testosterone to perimenopausal and menopausal women? A guide to prescribing testosterone for women in primary care'. *Br. J. Gen. Pract.*, 2020;70 (693):203–4.
10. The British Menopause Society (2019) 'BMS consensus statement – Bioidentical HRT'. www.thebms.org.uk/publications/consensus-state ments/bioidentical-hrt/.
11. Bodner-Adler, B. et al., 'Effectiveness of hormones in postmenopausal pelvic floor dysfunction – International Urogynecological Association research and development – committee opinion'. *Int. Urogynecol. J.*, 2020;31(8):1577–82.

12. Lin X.Y., 'An update on vaginal oestrogen for overactive bladder: reporting the literature'. *Australian and New Zealand Continence J.*, 2021;27(2):40–46.

13. Fournier, A., et al., 'Risk of breast cancer after stopping menopausal hormone therapy in the E3N cohort'. *Breast Cancer Research and Treatment*, 2014;145(2):535–43.

14. Mercier, J. et al., 'Pelvic floor muscle training: mechanisms of action for the improvement of genitourinary syndrome of menopause'. *Climacteric*, 2020 Oct;23(5):468–73, doi: 10.1080/13697137.2020.1724942.

15. Tosun, Ö.Ç. et al., 'Do stages of menopause affect the outcomes of pelvic floor muscle training?' *Menopause*, 2015 Feb;22(2):175–84.

16. Cacciari, L. et al., 'Never too late to train: the effects of pelvic floor muscle training on the shape of the levator hiatus in incontinent older women'. *Int. J. Environ. Res. Public Health*, 2022;19:11078.

17. Lee Jinju et al., 'Sleep disorders and menopause'. *J. Menopausal. Med.*, 2019 Aug;25(2):83–7.

18. Barber, T.M. et al., 'The health benefits of dietary fibre'. *Nutrients*, 2020;12(10):3209, https://doi.org/10.3390/nu12103209.

19. Barnard, N.D. et al., 'The Women's Study for the Alleviation of Vasomotor Symptoms (WAVS): a randomized, controlled trial of a plant-based diet and whole soybeans for postmenopausal women'. *Menopause*, 2021 Jul 12;28(10):1150–56, doi: 10.1097/GME.0000000000001812.

20. National Institute for Health and Care Excellence (2015), 'Menopause:diagnosis and management'. Published 12 November 2015. www.nice.org.uk/guidance/ng23.

CHAPTER 13 – MOVING THROUGH MENOPAUSE

1. Department of Health and Social Care (2019), 'Physical activity for adults and older adults', https://assets.publishing.service.gov.uk /government/uploads/system/uploads/attachment_data/file/1054541 /physical-activity-for-adults-and-older-adults.pdf.

2. The Royal Osteoporosis Society (2021), 'Life with Osteoporosis'. Accessed May 2023. www.theros.org.uk/latest-news/women-s-health -strategy-needs-to-go-big-on-osteoporosis-emergency-affecting-one-in-two -women-over-50/.

3. British Heart Foundation. 'Women and Heart Disease' www.bhf.org .uk/informationsupport/conditions/heart-attack/women-and-heart -attacks.

4. British Menopause Society (2021), 'Primary prevention of coronary heart disease in women', www.thebms.org.uk/publications/consensus -statements/primary-prevention-of-coronary-heart-disease-in-women/.

5. Volpi, E. et al., 'Muscle tissue changes with ageing'. *Curr. Opin. Clin. Nutr. Metab. Care*, 2004 Jul;7(4):405–10.

6. Smith-Ryan, A.E. et al., Menopause Transition - A Cross-Sectional Evaluation on Muscle Size and Quality. Med Sci Sports Exerc. 2023 Feb 24. doi: 10.1249/MSS.0000000000003150. Epub ahead of print. PMID: 36878186.

7. Buckinx, F. and Aubertin-Leheudre, M., 'Sarcopenia in menopausal women: current perspectives'. *Int. J. Women's Health*, 2022;14:805–19.

8. Gould, L. M. et al., 'Metabolic effects of menopause: a cross-sectional characterization of body composition and exercise metabolism'. *Menopause*, 2022 Apr;29(4):377–89.

9. Kim Y.J.et al., 'Association between menopausal hormone therapy and risk of neurodegenerative diseases: implications for precision hormone therapy'. *Alzheimer's Dement.*, 2021;7:e12174, https://doi.org/10.1002 /trc2.12174.

10. Hong A.R. and Kim S.W., 'Effects of resistance exercise on bone health'. *Endocrinol. Metab. (Seoul)*, 2018 Dec;33(4):435–44, doi: 10.3803/EnM .2018.33.4.435.

11. Department of Health and Social Care (2019), 'Physical activity for adults and older adults', https://assets.publishing.service.gov.uk /government/uploads/system/uploads/attachment_data/file/1054541 /physical-activity-for-adults-and-older-adults.pdf.

12. Benedetti, M.G. et al., 'The effectiveness of physical exercise on bone density in osteoporotic patients'. *Biomed. Res. Int.*, 2018 Dec 23;2018:4840531, doi: 10.1155/2018/4840531.

13. Sport England, 'Active Lives', 2017, https://activelives.sportengland.org.

14. Dakic, J.G. et al., 'Pelvic floor symptoms are an overlooked barrier to exercise participation: a cross-sectional online survey of 4556 women who are symptomatic'. *Phys. Ther.*, 2022 Mar 1;102(3):pzab284, doi: 10.1093 /ptj/pzab284.

15. Lu C.B. et al, 'Musculoskeletal pain during the menopausal transition: a systematic review and meta-analysis'. *Neural. Plast.*, 2020 Nov 25;2020:8842110, doi: 10.1155/2020/8842110.

16. Mellor, R. et al., 'Education plus exercise versus corticosteroid injection use versus a wait and see approach on global outcome and pain from gluteal tendinopathy: prospective, single blinded, randomised clinical trial'. *BMJ*, 2018;361:k1662, doi:10.1136/bmj.k1662.

17. NHS Website (2021) 'Falls: Overview' www.nhs.uk/conditions/falls/
18. Thomas, E. et al., 'Physical activity programs for balance and fall prevention in elderly: a systematic review'. *Medicine (Baltimore)*, 2019 Jul;98(27):e16218, doi: 10.1097/MD.0000000000016218.
19. Papalia, G.F. et al., 'The effects of physical exercise on balance and prevention of falls in older people: a systematic review and meta-analysis'. *J. Clin. Med.*, 2020;9:2595.
20. Moon S. et al. 'The impact of urinary incontinence on falls: a systematic review and meta-analysis', *PLoS ONE*, 2021;16(5):e0251711, https://doi .org/10.1371/journal.pone.0251711.
21. Szabo, S.M. et al., 'The association between overactive bladder and falls and fractures: a systematic review'. *Adv. Ther.*, 2018 Nov;35(11):1831-41, doi: 10.1007/s12325-018-0796-8.
22. Parkkari, J. et al., 'Majority of hip fractures occur as a result of a fall and impact on the greater trochanter of the femur: a prospective controlled hip fracture study with 206 consecutive patients'. *Calcif. Tissue Int.*, 1999 Sep;65(3):183-7, doi: 10.1007/s002239900679.

Helpful Resources

Chapter 1 – Dear Body
The Gut Stuff – www.thegutstuff.com

Chapter 2 – Pelvic Floor Foundations
Squeezy App – www.squeezyapp.com

Chapter 3 – Where Did It All Begin?
ERIC The Children's Bladder and Bowel Charity –
    www.eric.org.uk
The Day I Learned reading and activity books – available from
    www.drleafeghali.com/order-books
The Gentle Potty Training Book by Sarah Ockwell-Smith
    (Piatkus, 2017)

Chapter 4 – A Defining Season
The Vaginismus Network – www.thevaginismusnetwork.com
The IBS Network – www.theibsnetwork.org

Chapter 5 – Some Key Pelvic Health Players
Endometriosis UK – www.endometriosis-uk.org
Vulval Pain Society - www.vulvalpainsociety.org

Eve Appeal, offers support for women with gynaecological
cancers – www.eveappeal.org.uk
The Vaginismus Network – www.thevaginismusnetwork.com

Chapter 6 – Bump – An Introduction
Posture Fitting Website – www.posturefittingphysio.com
Pregnancy Sickness Support –
www.pregnancysicknesssupport.org.uk
Pelvic Girdle Pain Advice Booklet – available from
www.thepogp.co.uk

Chapter 7 – Bump – To Care and Prepare
Active Pregnancy Foundation –
www.activepregnancyfoundation.org
Bumps and Burpees – www.bumpsandburpees.com
Maternal Mental Health Alliance –
www.maternalmentalhealthalliance.org
MASIC Foundation, supports women who have suffered OASIs
during childbirth – www.masic.org.uk
Doula UK – www.doula.org.uk
Tell Me a Good Birth Story – www.tellmeagoodbirthstory.com

Chapter 8 – Birth Recovery
The Mindful Birth Group® – www.themindfulbirthgroup.com
The Royal College of Obstetricians and Gynaecologists –
www.rcog.org.uk

Chapter 9 – Beyond
Birth Trauma Association – www.birthtraumaassociation.org.uk
Make Birth Better – www.makebirthbetter.org
Lulu Adams Coaching – www.luluadams.co

PANDAS, support with perinatal mental illness – www.pandas
  foundation.org.uk
Anna Mathur courses and books – www.annamathur.com
The Birth Debrief by Illiyin Morrison (Quercus, 2023)

Chapter 10 – What Is This I Am Feeling?
Pelvic Obstetric and Gynaecological Physiotherapy –
  www.thepogp.co.uk
Hypopressives with Alice – www.alicehousman.co.uk
Qufora Rectal Irrigation – www.qufora.com

Chapter 11 – Sex – Nothing is TMI
*Mind the Gap: The Truth About Desire and How to
  Futureproof Your Sex Life* by Dr Karen Gurney (Headline
  Home, 2020)
Get Your Mojo Back: Sex, Pleasure and Intimacy After Birth
  by Clio Wood (Watkins, 2023)
The Sexual Wellness Sessions Podcast by Kate Moyle
Pain to Pleasure Course by Candice Langford –
  www.nurturepelvichealth.com

Chapter 12 – Menopause Matters
Menopause Charity symptom checker –
  www.themenopausecharity.org
Balance Menopause App and Website –
  www.balance-menopause.com
Positive Pause – www.positivepause.co.uk
Menopausing by Davina McCall and Dr Naomi Potter
  (HQ, 2022)
The Perimenopause Solution by Dr Shahzadi Harper and Emma
  Bardwell (Vermilion, 2021)

Chapter 13 – Moving Through Menopause
Menopause Movement – www.menopausemovement.co
Owning your Menopause – www.owningyourmenopause.com
Own Your Goals Davina – www.ownyourgoalsdavina.com

OTHER HELPFUL RESOURCES

Pelvic, Obstetric and Gynaecological Physiotherapy
Pelvic floor muscle exercises and advice - A guide for trans men,
   trans masculine and non-binary people (who were assigned
   female at birth).
   www.thepogp.co.uk/Resources/140/pelvic_floor_muscle
   _exercises_and_advice_a_guide_for_trans_men_trans_masculine
   _and_nonbinary_people_who_were_assigned_female_at_birth

Pelvic Obstetric and Gynaecological Physiotherapy:
   Find a Physiotherapist in the UK
   www.thepogp.co.uk/patients/physiotherapists/

Acknowledgements

This book would not be here without a whole range of wonderful people that have supported, guided and helped me to bring it to life. First, I really want to thank all the women and men that I have worked with over the years; you have taught me so much and allowed me to become the physiotherapist that I am today. To my Instagram community, I turned to you in the depths of a pandemic, with a newborn, a toddler, and a medical husband, when I was the loneliest I had ever felt. Sharing bitesize pelvic health information brought focus and distraction during a really hard time, and I am for ever thankful that a challenging time for us all has given me not only a wonderful community of friends, but also opportunities I never dreamed of.

A massive thank you goes to Anya Hayes who first suggested I should consider writing a book, it was in our discussions that the idea of *Strong Foundations* was born. Thank you for encouraging me throughout the whole writing process.

A big thank you goes to Eve White and Ludo Cinelli, my literary agents, for believing in me and my vision for this book. Your encouragement at every step has been really appreciated.

To my editor, Lydia, thank you for being a dream to work with. For getting behind the vision and for really understanding my passion, as well as being patient with me when life got rather hectic for a while. I am so glad that you, and the team at HarperCollins, were willing to be part of the mission to get more people talking about pelvic health.

There are three women that need a special mention. Lucia Berry, Camilla Lawrence and Charlotte Barton: thank you for being the most amazing team who took me under your wings 14 years ago, in my first ever job in pelvic health. I'm delighted to still call you my friends and mentors, who always have my back and have supported me endlessly over the years. Extended thanks go to Lucia and Camilla who have provided their expert review of multiple sections of this book and have always been at the end of the phone when I have needed them.

A special thanks goes to the many experts who have contributed throughout this book and have really made it what it is. Candice Langford, Dr Anna Cantlay, Dr Sula Windgassen, Lulu Adams, Lucy Allen, Tessa van der Vord, Charlie Launder, Crystal Miles, Kristy Coleman, Illy Morrison, Anna Mathur, Kate Rowe-Ham, Alice Housman, Emiliana Hall, Kate Moyle, Hannah Poulton, Jacqueline Hooton, Siobhan O'Donovan, Tracey Matthews, Dr Stephanie Ooi, Clio Wood and Emma Armstrong. I am also so grateful for the expert review of other physiotherapist and medical professionals of different sections of this book. Sarah Fellows, Dr Lea Feghali, Alex Frankham, Aby Tobin, Grainne Donnelly, Amanda Savage, Dr Brooke Vandermolen and Nichola Ludlam-Raine – I so appreciate the time you have given to review and provide feedback and words of encouragement.

Finally, to my family and friends, thank you doesn't really cut it. First of all to my husband, David, who is a big reason this book even exists. He encouraged me to explore the idea of writing a book when it was initially suggested to me and I didn't think I could do it. He has held the fort at home in more ways than one, has read through each chapter as I have written it, made me countless cups of tea, encouraged me when exhausted and taken care of the kids so I could bring this book to life. To my beautiful kids, Poppy and Jonas, thank you for inspiring me every day, for understanding that Mummy has had to work a lot and reminding me that it is exciting that 'Mummy has written a book!' Though you won't know it, becoming your mum has been the reason I could write this book, in more ways than one. To my amazing parents, who provided me with so much growing up, including a wonderful education. They are a constant sounding board and have been cheering me on for 35 years, as well as taking care of our kids on a weekly basis so that we can work and progress our careers. Thank you for your endless love, support and sacrifice. To my loving in-laws who support us as a family, providing childcare and endless meals as we have navigated one of the busiest seasons of our lives. Finally, to my friends; there are really too many to mention, but special thanks go to Tessa, Sarah, Charley, Sheena, Katy, Lulu, Anna and Charlie, who have been on the end of a phone so many times over recent years and months, and have picked me up with pep talks and encouragement.

Index